A-Z NORTHAMPTON

C000179715

CONTENTS

Key to Map Pages	2-3
Large Scale Town Centre	4-5
Map Pages	6-65

Ind...
Vill...
and...

REFERENCE

Motorway	**M1**
A Road	**A428**
B Road	**B571**
Dual Carriageway	
One-way Street Traffic flow on A Roads is also indicated by a heavy line on the driver's left	
Road Under Construction Opening dates are correct at the time of publication	
Proposed Road	
Restricted Access	
Pedestrianized Road	
Track / Footpath	
Residential Walkway	
Railway	Level Crossing / Station / Tunnel
Built-up Area	HIGH ST.
Local Authority Boundary	
Posttown Boundary	
Postcode Boundary (within Posttown)	
Map Continuation	**20**
Large Scale Town Centre	**5**

Car Park (selected)	P
Church or Chapel	†
Cycleway (selected)	🚲
Fire Station	■
Hospital	H
House Numbers (A & B Roads only)	298 77
Information Centre	i
National Grid Reference	495
Police Station	▲
Post Office	★
Safety Camera with Speed Limit Fixed cameras and long term road works cameras. Symbols do not indicate camera direction	(30)
Toilet: without facilities for the Disabled with facilities for the Disabled	▽ ▽
Educational Establishment	▢
Hospital or Healthcare Building	▢
Industrial Building	▢
Leisure or Recreational Facility	▢
Place of Interest	▢
Public Building	▢
Shopping Centre or Market	▢
Other Selected Buildings	▢

SCALE

Map Pages 6-65
1:15,840 4 inches to 1 mile

0 — ¼ — ½ Mile
0 — 250 — 500 — 750 Metres
6.31 cm to 1km   10.16 cm to 1 mile

Map Pages 4-5
1:7,920 8 inches to 1 mile

0 — ⅛ — ¼ Mile
0 — 100 — 200 — 300 Metres
12.63 cm to 1km   20.32 cm to 1 mile

Copyright of Geographers' A-Z Map Company Limited

Fairfield Road, Borough Green, Sevenoaks, Kent TN15 8PP
Telephone: 01732 781000 (Enquiries & Trade Sales)
01732 783422 (Retail Sales)

www.az.co.uk

 **Ordnance Survey®**

This product includes mapping data licensed from Ordnance Survey® with the permission of the Controller of Her Majesty's Stationery Office.

Copyright © Geographers' A-Z Map Co. Ltd.

EDITION 5 2013

© Crown Copyright 2012. All rights reserved. Licence number 100017302

Safety camera information supplied by www.PocketGPSWorld.com
Speed Camera Location Database Copyright 2012 © PocketGPSWorld.com

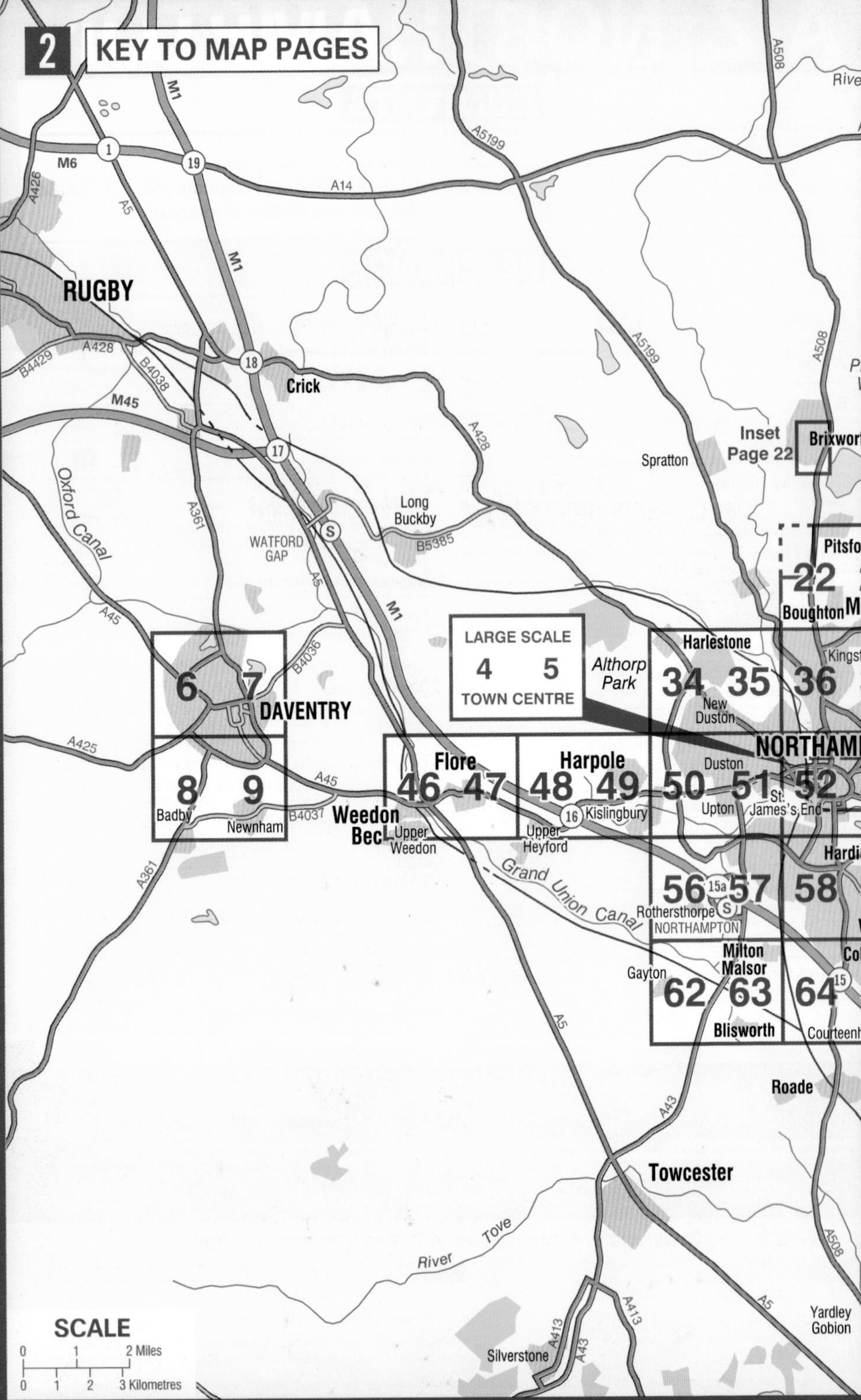

KEY TO MAP PAGES

2

LARGE SCALE
4   5
TOWN CENTRE

SCALE
0   1   2 Miles
0   1   2   3 Kilometres

M6
M1
M45
A5
A14
A428
A426
A428
B4429
A5199
A5199
A508
A508
A14

RUGBY
Crick
Long Buckby
B5385
WATFORD GAP
Oxford Canal
A361
A45
B4036
DAVENTRY
A425
A361
A45
B4037
6   7
8   9
Badby
Newnham
Weedon Bec
Upper Weedon
Flore
46   47
Upper Heyford
48
Harpole
49   50
Kislingbury
16
Spratton
Inset Page 22
Brixworth
Pitsfo
Harlestone
Althorp Park
34   35   36
New Duston
Kingst
Boughton
M
22
Duston
NORTHAMP
51   52
Upton
St. James's End
Hardir
56   57   58
15a
Rothersthorpe
NORTHAMPTON
Col
W
Milton Malsor
Gayton
62   63   64
Blisworth
Courteenh
15
Roade
Towcester
Grand Union Canal
River Tove
A43
A413
A413
A5
A43
A508
A5
Silverstone
Yardley Gobion

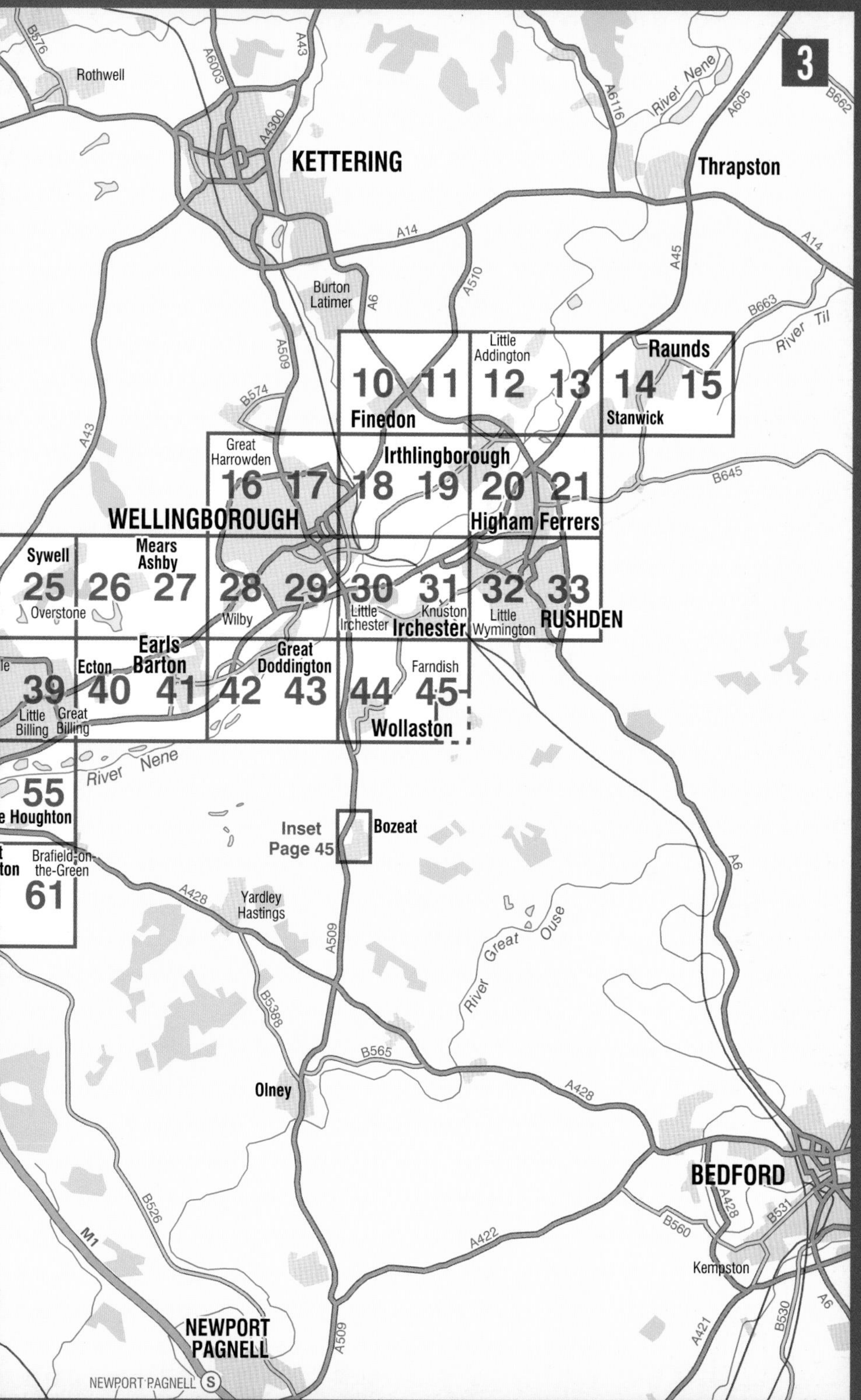

3

Rothwell

B576

A6003

A4300

A43

KETTERING

Thrapston

River Nene

A6116

A605

B662

A14

B663

River Til

A510

A45

A14

Burton
Latimer

A6

A509

B574

Little
Addington

Raunds

10 **11** **12** **13** **14** **15**

Finedon

Stanwick

Great
Harrowden

Irthlingborough

16 **17** **18** **19** **20** **21**

WELLINGBOROUGH

Higham Ferrers

B645

Mears
Ashby

Sywell

25 **26** **27** **28** **29** **30** **31** **32** **33**

Overstone

Wilby

Little
Irchester

Knuston

Little
Wymington

RUSHDEN

Irchester

Earls
Barton

Ecton

Great
Doddington

Farndish

39 **40** **41** **42** **43** **44** **45**

Little
Billing

Great
Billing

Wollaston

River Nene

55

e Houghton

Inset
Page 45

Bozeat

Brafield-on-
the-Green

ton

61

A428

Yardley
Hastings

A509

River Great Ouse

A6

B5388

B565

A428

Olney

A428

BEDFORD

A428

A421

B531

B560

M1

B526

A422

A509

Kempston

A6

B530

A421

**NEWPORT
PAGNELL**

NEWPORT PAGNELL **S**

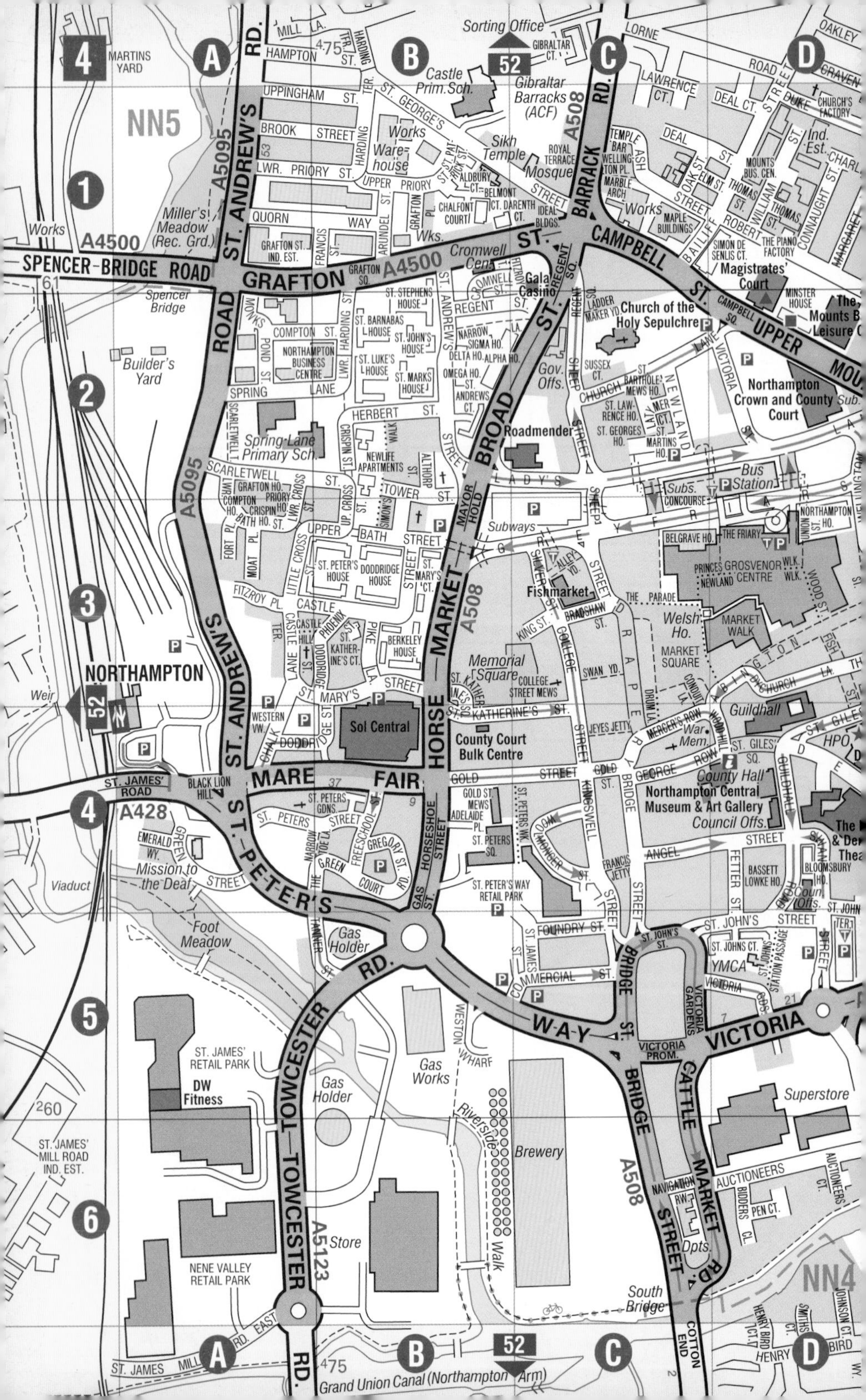
4
A
B
C
D
1
2
3
4
5
6
NN5
NN4
52
Sorting Office
Gibraltar Barracks (ACF)
Castle Prim.Sch.
Sikh Temple
Mosque
SPENCER-BRIDGE ROAD
GRAFTON ST.
A4500
A5095
A508
A428
A5123
ST. ANDREW'S RD.
BARRACK RD.
CAMPBELL ST.
UPPER MOUNTS
BROAD ST.
HORSE MARKET
MARE FAIR
ST. PETER'S WAY
TOWCESTER RD.
VICTORIA
BRIDGE ST.
CATTLE MARKET RD.
NORTHAMPTON
Spencer Bridge
Builder's Yard
Miller's Meadow (Rec. Grd.)
Spring Lane Primary Sch.
Church of the Holy Sepulchre
Magistrates' Court
Northampton Crown and County Court
Roadmender
Bus Station
Gov. Offs.
Grosvenor Centre
Fishmarket
Memorial Square
Market Square
Welsh Ho.
Market Walk
Guildhall
Sol Central
County Court Bulk Centre
County Hall
Northampton Central Museum & Art Gallery
Council Offs.
Mission to the Deaf
Viaduct
Foot Meadow
Gas Holder
Gas Works
Brewery
Riverside Walk
St. James' Retail Park
DW Fitness
St. James' Mill Road Ind. Est.
Nene Valley Retail Park
Store
Superstore
South Bridge
Grand Union Canal (Northampton Arm)
St. James Mill Rd. East
Cotton End
YMCA
Weir
Works
Brewery

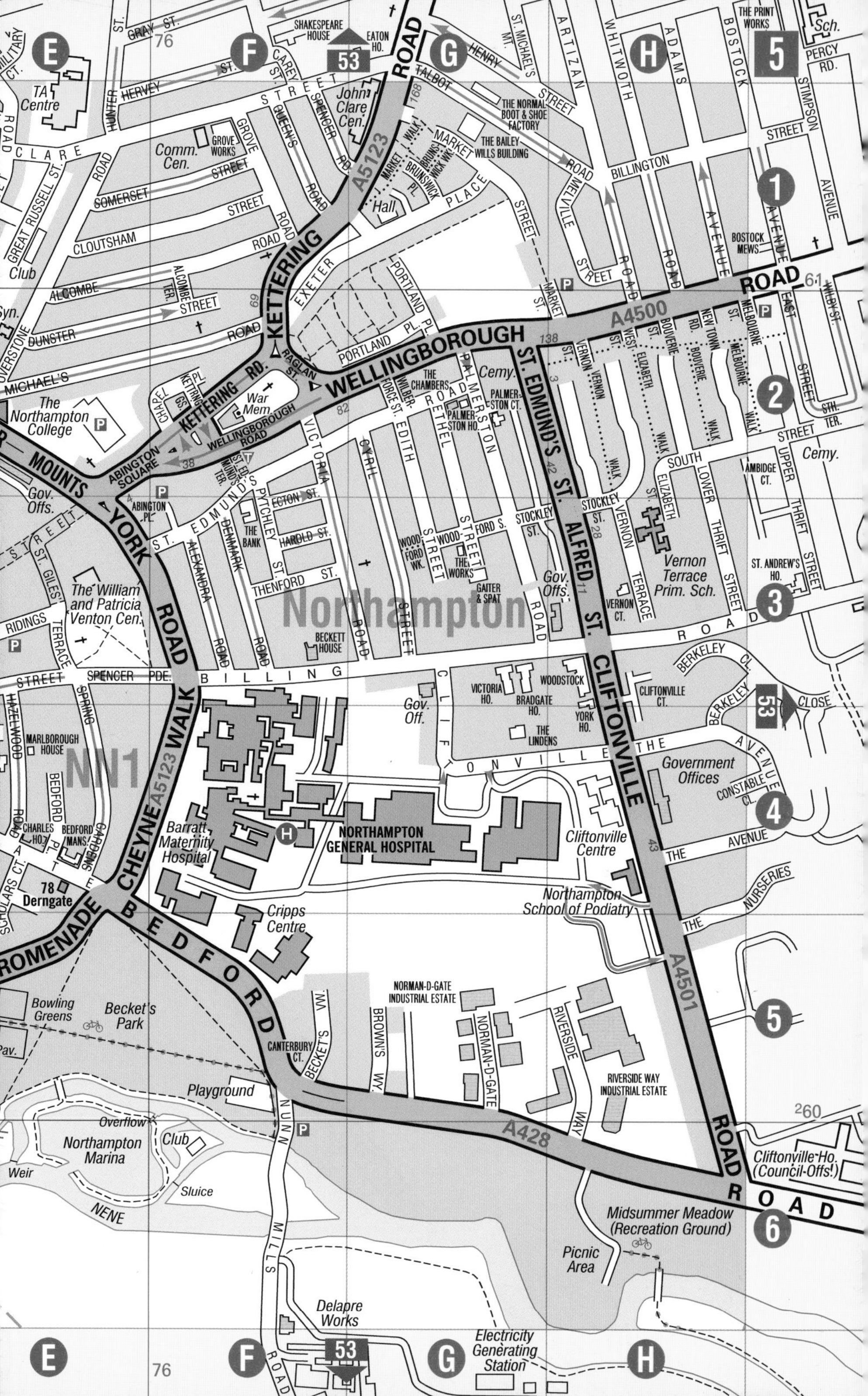

Northampton
NN1
E
F
G
H
5
1
2
3
4
5
6
53
76
KETTERING ROAD
WELLINGBOROUGH ROAD
A5123
A4500
A4501
A428
ST. EDMUND'S ST.
ALFRED ST.
CLIFTONVILLE ROAD
BILLING ROAD
YORK ROAD
CHEYNE WALK
BEDFORD ROAD
MOUNTS
The Northampton College
Gov. Offs.
The William and Patricia Venton Cen.
War Mem.
ABINGTON SQUARE
Comm. Cen.
TA Centre
John Clare Cen.
SHAKESPEARE HOUSE
EATON HO.
THE PRINT WORKS
Sch.
THE NORMAL BOOT & SHOE FACTORY
THE BAILEY WILLS BUILDING
Hall
Cemy.
Vernon Terrace Prim. Sch.
NORTHAMPTON GENERAL HOSPITAL
Barratt Maternity Hospital
Cliftonville Centre
Northampton School of Podiatry
Cripps Centre
Government Offices
NORMAN-D-GATE INDUSTRIAL ESTATE
RIVERSIDE WAY INDUSTRIAL ESTATE
Becket's Park
Bowling Greens
Playground
Northampton Marina
Overflow
Club
Weir
Sluice
NENE
Midsummer Meadow (Recreation Ground)
Picnic Area
Delapre Works
Electricity Generating Station
Cliftonville Ho. (Council-Offs!)
78 Derngate
MARLBOROUGH HOUSE
BECKETT HOUSE
GAITER & SPAT
VICTORIA HO.
BRADGATE HO.
WOODSTOCK
YORK HO.
THE LINDENS
CLIFTONVILLE CT.
ST. ANDREW'S HO.
VERNON CT.
THE BANK
THE WORKS
THE CHAMBERS
PALMERSTON CT.
PALMERSTON HO.
CANTERBURY CT.
ROMENADE

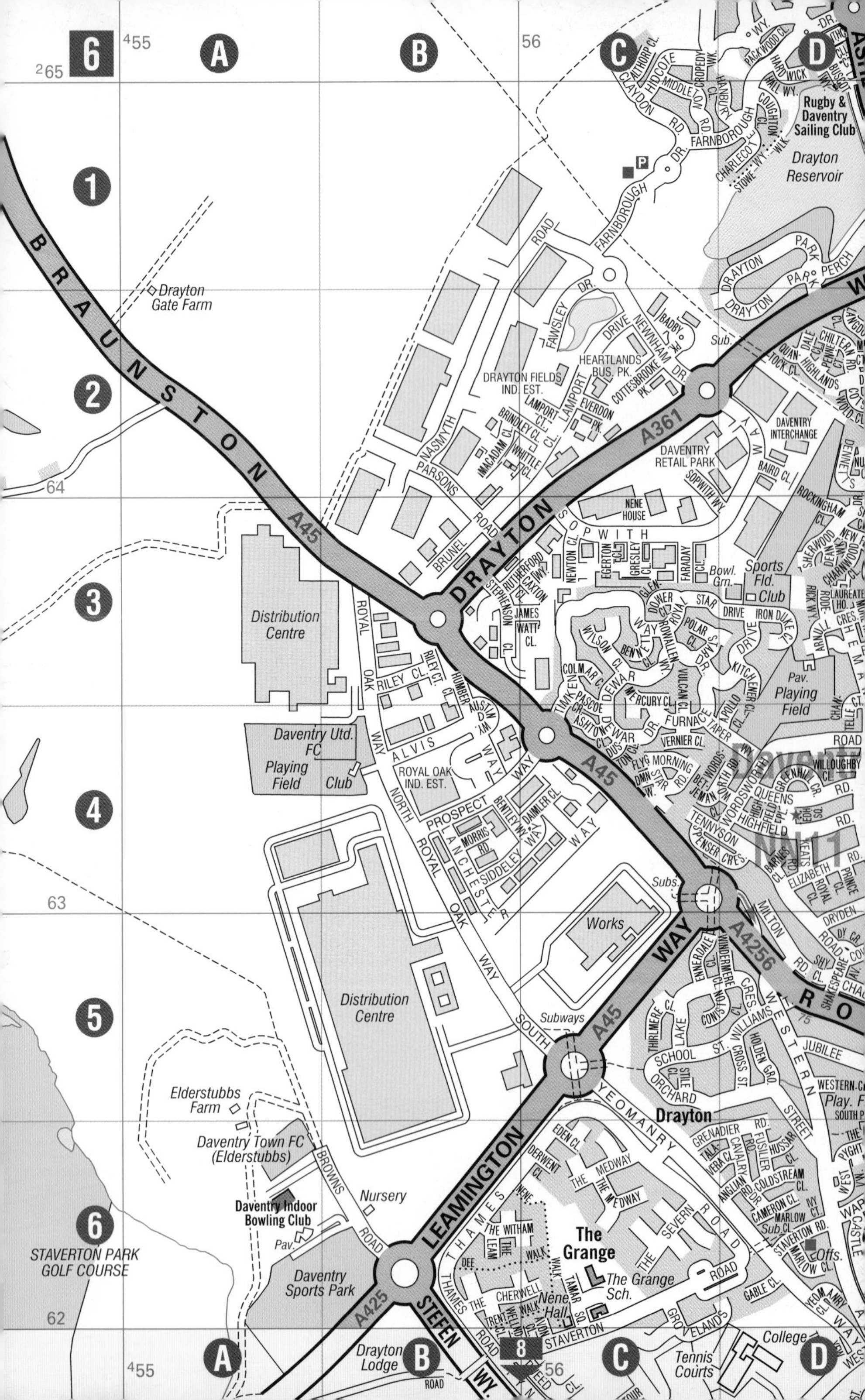

Drayton Gate Farm
BRAUNSTON
A45
DRAYTON WAY
A361
A4256
A425
LEAMINGTON
STEFFEN WY.
Distribution Centre
Daventry Utd. FC
Playing Field
Club
ROYAL OAK IND. EST.
DRAYTON FIELDS IND. EST.
HEARTLANDS BUS. PK.
DAVENTRY RETAIL PARK
DAVENTRY INTERCHANGE
NENE HOUSE
Rugby & Daventry Sailing Club
Drayton Reservoir
Sports Fld. Club
Pav. Playing Field
Works
Subways
Elderstubbs Farm
Daventry Town FC (Elderstubbs)
Daventry Indoor Bowling Club
Nursery
Daventry Sports Park
STAVERTON PARK GOLF COURSE
Drayton
The Grange
The Grange Sch.
Nene Hall
Drayton Lodge
Tennis Courts
College
NN11

8

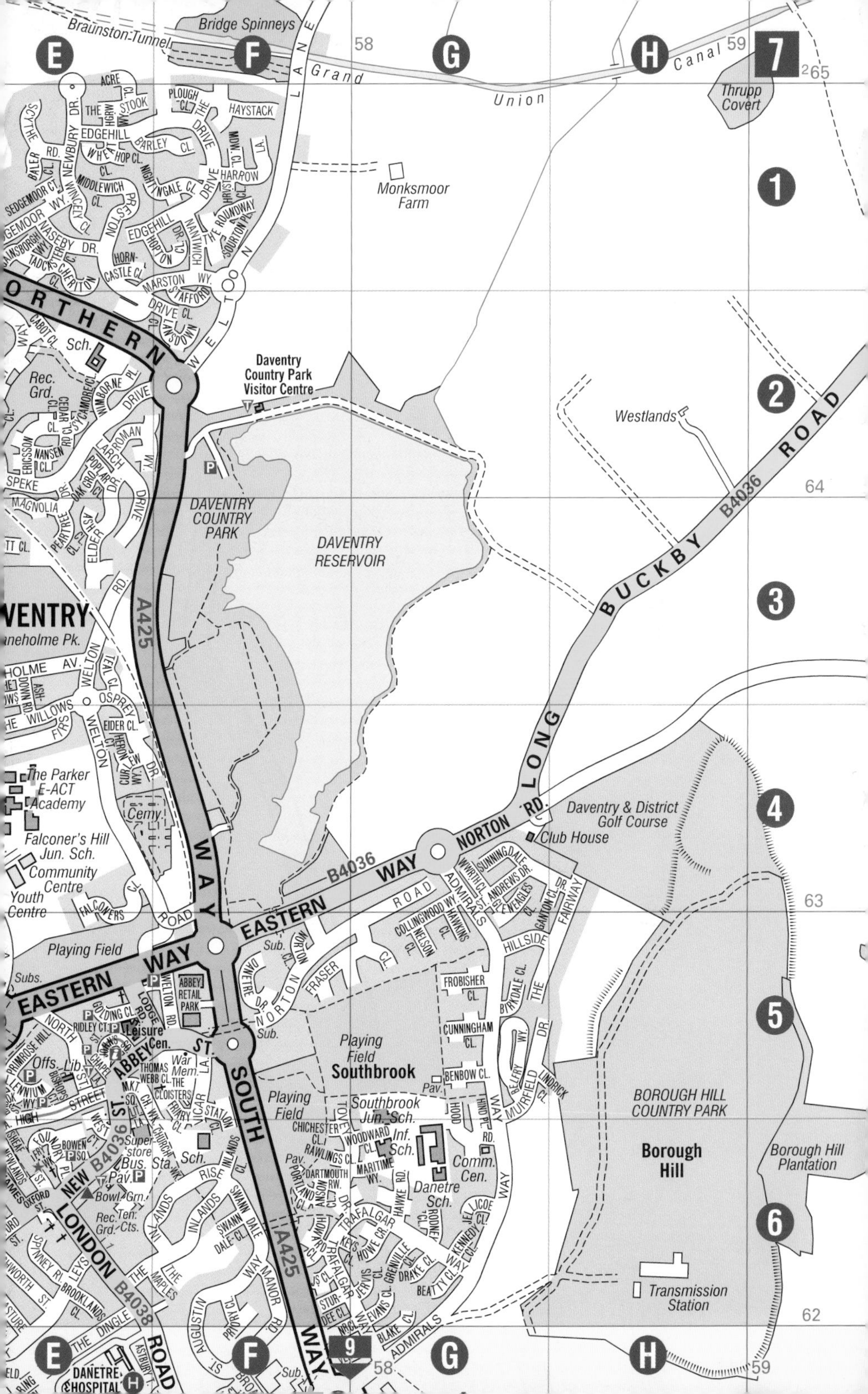
7
Braunston Tunnel
Bridge Spinneys
Grand Union Canal
Thrupp Covert
Monksmoor Farm
Daventry Country Park Visitor Centre
DAVENTRY COUNTRY PARK
DAVENTRY RESERVOIR
Westlands
LONG BUCKBY ROAD
B4036
NORTHERN WAY
A425
WELTON LANE
EASTERN WAY
NORTON RD.
Daventry & District Golf Course
Club House
The Parker E-ACT Academy
Falconer's Hill Jun. Sch.
Community Centre
Youth Centre
Playing Field
Southbrook
Southbrook Jun. Sch.
Danetre Sch.
Comm. Cen.
BOROUGH HILL COUNTRY PARK
Borough Hill
Borough Hill Plantation
Transmission Station
SOUTH WAY
LONDON ROAD
B4038
DANETRE HOSPITAL
Leisure Cen.
Abbey Retail Park
9

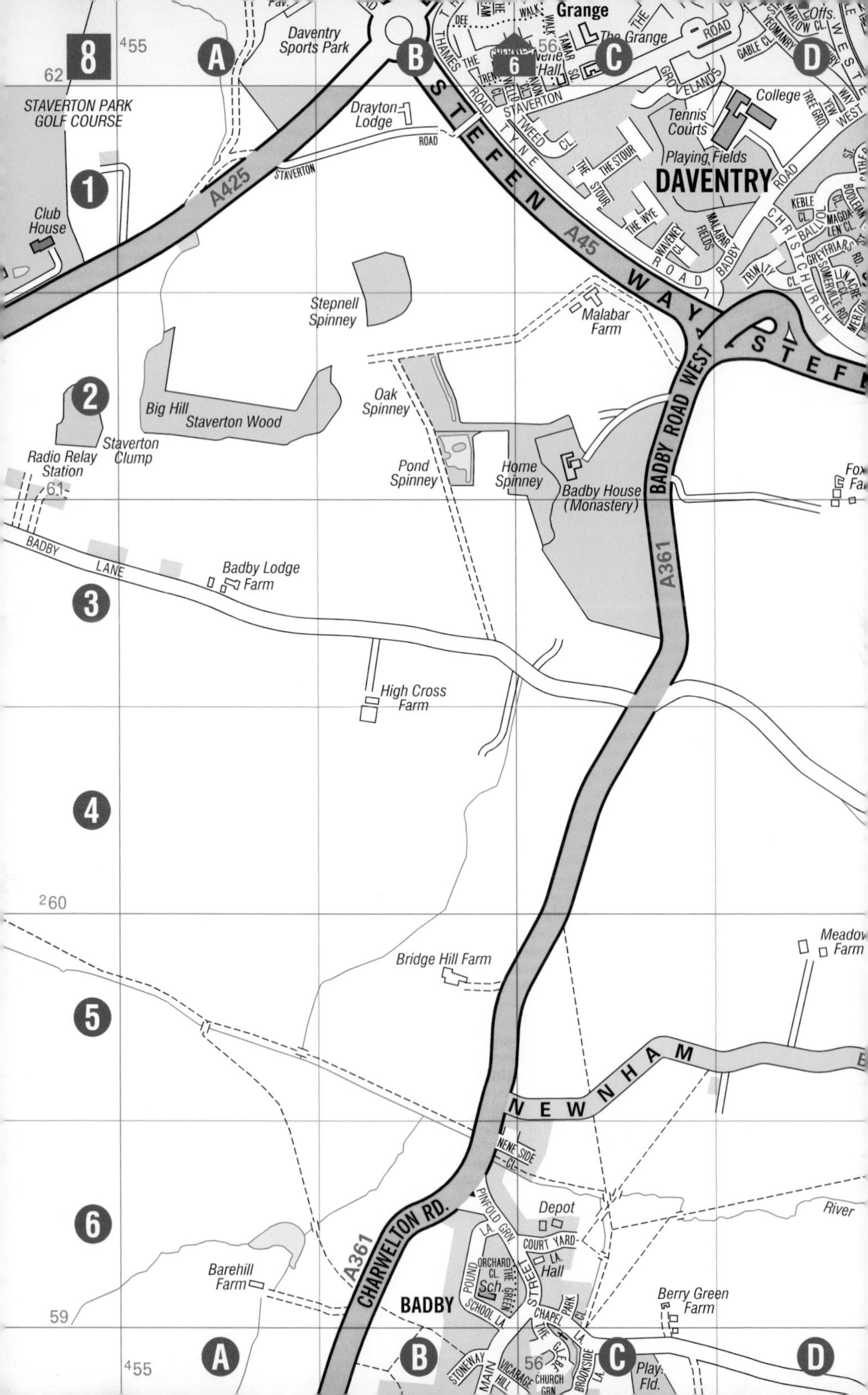
8
Daventry Sports Park
Grange
The Grange
College
Tennis Courts
Playing Fields
DAVENTRY
STAVERTON PARK GOLF COURSE
Club House
Drayton Lodge
STAVERTON ROAD
A425
STEFEN WAY
A45
Stepnell Spinney
Malabar Farm
Big Hill
Staverton Wood
Staverton Clump
Radio Relay Station
Oak Spinney
Pond Spinney
Home Spinney
Badby House (Monastery)
BADBY ROAD WEST
BADBY LANE
Badby Lodge Farm
High Cross Farm
A361
Bridge Hill Farm
Meadow Farm
NEWNHAM
NENE SIDE CL.
CHARWELTON RD.
Depot
River
Barehill Farm
Hall
Sch.
BADBY
Berry Green Farm
Play Fld.
A
B
C
D
1
2
3
4
5
6
455
456
260
259
62
61

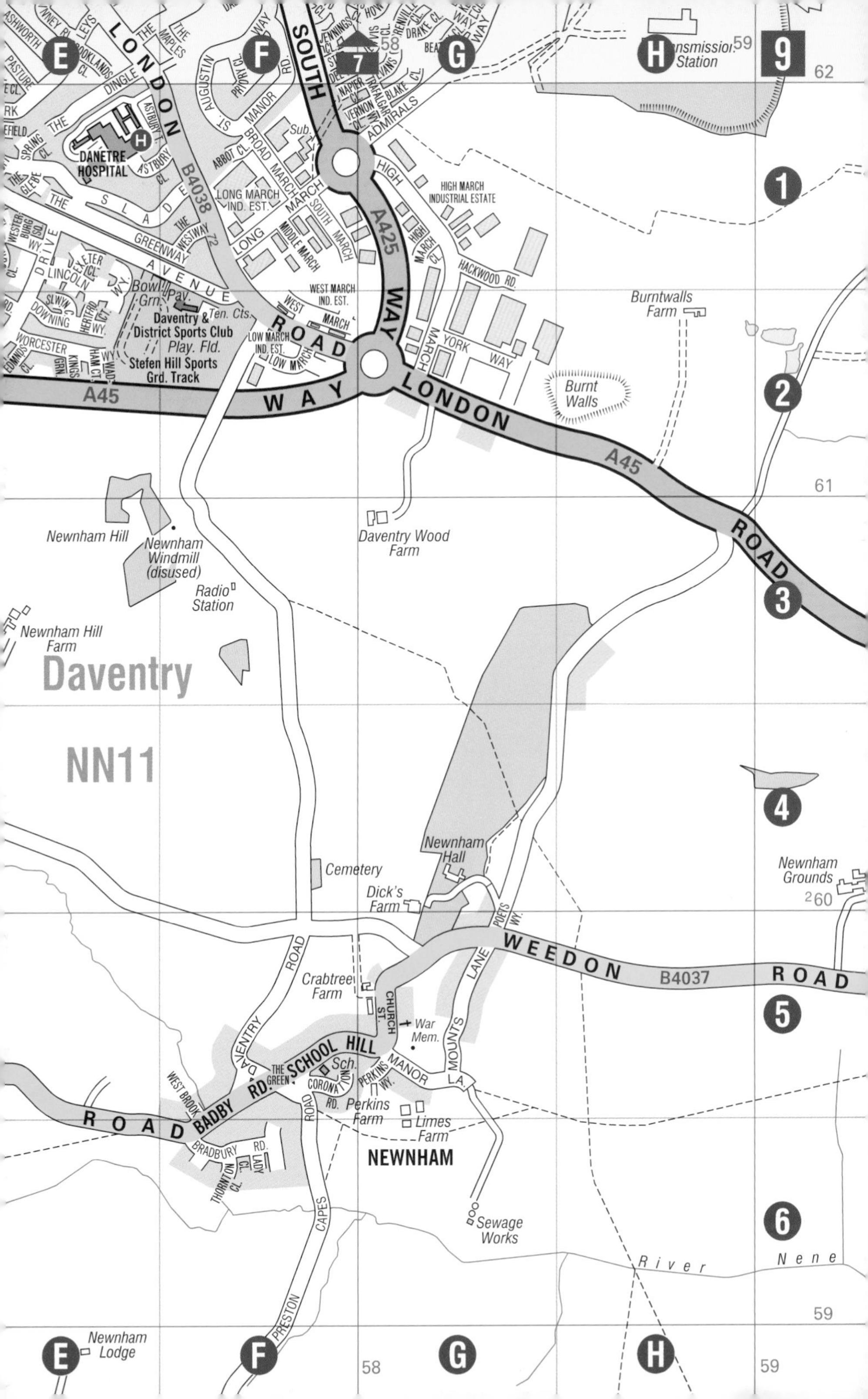

9
Daventry
NN11
DANETRE HOSPITAL
LONG MARCH IND. EST.
HIGH MARCH INDUSTRIAL ESTATE
WEST MARCH IND. EST.
LOW MARCH IND. EST.
Daventry & District Sports Club
Stefen Hill Sports Grd. Track
Transmission Station
Burntwalls Farm
Burnt Walls
Newnham Hill
Newnham Windmill (disused)
Radio Station
Newnham Hill Farm
Daventry Wood Farm
Newnham Hall
Cemetery
Dick's Farm
Crabtree Farm
Newnham Grounds
Perkins Farm
Limes Farm
NEWNHAM
Sewage Works
River Nene
Newnham Lodge
LONDON ROAD
LONDON WAY
SOUTH WAY
WEEDON ROAD
BADBY ROAD
SCHOOL HILL
DAVENTRY RD.
PRESTON CAPES ROAD
A45
A425
B4038
B4037

A
B
C
D
1
2
3
4
5
6
490
91
74
73
72
71
Kettering NN15
Wellingborough NN9
FINEDON
HIGHAM RD.
QUEENSWAY
HILL CREST AV.
FINEDON ROAD
A6
BURTON
Buccleuch Farm
Ashmeads School
Barnfield Lodge Farm
KETTERING
WELLINGBOROUGH
FINEDON STATION RD.
STATION
Isebrook Bridge
Warehouses
Westfield Lodge
LANE
Piggery
River Ise
MILL
Cemy.
Pav.
Cricket Ground
ROAD
CHURCH HILL
AVENUE RD.
ORCHARD
T.H. & Lib.
Sch.
HIGH ST.
CHURCH ST.
Graveyard
FINEDON HALL
MACKWORTH DR.
HOLLY WLK.
DOLBEN CL.
STOCKS HILL
REGENT ST.
BELL HILL
WY. LA.
A510
CROMER
MILNER
EWENFIELD RD.
KENMUIR RD.
ROAD
DRIVE
HALL
GROVE WY.
LANE
WELLINGBOROUGH
Finedon Cally Banks Nature Reserve
THE SLIPS
HARROWDEN
Hillside Farm
RYEBURY HILL
18

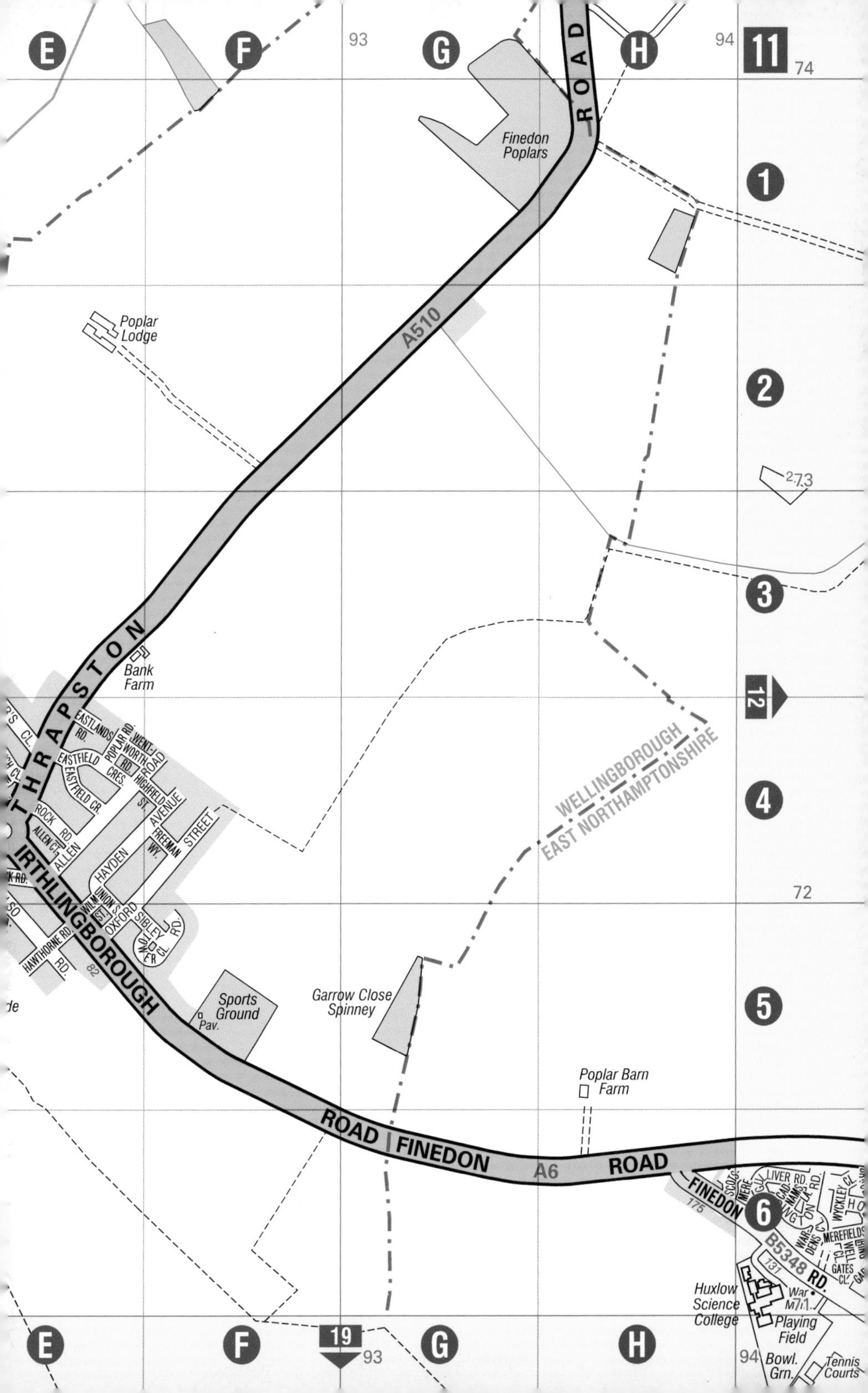

ROAD

1

Finedon Poplars

A510

2

2·73

Poplar Lodge

3

Bank Farm

12 ▶

THRAPSTON

EASTLANDS RD
EASTFIELD CR
EASTFIELD CRES.
POPLAR RD
WENT RD
WORTH RD
HIGHFIELD CRES.
ROCK RD
ALLEN CL
AVENUE
FREEMAN STREET
ALLEN WY.
ST.
HAYDEN
LINDA
OXFORD
SIBLEY RD.
ER
TOWER CL.
4

WELLINGBOROUGH
EAST NORTHAMPTONSHIRE

72

IRTHLINGBOROUGH

HAWTHORNE RD.
82

5

Sports Ground
Pav.

Garrow Close Spinney

Poplar Barn Farm

ROAD   FINEDON   A6   ROAD

FINEDON
175
LIVER RD.
WYCKLEY CL.
MEREFIELDS
WELL GATES CL.
B5348 RD.
6

Huxlow Science College

War Mem.

Playing Field

Wellingborough
NN9

12

A B C D

94 495

74

1

2

²73

3

←11

4

72

5

Bar Barn Farm

6

ROAD

FINEDON

Huxlow Science College

War Mem.

B5348

Playing Field

71

94 Bowl. Grn.

Tennis Courts

A B C D

SEDGE LIVER RD. LONG ACRES DR. MIDDLE GRASS A6

WARD HARRINGTON RD. MCCLXKY BRACK. BUNGBUNG CL. DRAYTON MOUNTFIELD RD. PORTLAND RD. KNIGHTLANDS WILLIAM RD.

DENS CL. INGRE MEREFIELDS WELL GATES BARROW CL. ROBB CL. SCHARPWELL DRAYTON KNIGHTLANDS ROAD

BUSH CLOSE PEPYS CLOSE FERNMOOR CL. D RD.

By Pass Farm

Crow Hill

ADDINGTON ROAD

DIAMONDS BUSINESS CENTRE

HARTLEY

20

495

Wks.

DIAMOND WY.

Football Pitches

MARSH

RIVER

Kettering Town FC (Nene Park)

FINEDON RD. ADDINGTON RD. B571 B5348 RD.

Burrows Farm

Burrows Fm. La.

The Gin Chapel

Back Hill

Bare Hill

Cotes Eve.

Green

Hill Farm

Freestones Farm

Playing Field

Rugby Dr.

WELFORD CL. OXFORD CL. RIVAL CL. CHURCHILL GARDEN FIELDS CL. LANGLEY CRES. FETTLE DINE Cor. C.

NOBLE AV. ALEXANDER PL. ALEXANDER RD.

WELFORD

THE SHORTLANDS CLARKE PALMER AV.

Sports Hall

Knightlands

Crow Hill Farm

E
F
G
H
97
98
74
1
2
3
4
5
6
73
72
71
Sewage Works
AMEN CORNER
WOODFORD RD.
Hillside Farm
Kettering
NN14
TTLE
NGTON
HILL FARM ESTATE
Mallows Cotton
Hog Dyke
Sub.
MEADOW
LANE
A45
RIVER
NENE
14
Sewage Works
LANE
STANWICK LAKES
Stanwick Lakes Visitor Centre
Sewage Works
COTTON
WEST
STANWICK
NEEDHAM RD.
ALFRED ST.
ST. LAURENCE WY.
RECTORY CL.
JOHN ST. EAGLE CL.
MANSFIELD CL.
DOLBEN AV.
GREEN LA.
PARKLANDS
Factory
STREET
SPENCER PDE.
RAUNDS
FLEET
Sch.
CHURCH
MANOR GDS.
COURTWOOD
STR
CHAPEL
ST.
THE BROOK
SAMUELS
HIGH
HILL HOUSE GDS.
GRANGE
HIGHAM
ROAD
NEW BRIDGE LA.
SIDE
ROAD EAST
MARKS CL.
Orcha Farm
Hall Farm
ADAMS
CASTERTON CL.
COLLINGHAM
COURTMAN RD.
MANNINGHAM RD.
CLEBURNE CL.
POTTER CT.
LOVELL CL.
WETENHALL RD.
CUMBERLAND AV.
ROAD
21

RAUNDS
STANWICK
Raunds Town FC (Kiln Park)
BRICK KILN
B663
A45
LONDON RD.
LONDON ROAD
WARTH PARK WAY
WARTH HOUSE
Cemy.
Windmill Prim. Sch.
Scalley Farm
MEADOW LANE
MARSHALL'S ROAD
Works
Yala Poultry Farm
Rec Grd.
Pav. Ckt. Grd.
Smith's Bridge
Sewage Works
Nursery
Playing Field
TITTY HO
GROVE
WELLINGTON RD.
CHELVESTON ROAD
STANWICK ROAD
Factory
Darsdale Farm
Orchard Farm
Cemetery
CHELVESTON ROAD
Hall
ST. THORPE
BROOK ST.
Sch.
HIGH STREET
CHURCH ST.
EAST STREET
GRANGE RD.
THE AVENUE
SPENCER PDE.
NEEDHAM RD.
13

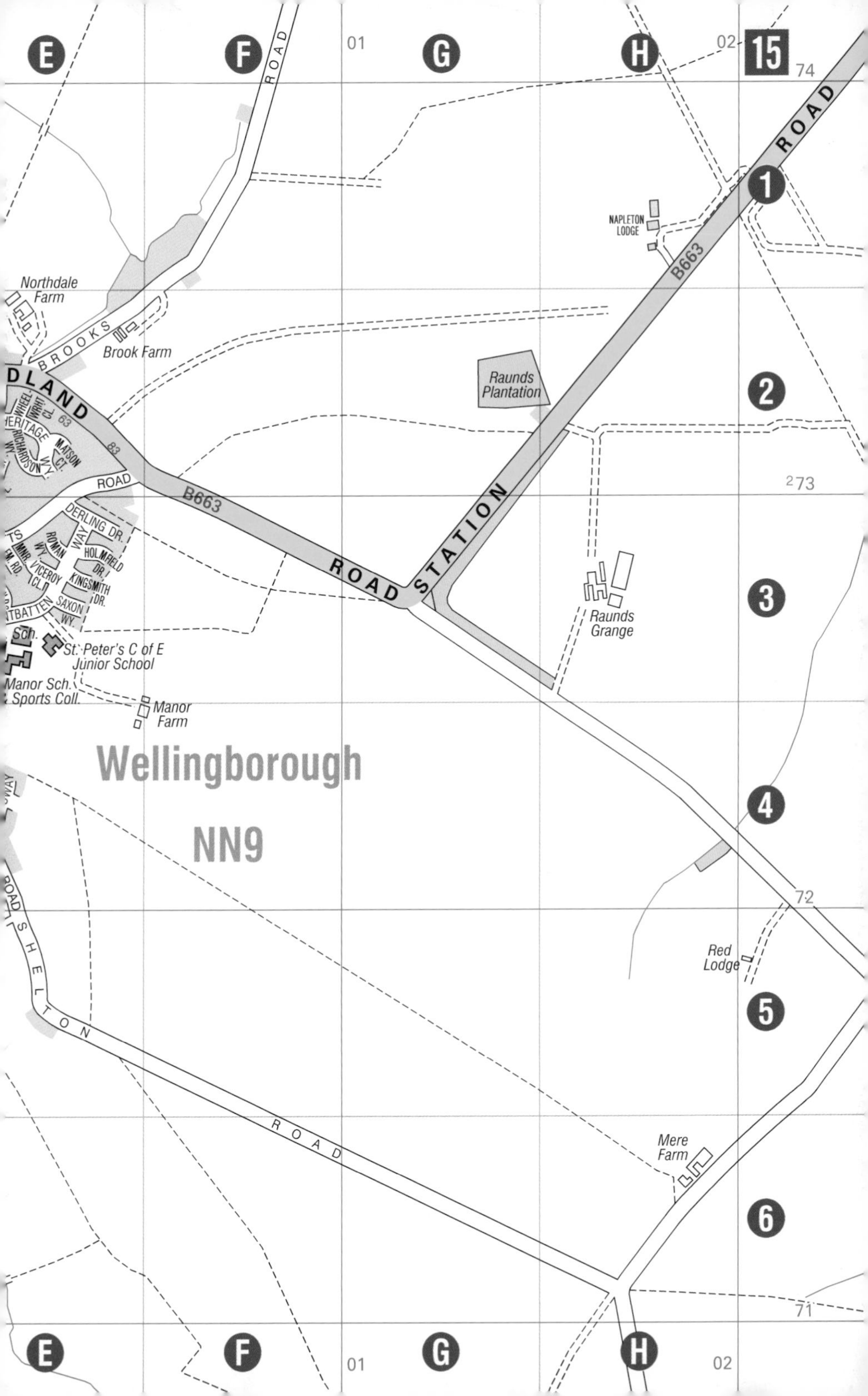
E
F
G
H
01
02
74
73
72
71
1
2
3
4
5
6
ROAD
B663
STATION
NAPLETON LODGE
Northdale Farm
BROOKS
Brook Farm
Raunds Plantation
DLAND
WHEEL-WRIHT CL.
HERITAGE
RICHARDSON WY.
MATSON CT.
ROAD
DERLING DR.
ROWAN WY.
HOLMFIELD DR.
VICEROY CL.
KINGSMITH DR.
SAXON WY.
Raunds Grange
Sch.
St. Peter's C of E Junior School
Manor Sch. Sports Coll.
Manor Farm
Wellingborough
NN9
SHELTON ROAD
Red Lodge
Mere Farm

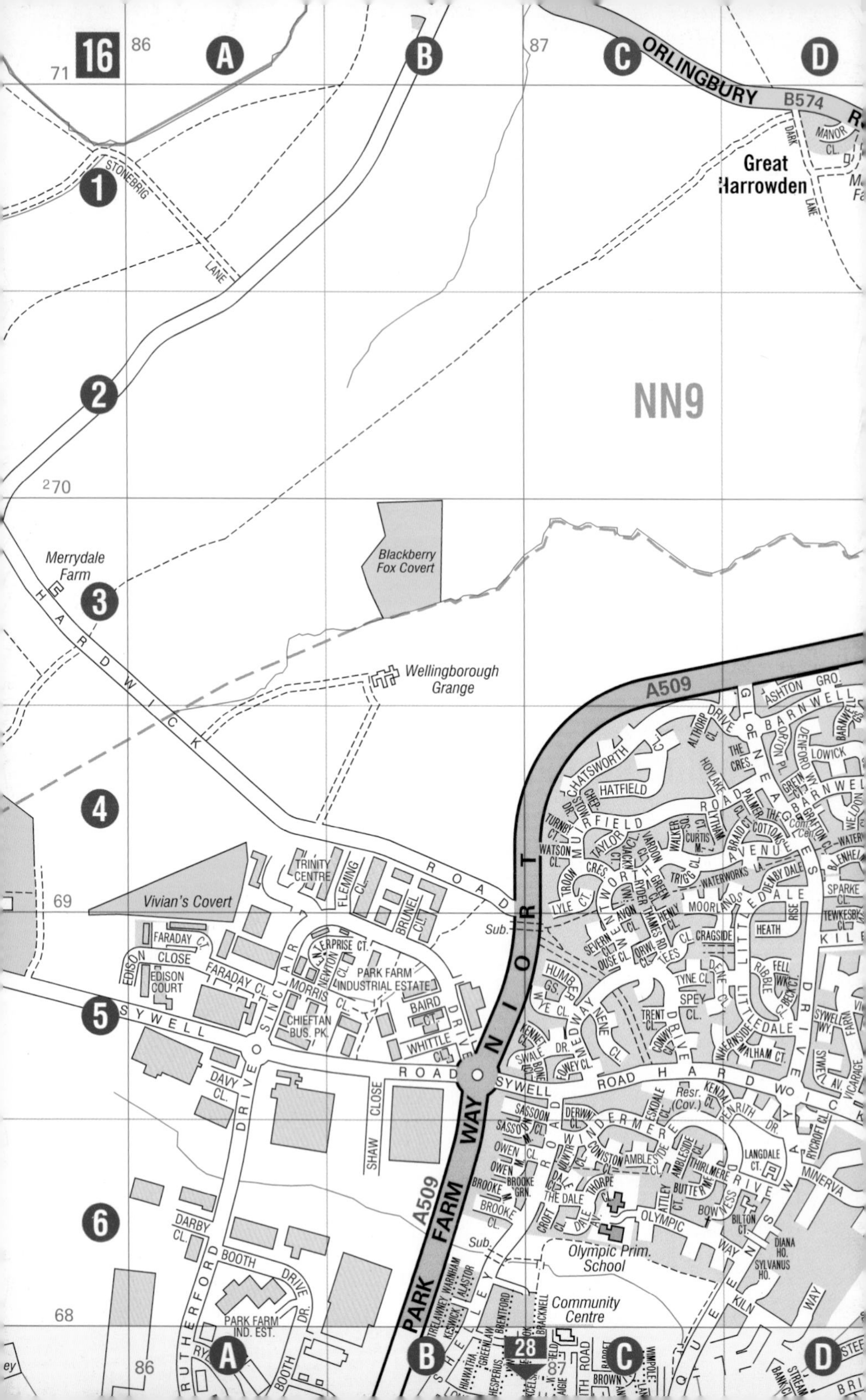
A
B
C
D
1
2
3
4
5
6
ORLINGBURY
B574
Great Harrowden
MANOR CL.
DARK LANE
STONEBRIG LANE
NN9
Merrydale Farm
HARDWICK ROAD
Blackberry Fox Covert
Wellingborough Grange
A509
Vivian's Covert
TRINITY CENTRE
FLEMING CL.
BRUNEL CL.
FARADAY CT.
EDISON CLOSE
EDISON COURT
FARADAY CL.
SINCLAIR DRIVE
ENTERPRISE CT.
NEWTON CL.
MORRIS CL.
PARK FARM INDUSTRIAL ESTATE
CHIEFTAN BUS. PK.
BAIRD CT.
WHITTLE CL.
SYWELL ROAD
DAVY CL.
SHAW CLOSE
NIORT WAY
PARK FARM WAY
DARBY CL.
BOOTH DRIVE
RUTHERFORD DR.
PARK FARM IND. EST.
Sub.
ASHTON GRO.
BARNWELL
CHATSWORTH
HATFIELD
ALTHORP CL.
THE CRES.
LOWICK
MUIRFIELD ROAD
TAYLOR
WATSON CL.
TURNBY CT.
TROON
LYLE CT.
WENTWORTH AVENUE
VARDON
WALKER SQ.
CURTIS M.
TRIGG CL.
WATERWORKS LA.
DENBY DALE
MOORLANDS
LITTLEDALE
HEATH
CRAGSIDE
SEVERN CL.
OUSE CL.
AVON CL.
TEES
TYNE CL.
SPEY CL.
HUMBER GS.
MEDWAY
WYE CL.
NENE CL.
TRENT CL.
SWALE DR.
FOWEY CL.
WHERNSIDE
MALHAM CT.
HARDWICK
SPARKE CL.
TEWKESBURY CL.
SYWELL AV.
VICARAGE
DERWENT CL.
ESKDALE
KENDAL CL.
PENRITH DR.
Resr. (Cov.)
WINDERMERE
SASSOON CL.
OWEN CL.
OWEN M.
CONISTON CL.
AMBLESIDE CL.
THIRLMERE DRIVE
BUTTERMERE
LANGDALE CT.
RYCROFT CL.
MINERVA WAY
BROOKE GRN.
BROOKE CL.
THE DALE
CROFT CL.
DALE AV.
THORPE
BOWNESS
OLYMPIC WAY
BILTON CT.
DIANA HO.
SYLVANUS HO.
Olympic Prim. School
Community Centre
QUEENSWAY
KILN WAY
SHELLEY
TRELAWNEY
WARNHAM
ALASTOR
KESWICK
BRENTFORD
BRACKNELL
BROWN
WIMPOLE
28
86
87
71
70
69
68

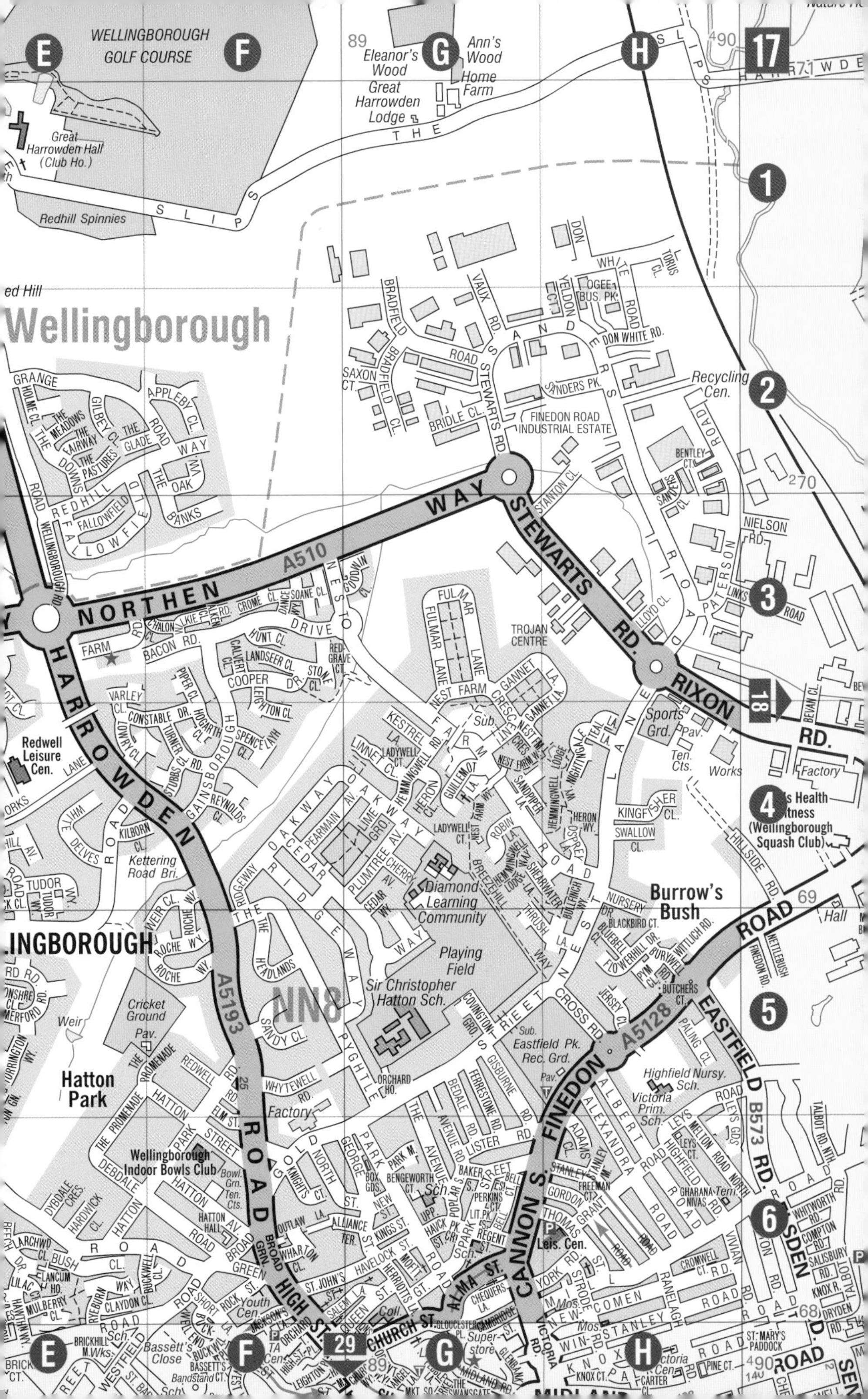

17
18
29
Wellingborough
WELLINGBOROUGH GOLF COURSE
Great Harrowden Hall (Club Ho.)
Redhill Spinnies
Eleanor's Wood
Ann's Wood
Home Farm
Great Harrowden Lodge
FINEDON ROAD INDUSTRIAL ESTATE
Recycling Cen.
TROJAN CENTRE
Redwell Leisure Cen.
Kettering Road Bri.
Diamond Learning Community
Playing Field
Sir Christopher Hatton Sch.
NN8
Burrow's Bush
Sports Grd.
Cricket Ground
Hatton Park
Wellingborough Indoor Bowls Club
Eastfield Pk. Rec. Grd.
Highfield Nursy. Sch.
Victoria Prim. Sch.
Leis. Cen.
Super-store
NORTHEN WAY
STEWARTS RD.
RIXON RD.
HARROWDEN ROAD
HIGH ST.
CHURCH ST.
CANNON S.
FINEDON
EASTFIELD RD.
A510
A5193
A5128
B573

18
HARROWDEN LANE
NN9
Hillside Farm
RYEBURY HILL ROAD
A510
Ryebury Farm
WELLINGBOROUGH ROAD
SIDEGATE
Carrol Spring Farm
Works
Finedon Bridge
Neilson's Sidings
ISE VALLEY IND. EST.
MEADOW CLOSE
Finedonhill Farm
PATERSON ROAD
BENTLEY CT.
NIELSON RD.
LINKS ROAD
BEVAN CT.
BEVAN CL.
RIXON ROAD
Depot
Factory
Sports Grd.
Pav.
Ten. Cts.
Works
Diana's Health & Fitness (Wellingborough Squash Club)
Wellingborough
Burrow's Bush
HILLSIDE RD.
FINEDON ROAD
A5128
Hall
MIDLAND BUSINESS UNITS
NETTLEBUSH
FINEDON RD.
Engine Shed
River Ise
NN8
South Hill Farm
B571
MILL ROAD INDUSTRIAL ESTATE
MIDLAND WORKS BUS. CEN.
ROAD
Works
IRTHLINGBOROUGH ROAD
Pumping Station
Irthlingborough Grange
EASTFIELD B573 RD.
ELSDEN RD.
TALBOT RD. NTH.
WHITWORTH RD.
COMPTON RD.
SALISBURY RD.
KNOX R.
DRYDEN
TALBOT RD.
Wellingborough
Warehouse
ST. MARY'S PADDOCK
MIDLAND
Highfield Nursy. Sch.
Victoria Prim. Sch.
LEYS ROAD
LEYS GDS.
LEYS CT.
MELTON ROAD NORTH
HIGHFIELD
GHARANA NIVAS
Tem.
MELTON RD.
VIVIAN RD.
CROMWELL CT.
MILL ROAD
KNOX ROAD
ROAD
TORUS CL.
WHITE RD.
LLOYD CL.
KINGFISHER CL.
SWALLOW CL.
BLACKBIRD CT.
WITTLICH RD.
BURYWELL RD.
PYM CL.
BUTCHERS CT.
PALING CL.
Victoria Cen.
PINE CT.
CARTER CL.
B572
10
30
17
A B C D
1 2 3 4 5 6

E
F
G
H
11
93
94
19
Huxlow Science College
Playing Field
Bowl. Grn.
Pav.
Recreation Ground
Sports Ground
Reservoir (Covered)
Pav.
Cricket Ground
MUSSON
QUEEN ST.
JUBILEE ST.
WINDMILL RD.
CRISPIN CT.
GEORGE ST.
VICTORIA
Works
ROAD
HIGH
WHITES RD.
SPENCER RD.
ALLEN RD.
WHITLEY CL.
PRESLAND WY.
GREEN CL.
VALE
ALLEN ROAD
270
THOMAS FLAWN RD.
DIAMOND
MARRIOTT CL.
EXPRESS CL.
PERKINS RD.
PREMYER WY.
WILM
TRIGG
BRIGHTWELL WLK.
McGIBBN WK.
THOMAS FLAWN
EVENSFORD
THE WLK.
SIDINGS
LUCAS CL.
VALE
HOME CL.
LAKESIDE
LODGE
LODGE WY.
20
WELLINGBOROUGH EAST NORTHAMPTONSHIRE
NN9
B571
WELLINGBOROUGH
West Field Lodge
Cemetery
Stone Cross Farm
Broadholme
ROAD
MILL
ROAD
LANE
DITCHFORD
69
Sewage Works
Drain
South View Farm
LANE
DITCHFORD
RIVER NENE
Ditchford Bridge
Weir
River Nene Navigation
Ditchford Lock
NN10
Skew Bridge Ski Lake
NENE
Ditchford Mill
Weir
ROAD
RIVER
68
31
93
94
Skew Bridge
1
2
3
4
5
6

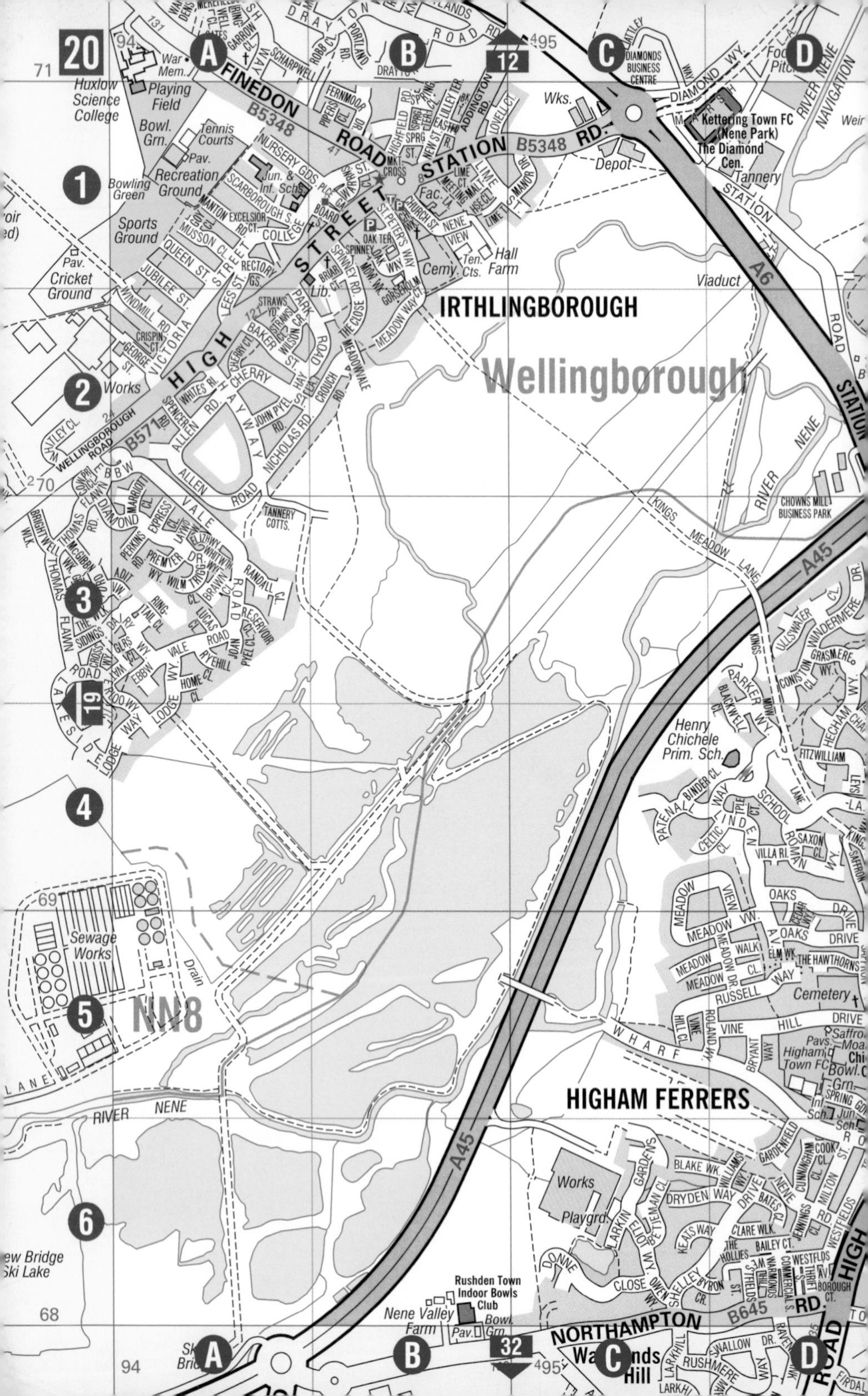
IRTHLINGBOROUGH
Wellingborough
HIGHAM FERRERS
NN8
FINEDON ROAD
B5348
STATION RD.
HIGH STREET
WELLINGBOROUGH ROAD
B571
A6
A45
RIVER NENE
NENE NAVIGATION
Huxlow Science College
Playing Field
Bowl. Grn.
Tennis Courts
Pav.
Recreation Ground
Bowling Green
Sports Ground
Cricket Ground
Works
Jun. & Inf. Sch.
MKT. CROSS
Lib.
Cemy.
Hall Farm
Ten. Cts.
Fac.
Wks.
Depot
DIAMONDS BUSINESS CENTRE
Kettering Town FC (Nene Park)
The Diamond Cen.
Tannery
Viaduct
CHOWNS MILL BUSINESS PARK
KINGS MEADOW LANE
TANNERY COTTS.
Sewage Works
Drain
Henry Chichele Prim. Sch.
Cemetery
Higham Town FC
WHARF
Playgrd.
Rushden Town Indoor Bowls Club
Nene Valley Farm
Bowl. Grn.
Pav.
NORTHAMPTON RD.
B645
New Bridge Ski Lake
12
19
32
A
B
C
D
1
2
3
4
5
6
71
70
69
68
94
495

E
F
13
97
G
Hall Farm
H
98
71
1
2
3
4
5
6
NN9
A45
Redlands Farm
Hillstone Farm
HIGHAM ROAD
STANWICK ROAD
Glebe Farm
Chelveston Lodge
270
RUSHDEN AND HIGHAM FERRERS BY-PASS
A6
Rushden
NN10
Lancaster Farm
B645
CHELVESTON ROAD
Duchy Farm
New Buildings Farm
Club House
69
RUSHDEN GOLF COURSE
NEWTON ROAD
BOLTON ROAD
MIDLAND ROAD
Works
Warehouse
Bury Close
Lib.
The Ferrers Specialist Arts College
Sports Hall
68
33

22
A
B
C
D
1
2
3
4
5
6
INSET
BRIXWORTH
Northampton
NN6
PITSFORD
Pitsford School
The Poplars
Collyweston House
Nursery
Longman's Hill
Tennis Courts
Rec. Grd.
Pav.
Stone Quarry
Long Clump
Fox Covert Hall
Grotto Spinney
Brixworth Country Park
Visitor Centre
HARBOROUGH ROAD
A508
Brickhill Spinney
Little Brickhill Spinney
Butcher's Spinney
BOUGHTON PARK
Cricket Grd.
Park Cottages
Hawking Lodge
Boughton House & Gardens
Weldon House
BOUGHTON
Playing Field
Boughton Prim. Sch.
Recreation Ground
NN2
Nursery Wood
Obelisk Spinney
Sports Ground
Ten. Cts.
The Obelisk Centre
Devonshire Obelisk
Boughton Grange
Grange Farm
Boughton Mill
BRAMPTON APARTMENTS
BRAMPTON COTTAGES
BRAMPTON VALLEY LA.
Rectory Farm
BRAMPTON LANE
Westview Farm
Kingsthorpe Bowling Club
Bowling Green
White Hills
Boughton Green
36
NORTH
MOULTON
SPRATTON ROAD
HOLCOT ROAD
HIGH STREET
CHURCH ST.
HUMFREY LANE
WYSE HOWARD
LYNTON AV.
TIVERTON AV.
OBELISK RISE
Comm. Cen. & Lib.
Sch.
Recycling Cen.
BRIXWORTH IND. EST.
BRIXWORTH HALL PARK

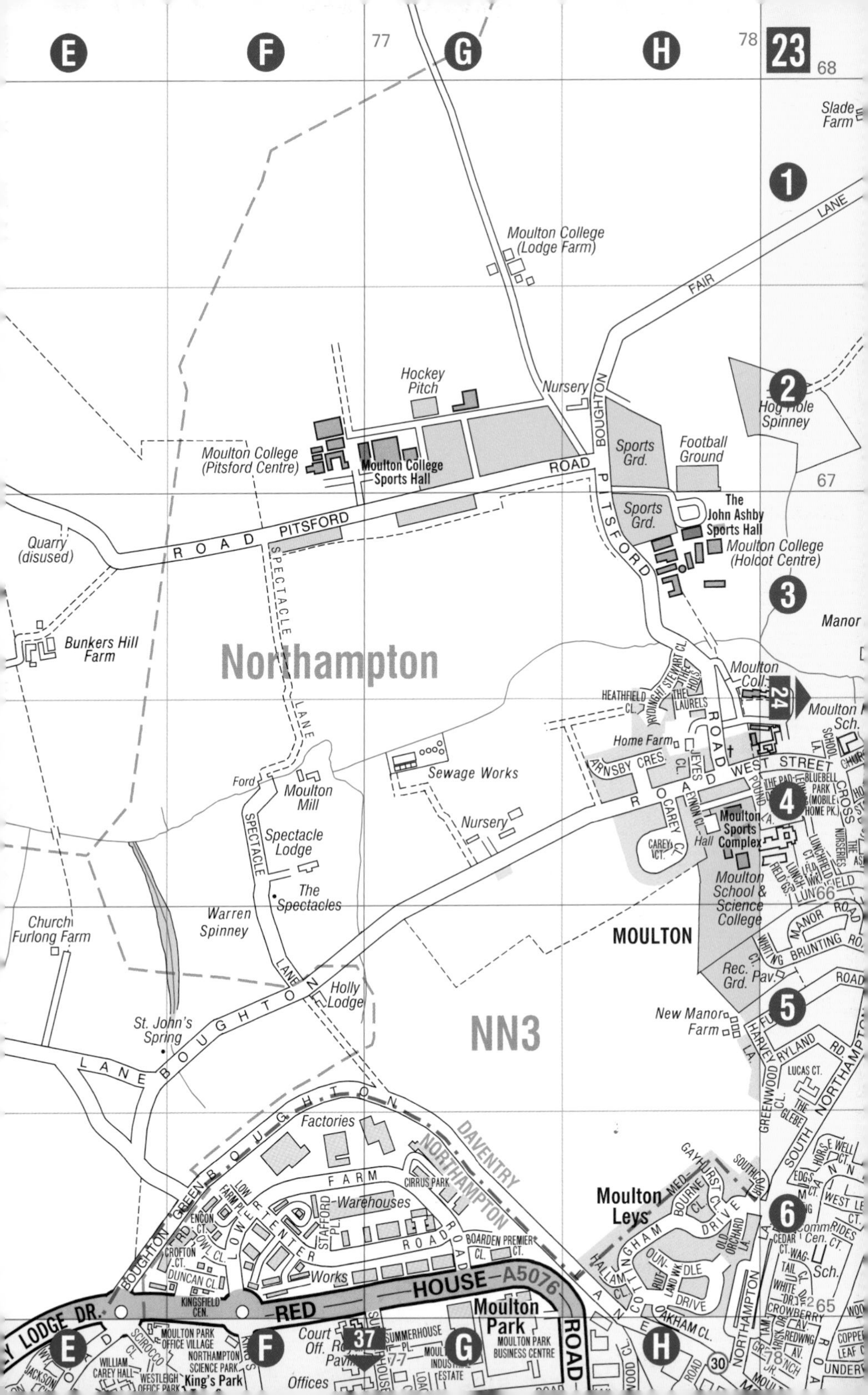
E
F
G
H
77
78
68
Slade Farm
Lane
Fair
Moulton College (Lodge Farm)
Hockey Pitch
Nursery
Boughton
Hog Hole Spinney
Moulton College (Pitsford Centre)
Moulton College Sports Hall
Road
Sports Grd.
Football Ground
67
Quarry (disused)
Pitsford
Road
Sports Grd.
The John Ashby Sports Hall
Moulton College (Holcot Centre)
Spectacle
Manor
Bunkers Hill Farm
Northampton
Moulton Coll.
Heathfield Cl.
The Laurels
Moulton Sch.
Home Farm
Arnsby Cres.
Jeyes Cl.
West Street
Sewage Works
Ford
Moulton Mill
Nursery
Moulton Sports Complex
Hall
Spectacle Lodge
The Spectacles
Carey Ct.
Carey Cl.
Moulton School & Science College
66
Church Furlong Farm
Warren Spinney
MOULTON
Manor Road
Brunting Ro.
Holly Lodge
Rec. Grd.
Pav.
Road
New Manor Farm
St. John's Spring
Boughton
NN3
Lane
Harvey La.
Ryland Rd.
Lucas Ct.
Greenwood Cl.
The Glebe
South
Northampton
Factories
Daventry
Northampton
Gayhurst Cl.
Farm
Cirrus Park
Moulton Leys
Warehouses
Boarden Cl.
Premier Ct.
Cedar Ct.
Crofton Ct.
Duncan Cl.
Works
Road
Red
House
A5076
Kingsfield Cen.
Moulton Park
Drive
Oakham Cl.
Lodge Dr.
Moulton Park Office Village
Northampton Science Park
Court Off.
Summerhouse
Moulton Park Business Centre
William Carey Hall
Westleigh Office Park
King's Park
Offices
Road
65
24
37
30

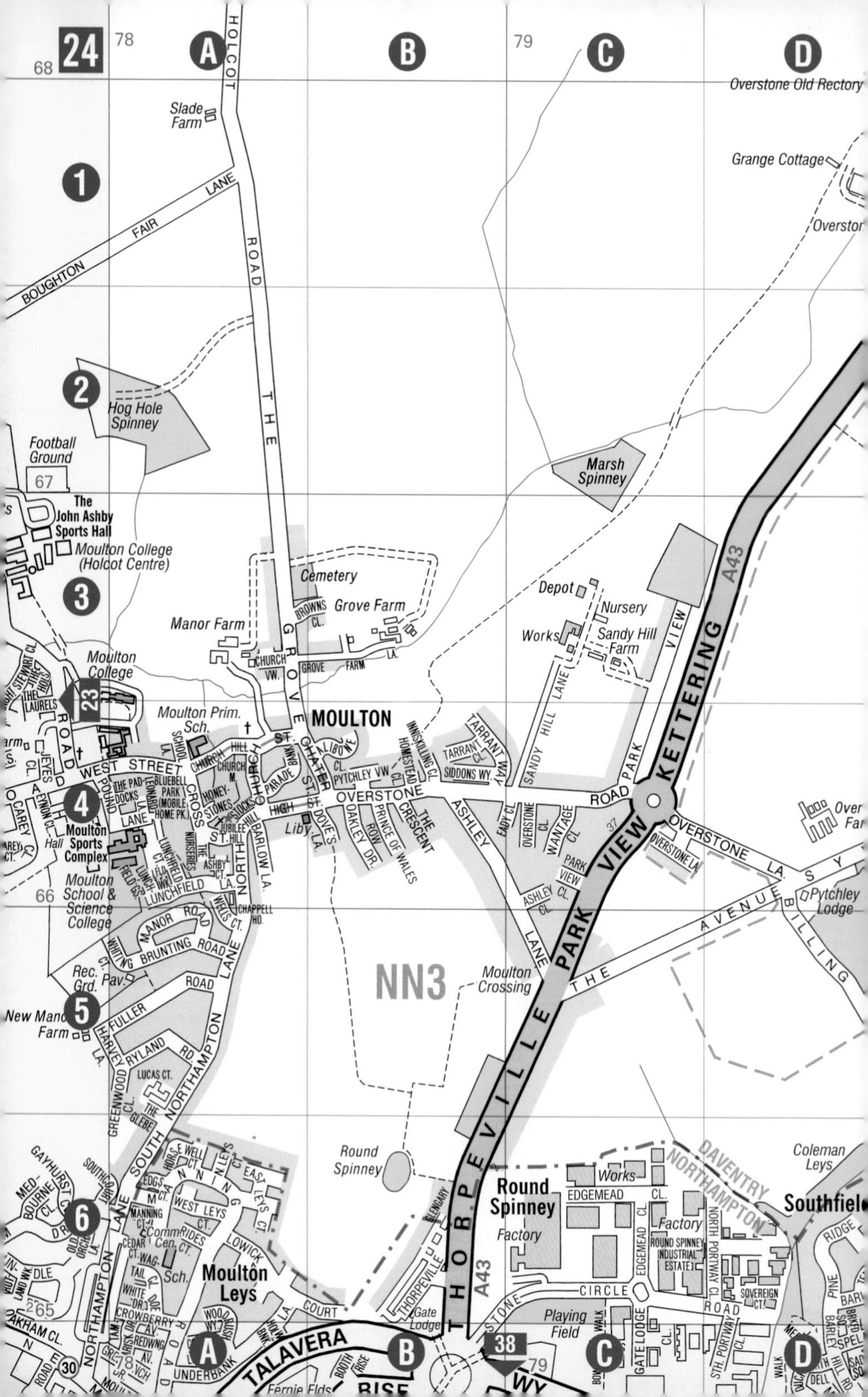

MOULTON
NN3
Moulton Leys
Round Spinney
Southfield
HOLCOT ROAD
THE GROVE
BOUGHTON FAIR LANE
KETTERING ROAD
THORPEVILLE
PARK VIEW
A43
TALAVERA
Hog Hole Spinney
Marsh Spinney
Slade Farm
Overstone Old Rectory
Grange Cottage
Football Ground
The John Ashby Sports Hall
Moulton College (Holcot Centre)
Moulton College
Cemetery
Grove Farm
Manor Farm
Depot
Nursery
Works
Sandy Hill Farm
Moulton Prim. Sch.
Moulton Sports Complex
Moulton School & Science College
Rec. Grd.
New Manor Farm
Moulton Crossing
Pytchley Lodge
Coleman Leys
Round Spinney
Factory
Playing Field
Gate Lodge
ROUND SPINNEY INDUSTRIAL ESTATE
DAVENTRY
NORTHAMPTON
WEST STREET
OVERSTONE ROAD
OVERSTONE LA.
THE AVENUE
BILLING
ASHLEY LANE
SANDY HILL LANE
NORTHAMPTON LANE SOUTH
NORTH
BRUNTING ROAD
MANOR ROAD
FULLER ROAD
RYLAND RD
EDGEMEAD CL.
CIRCLE
ROAD
WAGTAIL CL.

Rectory Farm
E
F
G
H
81
82
68
ROAD
A43
KETTERING ROAD
BELLMAN GA.
Industrial Estate
HOLCOT
1
Northampton
Rectory Farm
WEBBS
SYWELL
PALMER GRO.
STONELEA RD.
WESTLEA RD.
LANE
Park Pond
ROAD
2
Rec. Grd.
PIE CORNER
WELLINGBOROUGH
DAVENTRY
CHURCH LANE
The Rectory
Sports Grds.
OVERSTONE HGTS.
Sywell C of E Prim. Sch.
67
Spinney
Pav.
OVERSTONE
WOODFORD CHASE
PARK CL.
BREMBRIDGE CL.
ECTON
Bonfire Bank
3
Lavender Hill Farm
ROAD
Fox Covert
Ass Bank
Ferry Bank
26
New Pla
OVERSTONE
AVENUE
OVERSTONE CR.
WOODLAND
Highlands
Large Quarter
Overstone Prim. Sch.
NN6
Parson's Wood
Young Spinney
WOODSIDE
PINE
AVENUE
4
ASHDALE CL.
PINE CRES.
PARKLANDS
HIGHWOODS
Church Farm
66
Pond Spinney
Hayes Belt
OVERSTONE SOLARIUM RESIDENTIAL PARK
OVERSTONE PARK
Round Clump
5
Overstone Solarium
CHERRYTREE WK.
Hayes Lodge
KINGFISHER CT.
SYCAMORE DR.
Overstone Park Sch.
Overstone Park
Upper Pond
Warren Belt
Court Lodge
Court Ho.
CEDAR CL.
Ten. Cts.
Squash Cts.
TOWER COURT
Sports Field
WHISTLEFIELD COTTAGES
Club
ASH DRIVE
LANE
Pike Pond
Pondhead Spinney
LAKESIDE
Stone End Cottages
Icehouse Plantation
Ecton Belt
6
OVERSTONE PARK
GOLF COURSE
LUDLOW CL.
Ecton Field Plantation
Tennis Cts.
265
Bowling Green
Overstone Park
39
81
82
CRESCENT LODGE
FARMHILL
LANE
Ecton Belt

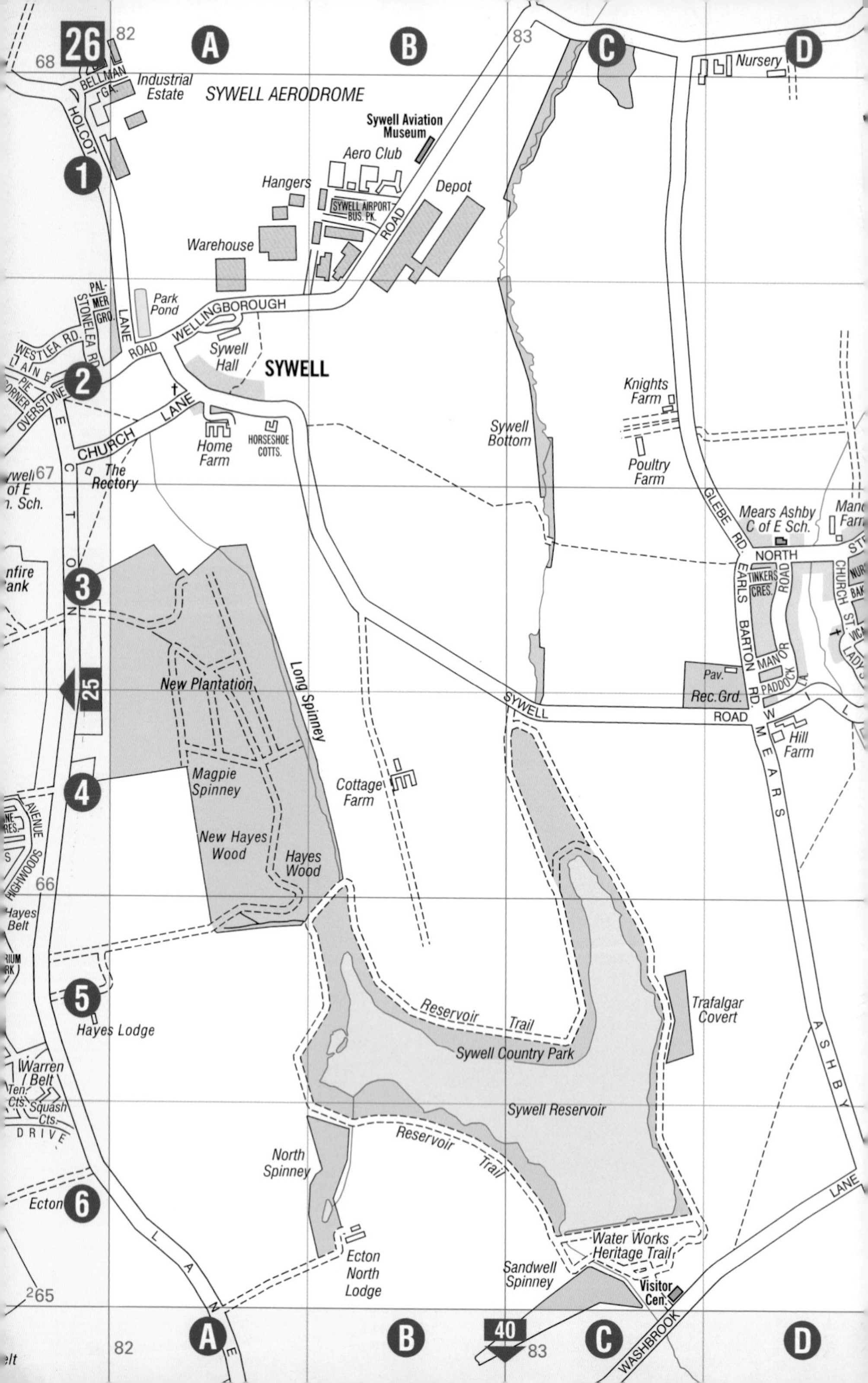

82
68

A **B** 83 **C** **D**

Nursery

Bellman
T.GA
Industrial
Estate
SYWELL AERODROME

HOLCOT

1

Sywell Aviation Museum

Aero Club

Hangers
SYWELL AIRPORT
BUS. PK.
Depot

Warehouse

ROAD

PAL-MER GRO.

Park Pond

LANE

STONELEA RD.

Knights Farm

WELLINGBOROUGH

ROAD

Sywell Hall

SYWELL

Sywell Bottom

Poultry Farm

WESTLEA RD.

TAIN

PIE

CORNER

OVERSTONE

2

STONE

CHURCH LANE

†

Home Farm

HORSESHOE COTTS.

Mears Ashby C of E Sch.

Mane Farm

ST

GLEBE RD.

well 67
of E
n. Sch.

The Rectory

NORTH

EARLS

TINKERS CRES.

CHURCH ST

VICAR

NURS

BAI

LADY

nfire
ank

3

MANOR

ROAD

New Plantation

Long Spinney

Sywell Bottom

Pav.
Rec. Grd.

PADDOCK

BARTON RD.

25

4

AVENUE

Magpie Spinney

Cottage Farm

SYWELL

ROAD

Hill Farm

MEARS

W

CRES.

New Hayes Wood

Hayes Wood

HIGHWOODS

66

ayes
Belt

RIUM
RK

5

Hayes Lodge

Reservoir   Trail

Sywell Country Park

Trafalgar Covert

Warren
Belt
en-
cts.
Squash
Cts.

D R I V E

North Spinney

Sywell Reservoir

ASHBY

6

Ecton

Reservoir   Trail

LANE

Ecton North Lodge

Water Works Heritage Trail

Sandwell Spinney

Visitor Cen.

265

A **B** 40 **C** **D**

82 83 WASHBROOK

E   F   485   G   H   86   **27**   68

Wilby Hall

The Rookery

Corrie's Spinney

PARK FARM
SOUTH

1

HUXLEY

RUTHERFORD

RYLE

RUTHERFORD

PARK IND

BOO

Wellingborough

NN8

Northampton

NN6

2   Cron
Spin

67

RS
BY

3

CHESS
END

Weir

R O A D   M E A R S   ASHBY   ROAD

Wilby
Spinney   Glebe
Barn

28

4

66

5

Field
Barn

Hockerhill
Farm

Wilby
Bridge

Brookhill
Ho.

Brookhill
Farm   ROAD

A4500   **6**

Sandpit
Barn   265

E   F   **41**   485   G   Main Road
Farm   MAIN   H   Quarry
(Dis.)   86

PARK FARM IND. EST.
DENCORA BUSINESS PARK
Health Club
PARK FARM SOUTH
Cromwell Spinney
PARK FARM WAY
A509
LONGFELLOW ROAD
BRICKHILL ROAD
Weavers Leisure Cen.
Olympic Prim. School
Comm. Centre
Jun. Sch.
Inf. Sch.
Rec. Grd.
Superstore
NORTHAMPTON ROAD
WILBY WAY
WILBY PARK MOBILE HOME PARK
Glebe Farm
MEARS ASHBY ROAD
Wilby C of E Prim. Sch.
The Farm
WILBY
A4500
Works
CHARLES PARTRIDGE CT.
MAIN ROAD
DODDINGTON ROAD
Wilby Bridge
Brookhill Ho.
Brookhill Farm
Sandpit Barn
Quarry (Dis.)
THROAT LANE
CUT
A45
WILBY LANE
Wellingborough FC

16
27
42

29
17
43
E
F
G
H
1
2
3
4
5
6
WELLINGBOROUGH
Wellingborough
NN8
NN29
OXFORD STREET
ROAD
CROYLAND ROAD
B571
BROADWAY
IRTHLINGBOROUGH RD.
B571
MIDLAND ROAD
B572
LONDON ROAD
A5193
30
Castle Fields
The Castle
Swanspool
Dale End Park
Croyland Park
Croyland Prim. Sch.
ISEBROOK HOSPITAL
Wellingborough School
Playing Field
Embankment Golf Course
Wellingborough Town Football Club
B573
ABBEY RD.
PRIORY ROAD
JUBILEE CRES.
Cemetery
DENINGTON INDUSTRIAL ESTATE
VICTORIA BUSINESS PARK
AMF Bowling
Superstore
A509
TURNELLS MILL LANE
HIGHAM RD.
MILL B573 LANE
TURNELLS RD.
A45
MILLERS PARK
Nene Wharf
River Nene Navigation
Weir
RIVER NENE
DODDINGTON ROAD
RIDGE
Poultry Farm
RIDGE GDS.
B573
THE STREET
GREAT DODDINGTON
GOODENS LANE
Pine Tree Farm
Warwick Primary Sch.
Wrenn Sch.
Friars Sch.
Croyland Hall
Tithe Barn
Fairlawn Cen.
Oxford Ho.
Bassett's Close
WESTFIELD ROAD
WINDSOR ROAD
BUTTS ROAD
VALLEY ROAD
SPUR RD.
489
490
265
66
67

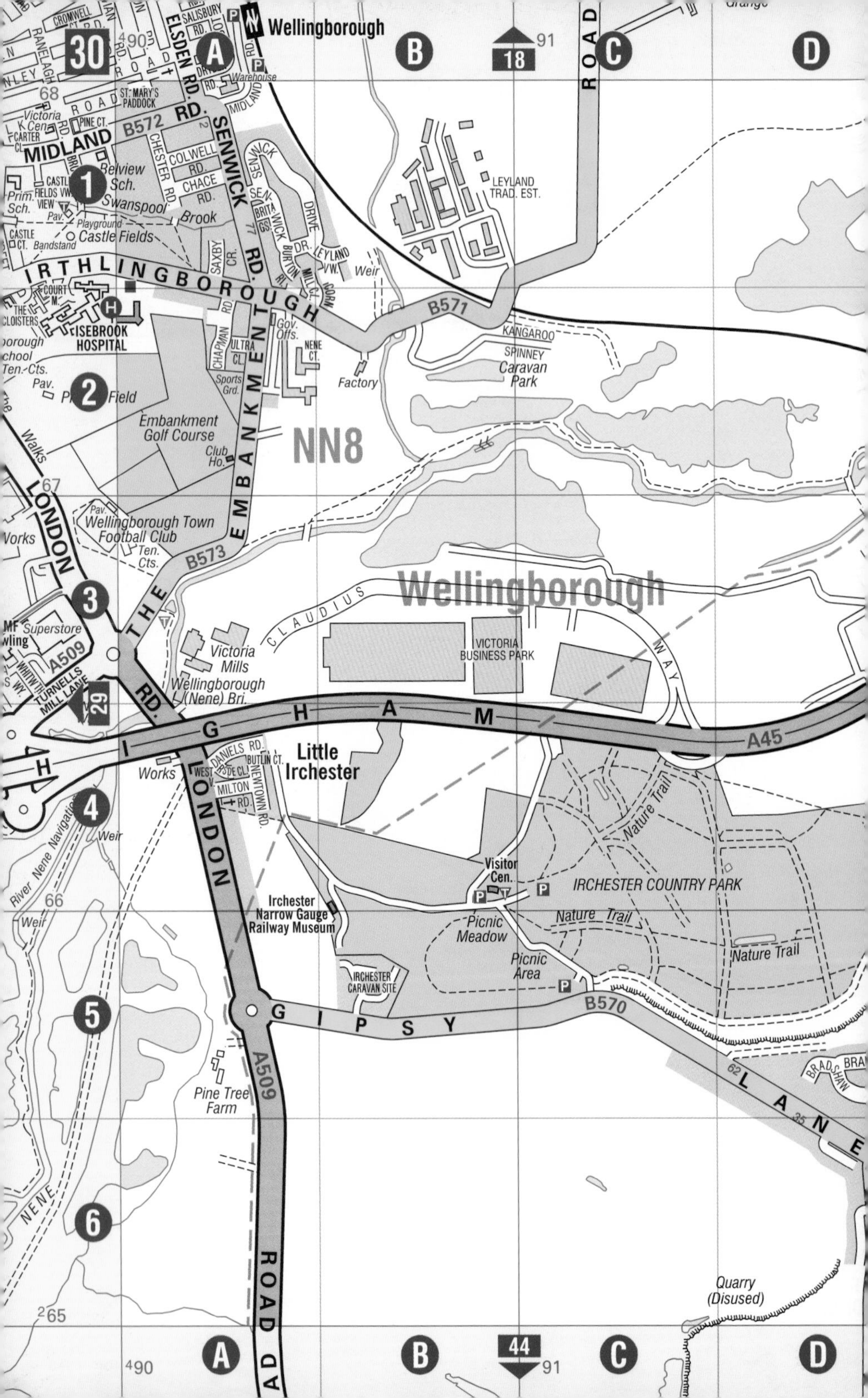
Wellingborough
A
B
C
D
18
91
490
MIDLAND RD.
B572
SENWICK RD.
IRTHLINGBOROUGH
B571
Belview Sch.
Swanspool Brook
Castle Fields
ISEBROOK HOSPITAL
LEYLAND TRAD. EST.
Weir
KANGAROO SPINNEY Caravan Park
Factory
Embankment Golf Course
NN8
THE EMBANKMENT
B573
Wellingborough Town Football Club
LONDON
Superstore
A509
TURNELLS MILL LANE
29
Wellingborough
CLAUDIUS WAY
VICTORIA BUSINESS PARK
Victoria Mills
Wellingborough (Nene) Bri.
HIGHAM
A45
Little Irchester
LONDON
River Nene Navigation
Visitor Cen.
IRCHESTER COUNTRY PARK
Nature Trail
Irchester Narrow Gauge Railway Museum
Picnic Meadow
Picnic Area
IRCHESTER CARAVAN SITE
GIPSY
B570
LANE
BRADSHAW
Pine Tree Farm
A509
NENE
ROAD
Quarry (Disused)
44
1
2
3
4
5
6
67
66
65
68

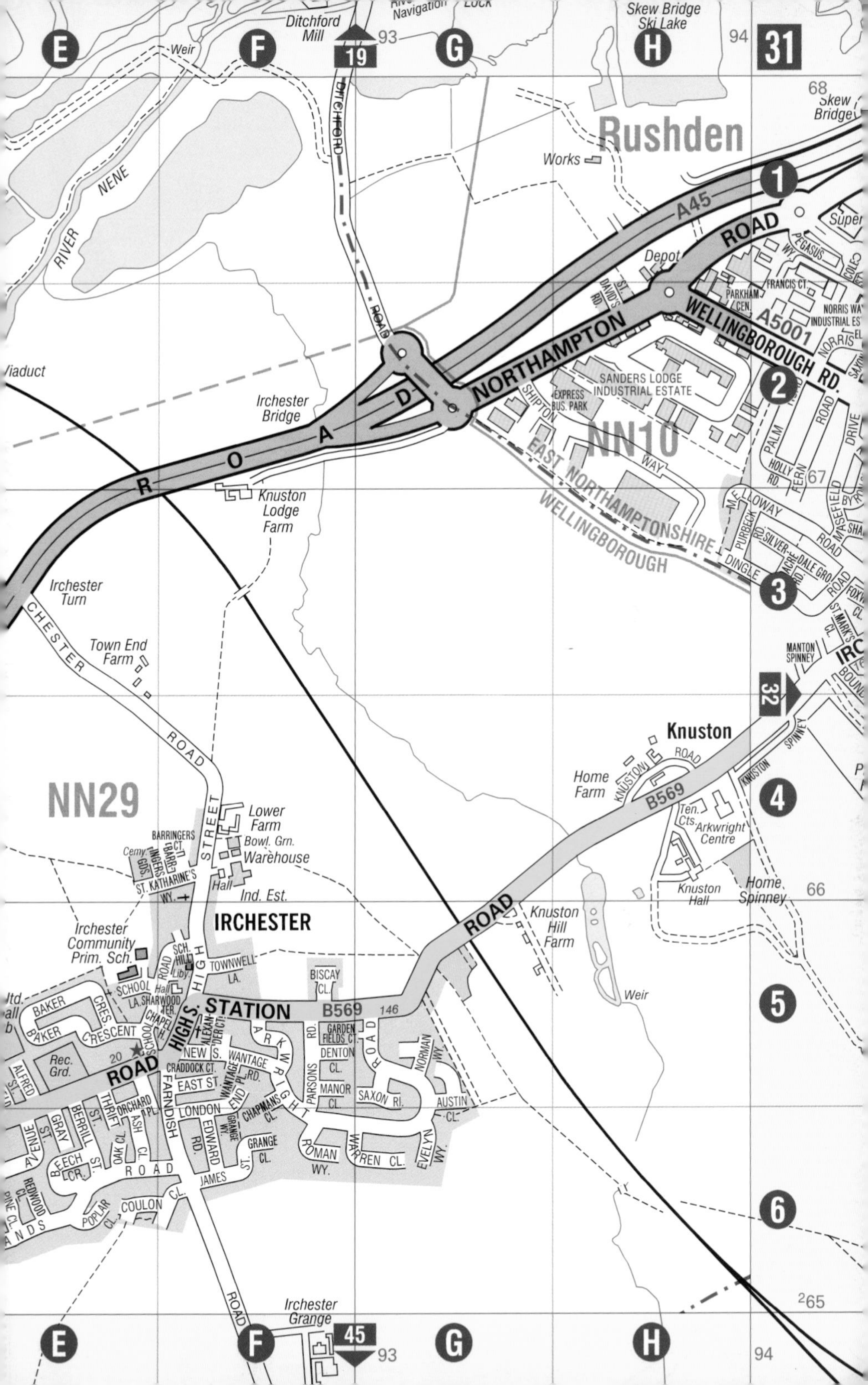
Ditchford Mill
Skew Bridge Ski Lake
Skew Bridge
Rushden
Works
Weir
RIVER NENE
DITCHFORD ROAD
A45
NORTHAMPTON ROAD
WELLINGBOROUGH RD.
A5001
Depot
PEGASUS WY.
FRANCIS CT.
PARKHAM CEN.
NORRIS WAY INDUSTRIAL EST.
SANDERS LODGE INDUSTRIAL ESTATE
EXPRESS BUS. PARK
SHIPTON WAY
NN10
EAST NORTHAMPTONSHIRE
WELLINGBOROUGH
Viaduct
Irchester Bridge
Knuston Lodge Farm
Irchester Turn
CHESTER ROAD
Town End Farm
MANTON SPINNEY
Knuston
KNUSTON ROAD
Home Farm
B569
Ten. Cts.
Arkwright Centre
Knuston Hall
Home Spinney
NN29
Lower Farm
Bowl. Grn.
Warehouse
Hall
Ind. Est.
IRCHESTER
BARRINGERS CT.
ST. KATHARINE'S WY.
Irchester Community Prim. Sch.
HIGH STREET
TOWNWELL LA.
BISCAY CL.
STATION ROAD
Knuston Hill Farm
Weir
BAKER CRES.
CRESCENT
SCHOOL LA.
SHARWOOD TER.
Rec. Grd.
ALFRED ST.
NEW S.
WANTAGE RD.
CRADDOCK CT.
EAST ST.
FARNDISH ROAD
ARKWRIGHT ROAD
GARDEN FIELDS CT.
DENTON CL.
PARSONS RD.
MANOR CL.
SAXON RI.
NORMAN WY.
AUSTIN CL.
THRIFT ST.
ORCHARD PL.
BERRILL ST.
GRAY ST.
AVENUE
LONDON RD.
EDWARD RD.
CHAPMANS CL.
GRANGE CL.
ROMAN WY.
WARREN CL.
EVELYN WY.
BEECH CR.
OAK CL.
ASH CL.
JAMES ST.
COULON CL.
POPLAR CL.
REDWOOD CL.
PINE CL.
Irchester Grange
E F G H
1 2 3 4 5 6
19 32 45
93 94
68 67 66 65

32
Rushden
NN10
Wellingborough
NN29
RUSHDEN
Knuston
Warmonds Hill
LITTLE WYMINGTON
NORTHAMPTON ROAD
WELLINGBOROUGH ROAD
IRCHESTER ROAD
WASHBROOK ROAD
HIGHAM ROAD
A45
A5001
A5028
B569
B645
Skew Bridge
Superstore
Playing Field
The Moors
Works
The Rushden Comm. Coll.
Recreation Ground
Splash Leisure Pool
The Pemberton Cen.
Rushden Hall
Hall Park
Knuston High Farm
Home Spinney
Arkwright Centre
Whitefriars Jun. & Inf. Schs.
South End Jun. Sch.
WELLINGBOROUGH
BEDFORD
EAST NORTHANTS

The Ferrers Specialist College
Sports Hall
RUSHDEN WAY
A5001
CLARK
A6
HIGHAM AND FERRERS BY-PASS
NEWTON ROAD
High Hayden Farm
Nursery
Knights Farm
Lodge Farm
Rectory Farm
Eastfields Farm
Cemetery
Spts. Grd.
Football Grd.
Jubilee Park
BEDFORD ROAD
A5028
Rushden & Higham RUFC (Manor Park)
Club
JOHN WHITE GOLF COURSE
HAYDEN ROAD
TRAFFORD ROAD
GRAFTON ROAD
OVAL RD.
HARBOROUGH RD.
BARRINGTON
SPRINGFIELD
QUEEN ST.
UPPER QUEEN ST.
ALEXANDRA RD.
97
98
68
67
66
65
21

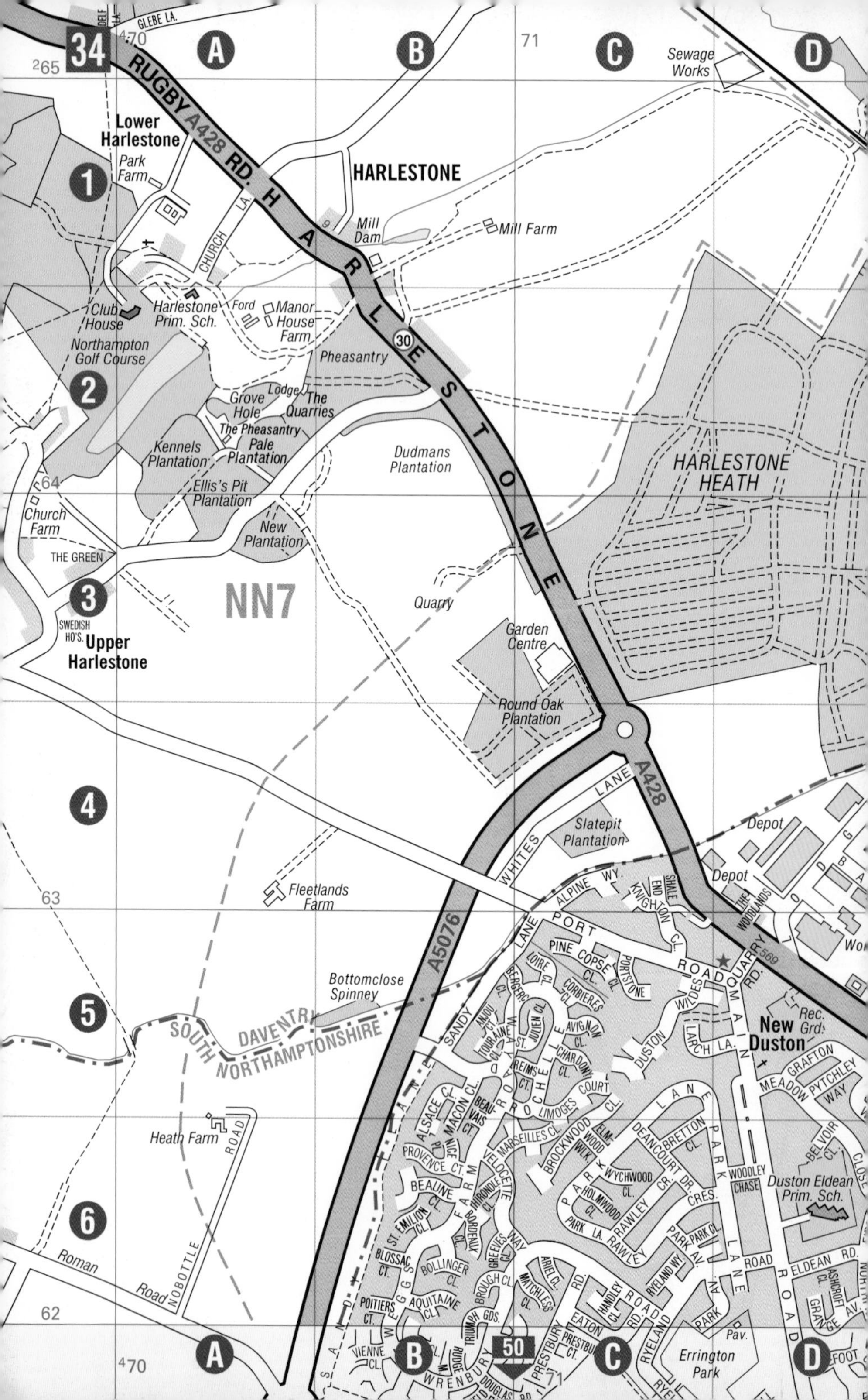
RUGBY A428 RD.
HARLESTONE
Lower Harlestone
Park Farm
HARLESTONE
CHURCH LA.
Mill Dam
Mill Farm
Sewage Works
Club House
Harlestone Prim. Sch.
Ford
Manor House Farm
Northampton Golf Course
Pheasantry
Lodge
Grove Hole
The Quarries
The Pheasantry
Pale Plantation
Kennels Plantation
Ellis's Pit Plantation
Dudmans Plantation
HARLESTONE HEATH
Church Farm
New Plantation
THE GREEN
NN7
Quarry
SWEDISH HO'S.
Upper Harlestone
Garden Centre
Round Oak Plantation
A428
WHITES LANE
Slatepit Plantation
Depot
Fleetlands Farm
A5076
PORT LANE
ALPINE WY.
KNIGHTON CL.
SHALE END
THE WOODLANDS
QUARRY RD.
ROAD
MAIN
PINE COPSE CL.
PORTSTONE
Bottomclose Spinney
SOUTH NORTHAMPTONSHIRE
DAVENTRY
New Duston
Rec. Grd.
LARCH LA.
DUSTON WILDES
GRAFTON
MEADOW
PYTCHLEY WAY
Heath Farm
ROAD
NOBOTTLE
Roman Road
BELVOIR CL.
Duston Eldean Prim. Sch.
WOODLEY CHASE
ELDEAN RD.
ASHCROFT CL.
GRANGE AV.
Errington Park
Pav.
50
A
B
C
D
1
2
3
4
5
6
470
71
265
64
63
62
569

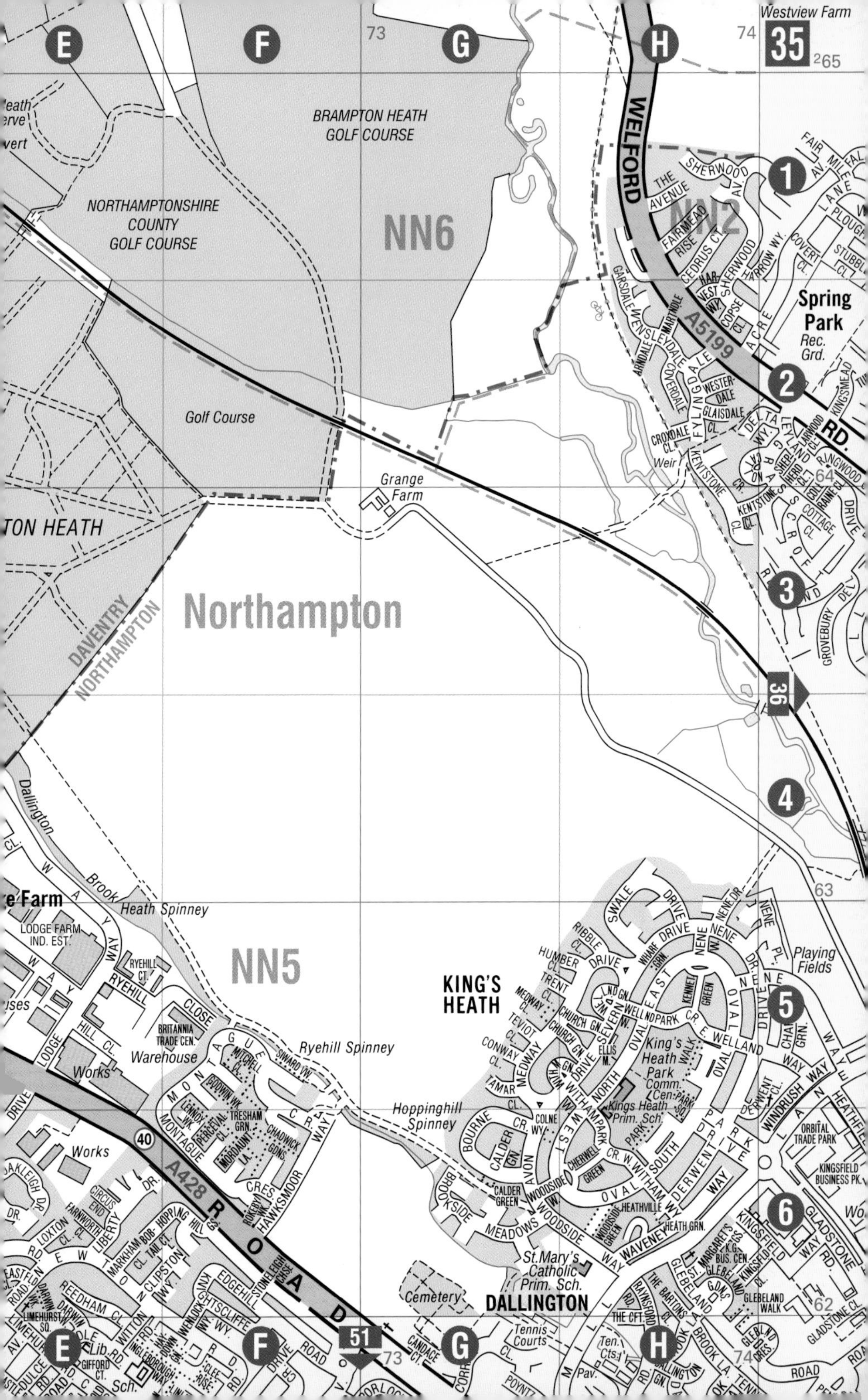
Westview Farm
BRAMPTON HEATH GOLF COURSE
NORTHAMPTONSHIRE COUNTY GOLF COURSE
NN6
Golf Course
Grange Farm
NN2
WELFORD RD.
A5199
Spring Park
Rec. Grd.
Northampton
DAVENTRY
NORTHAMPTON
Dallington Brook
Heath Spinney
LODGE FARM IND. EST.
NN5
KING'S HEATH
King's Heath Park Comm. Cen.
Kings Heath Prim. Sch.
Ryehill Spinney
Hoppinghill Spinney
BRITANNIA TRADE CEN.
Warehouse
Works
A428 ROAD
Playing Fields
ORBITAL TRADE PARK
KINGSFIELD BUSINESS PK.
K.G. BUS. CEN.
St.Mary's Catholic Prim. Sch.
Cemetery
DALLINGTON
Tennis Courts
Weir
36
51
40

Westview Farm
White Hills
Boughton Green
Spring Park
Hill Top
NN2
NN5
Kingsthorpe Mdws. Nature Reserve
Queens Park
KINGSTHORPE HOLLOW
Northgate School Arts College
Malcolm Arnold Academy
University of Northampton (Avenue Campus)
Kingsthorpe Cemetery
Northampton & District Indoor Bowling Association
Kingsthorpe Village Primary School

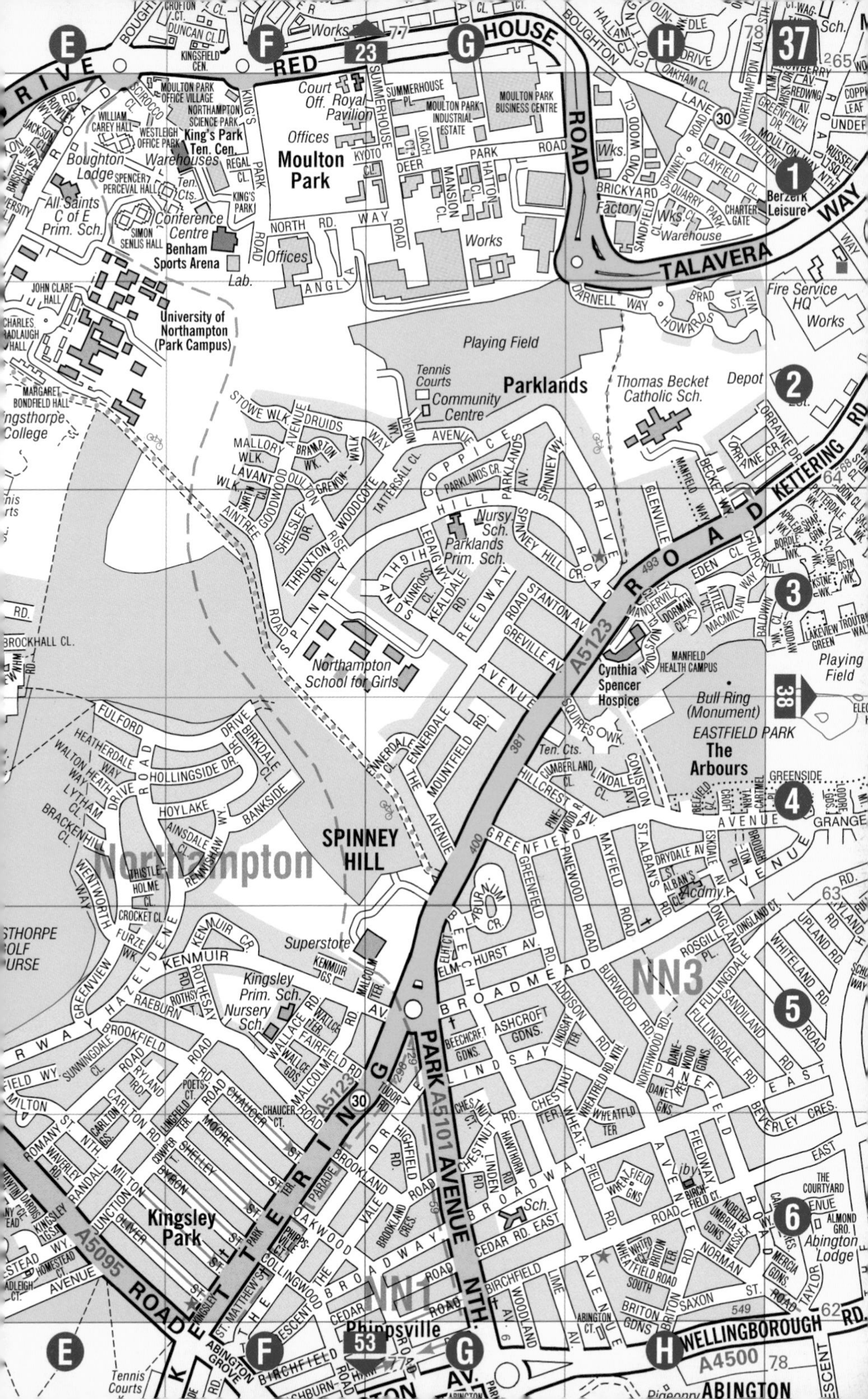
37
E
F
G
H
1
2
3
4
5
6
23
38
53
RED HOUSE ROAD
DRIVE
Moulton Park
Court
Off. Royal Pavilion
Offices
SUMMERHOUSE ROAD
SUMMERHOUSE PL.
MOULTON PARK INDUSTRIAL ESTATE
MOULTON PARK BUSINESS CENTRE
MOULTON PARK OFFICE VILLAGE
NORTHAMPTON SCIENCE PARK
WESTLEIGH OFFICE PARK
King's Park Ten. Cen.
Warehouses
KING'S PARK ROAD
REGAL CL.
KYOTO CL.
DEER PARK ROAD
LOACH CT.
MANSION CL.
HATTON CL.
NORTH RD.
WAY
ANGLIA WAY
Works
Offices
Lab.
Boughton Lodge
WILLIAM CAREY HALL
SPENCER PERCEVAL HALL
All Saints C of E Prim. Sch.
Conference Centre
SIMON SENLIS HALL
Benham Sports Arena
JOHN CLARE HALL
CHARLES BRADLAUGH HALL
MARGARET BONDFIELD HALL
University of Northampton (Park Campus)
Kingsthorpe College
SCIROCCO CL.
KINGSFIELD CEN.
DUNCAN CL.
CROFTON CT.
Wks.
POND WOOD CL.
BRICKYARD
Factory
Wks.
Warehouse
SANDFIELD CL.
QUARRY PARK
CHARTER GATE
SPINNEY
CLAYFIELD CL.
OAKHAM CL.
MOULTON LANE
NORTHAMPTON LANE
MOULTON WAY NTH.
Berzerk Leisure
TALAVERA WAY
BOUGHTON
HALLAM CL.
DARNELL WAY
BRAD ST.
HOWARDS
Fire Service HQ
Works
Playing Field
Tennis Courts
Community Centre
Parklands
Thomas Becket Catholic Sch.
Depot
LORRAINE DR.
LORRAINE CR.
BECKET WY.
MANFIELD WAY
GLENVILLE
KETTERING ROAD
STOWE WLK.
DRUIDS
MALLORY WLK.
LAVANT WLK.
BRAMPTON WK.
GRENON WALK
AINTREE
GOODWOOD
SHELSLEY DR.
THRUXTON DR.
WOODCOTE
TATTERSALL CL.
COPPICE
PARKLANDS CR.
PARKLANDS AV.
SPINNEY WY.
SPINNEY HILL CR.
HILL
Nursy. Sch.
Parklands Prim. Sch.
HIGHLANDS
LEDAIG WY.
KINROSS CL.
KEALDALE RD.
REEDWAY
STANTON AV.
GREVILLE AV.
SPINNEY HILL ROAD
Northampton School for Girls
A5123
493
EDEN CL.
CHURCHILL
ATTLEE CL.
MACMILLAN WAY
MANDERVILLE
DORMAN CL.
WOOLSTON
Cynthia Spencer Hospice
MANFIELD HEALTH CAMPUS
Bull Ring (Monument)
EASTFIELD PARK
The Arbours
Playing Field
LAKEVIEW GREEN
TROUTBECK
SQUIRES WK.
Ten. Cts.
CUMBERLAND CL.
LINDALE CL.
CONISTON AV.
GREENSIDE
AVENUE
GRANGE
HILLCREST AV.
PINE WOOD
GREENFIELD
PINEWOOD
MAYFIELD ROAD
ST. ALBAN'S RD.
DRYDALE AV.
ESKDALE AV.
Acdmy.
LONGLAND RD.
ROSGILL PL.
WHITELAND RD.
UPLAND RD.
FULLINGDALE RD.
SANDILAND ROAD
NN3
FULFORD DRIVE
HEATHERDALE WAY
WALTON HEATH WAY
LYTHAM CL.
BRACKENHILL CL.
HOLLINGSIDE DR.
BIRKDALE CL.
HOYLAKE
BANKSIDE
AINSDALE CL.
RENNISHAW WY.
Northampton
THISTLE HOLME CL.
WENTWORTH WAY
CROCKET CL.
SPINNEY HILL
ENNERDALE
MOUNTFIELD RD.
THE AVENUE
381
400
KINGSTHORPE GOLF COURSE
FURZE WK.
KENMUIR CR.
KENMUIR
ROTHESAY
Superstore
KENMUIR GS.
MALCOLM TER.
Kingsley Prim. Sch.
Nursery Sch.
WALLACE RD.
FAIRFIELD RD.
MALCOLM RD.
RAEBURN
BROOKFIELD ROAD
SUNNINGDALE CL.
GREENVIEW
HAZELDENE
LABURNUM CR.
BEECH
ELM
HURST AV.
BROADMEAD
ADDISON
BURWOOD RD.
NORTHWOOD RD.
DANEWOOD GDNS.
DANEFIELD
ASHCROFT GDNS.
BEECHCRFT GDNS.
LINDSAY
KETTERING
PARK A5101 AVENUE NTH.
A5123
30
CHAUCER CT.
CHAUCER
POETS CT.
RYLAND
CARLTON RD.
MILTON
ROMANY
WAVERLEY RD.
RANDALL
JUNCTION
OLIVER
MOORE
SHELLEY
BYRON
COWPER
LINGFIELD TER.
Kingsley Park
A5095 ROAD
AVENUE
HOMESTEAD WY.
Tennis Courts
ABINGTON GROVE
TUDOR
BROOKLAND
HIGHFIELD RD.
VALE
BROOKLAND CRES.
OAKWOOD
COLLINGWOOD
BROADWAY
ROAD
CHESTNUT RD.
HAWTHORN RD.
LINDEN
CHESTNUT TER.
WHEATFIELD RD. NTH.
WHEATFLD TER.
WHEATFIELD GNS.
Sch.
CEDAR RD. EAST
BIRCHFIELD
WOODLAND AV.
LIME AV.
ABINGTON CT.
BRITON GDNS.
SAXON ST.
NORMAN
WHEATFIELD ROAD SOUTH
FIELDWAY
BIRCHFIELD CT.
NORTHUMBRIA GDNS.
WESSEX WY.
MERCIA GDNS.
THE COURTYARD
ALMOND GRO.
Abington Lodge
TAYLOR
BEVERLEY CRES.
EAST
NN1
Phippsville
CEDAR
ST. MATTHEW'S
WELLINGBOROUGH RD.
A4500
549
ABINGTON
BIRCHFIELD
78
62
63
64
65

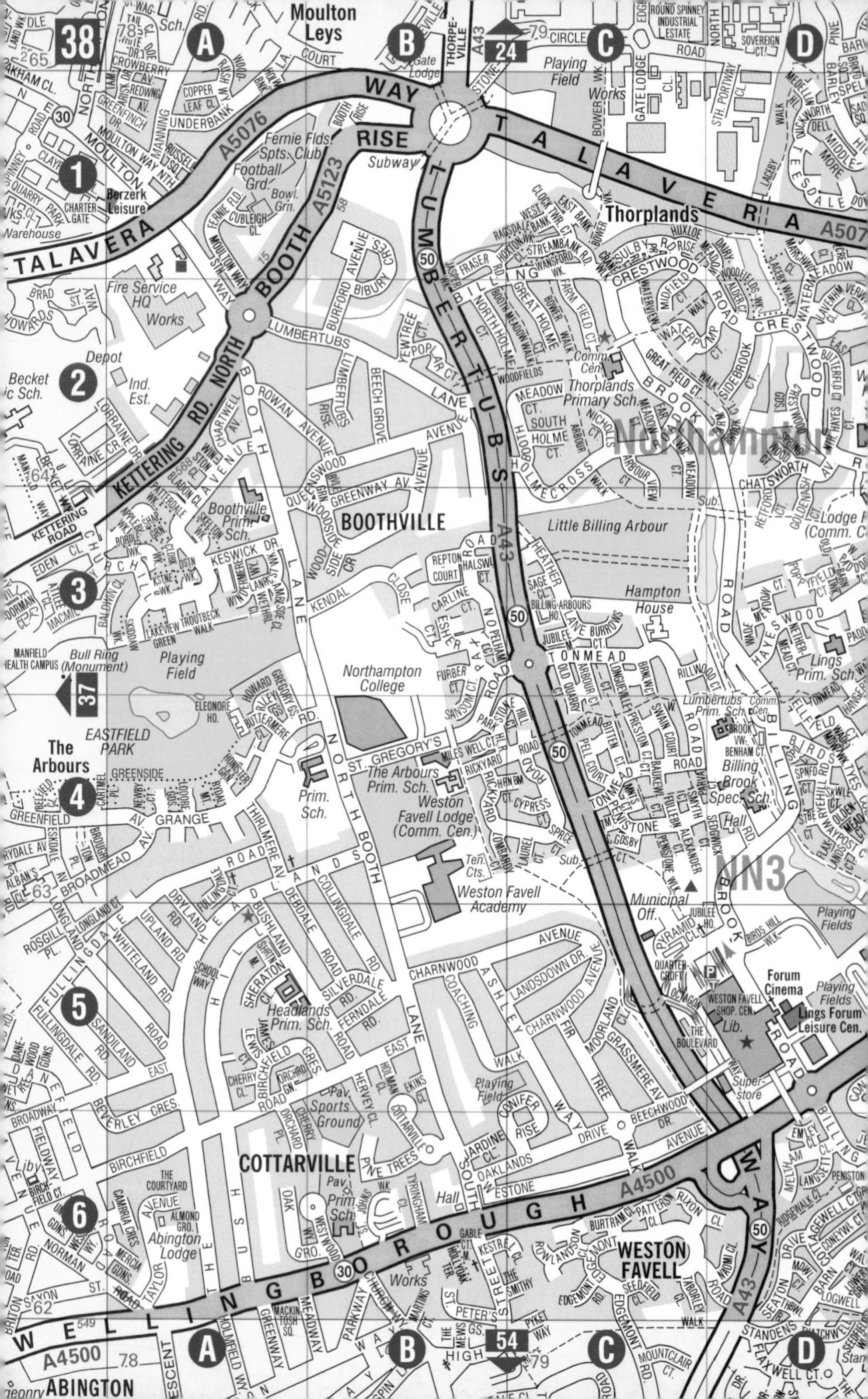
38
A
B
C
D
1
2
3
4
5
6
24
37
54
Moulton Leys
THORPEVILLE
Gate Lodge
CIRCLE
ROUND SPINNEY INDUSTRIAL ESTATE
SOVEREIGN CT.
Playing Field
Works
TALAVERA WAY
A5076
A5123
A43
A4500
BOOTH RISE
Fernie Flds. Spts. Club
Football Grd.
Bowl. Grn.
Subway
Berzerk Leisure
Warehouse
CHARTER GATE
MOULTON WAY NTH.
UNDERBANK
COPPER LEAF CL.
CROWBERRY AV.
REDWING AV.
GREENFINCH DR.
Thorplands
CRESTWOOD
HUXLOE RISE
MEADOW
WATERMEADOW
LACEBY
LUMBERTUBS WAY
LUMBERTUBS LANE
BOOTH LANE NORTH
KETTERING RD. NORTH
KETTERING ROAD
Fire Service HQ
Works
Depot
Ind. Est.
Becket
Sch.
LORRAINE CR.
LORRAINE DR.
BECKET WAY
BURFORD AVENUE
BIBURY CRES.
YEWTREE CT.
POPLAR CT.
LUMBERTUBS RISE
BEECH GROVE
ROWAN AVENUE
QUEENSWOOD AVENUE
GREENWAY AV.
WOODSIDE CR.
BOOTHVILLE
Boothville Prim. Sch.
KESWICK DR.
CHURCHILL AVENUE
EDEN CL.
Thorplands Primary Sch.
Comm. Cen.
WOODFIELDS
SOUTH HOLME CT.
HOLMECROSS WALK
BROOK ROAD
SIDEBROOK
GREAT FIELD CT.
Northampton
CHATSWORTH AV.
Lodge Farm (Comm. Cen.)
Little Billing Arbour
Hampton House
REPTON COURT
KENDAL CLOSE
CARLINE CT.
PAXTON ROAD
BILLING ARBOURS HO.
TONMEAD
JUBILEE CT.
HAYESWOOD ROAD
Lings Prim. Sch.
LAKEVIEW GREEN
TROUTBECK WALK
Playing Field
MANFIELD HEALTH CAMPUS
Bull Ring (Monument)
ELEONORE HO.
EASTFIELD PARK
The Arbours
GREENSIDE
GRANGE
Northampton College
ST. GREGORY'S RD.
Prim. Sch.
The Arbours Prim. Sch.
Weston Favell Lodge (Comm. Cen.)
Ten. Cts.
Weston Favell Academy
RICKYARD ROAD
CYPRESS CT.
Lumbertubs Prim. Sch.
Comm. Cen.
BENHAM CT.
Billing Brook Spec. Sch.
Hall
Municipal Off.
PENISTONE
ALEXANDER
NN3
BIRDS HILL WALK
Playing Fields
JUBILEE HO.
PYRAMID CL.
QUARTERCROFT
WESTON FAVELL SHOP. CEN.
Forum Cinema
Playing Fields
Lings Forum Leisure Cen.
Lib.
THE BOULEVARD
Super-store
BROADMEAD AV.
HEADLANDS
THIRLMERE AV.
DEBDALE ROAD
COLLINGDALE RD.
BUSHLAND
SHERATON CL.
Headlands Prim. Sch.
SILVERDALE RD.
FERNDALE RD.
CHARNWOOD AVENUE
LANDSDOWN DR.
COACHING WALK
ASHLEY WAY
MOORLAND CL.
GRASSMERE AV.
FIR TREE WALK
Playing Field
CONIFER RISE
BEECHWOOD DR.
OAKLANDS AVENUE
WESTONE
COTTARVILLE
Pav. Sports Ground
PINE TREES
JARDINE CL.
FULLINGDALE RD.
SANDILAND RD.
WHITELAND RD.
UPLAND RD.
ROSGILL PL.
BROADWAY
FIELDWAY
BEVERLEY CRES.
BIRCHFIELD ROAD EAST
THE COURTYARD
Abington Lodge
ALMOND RD.
NORMAN ST.
TAYLOR AVENUE
Liby.
Pav.
Prim. Sch.
WESTWOOD
Hall
Works
WELLINGBOROUGH ROAD
WESTON FAVELL
EDGEMONT RD.
SEEDFIELD CL.
TABORLEY WALK
STANDENS
FLAXWELL CT.
MOUNTCLAIR CT.
ST. PETER'S WAY
HIGH ST.
THE MEWS
MACKINTOSH SQ.
MEADWAY
GREENWAY
HOLMFIELD WY.
PARKWAY
ABINGTON
CRESCENT
BRITON
SAXON
RIDGEWALK CL.
PENISTON
COTTAGEWELL CT.
LOGWELL
SEATON
MELTHAM
EMLEY
30
50
65
64
63
62
78
79

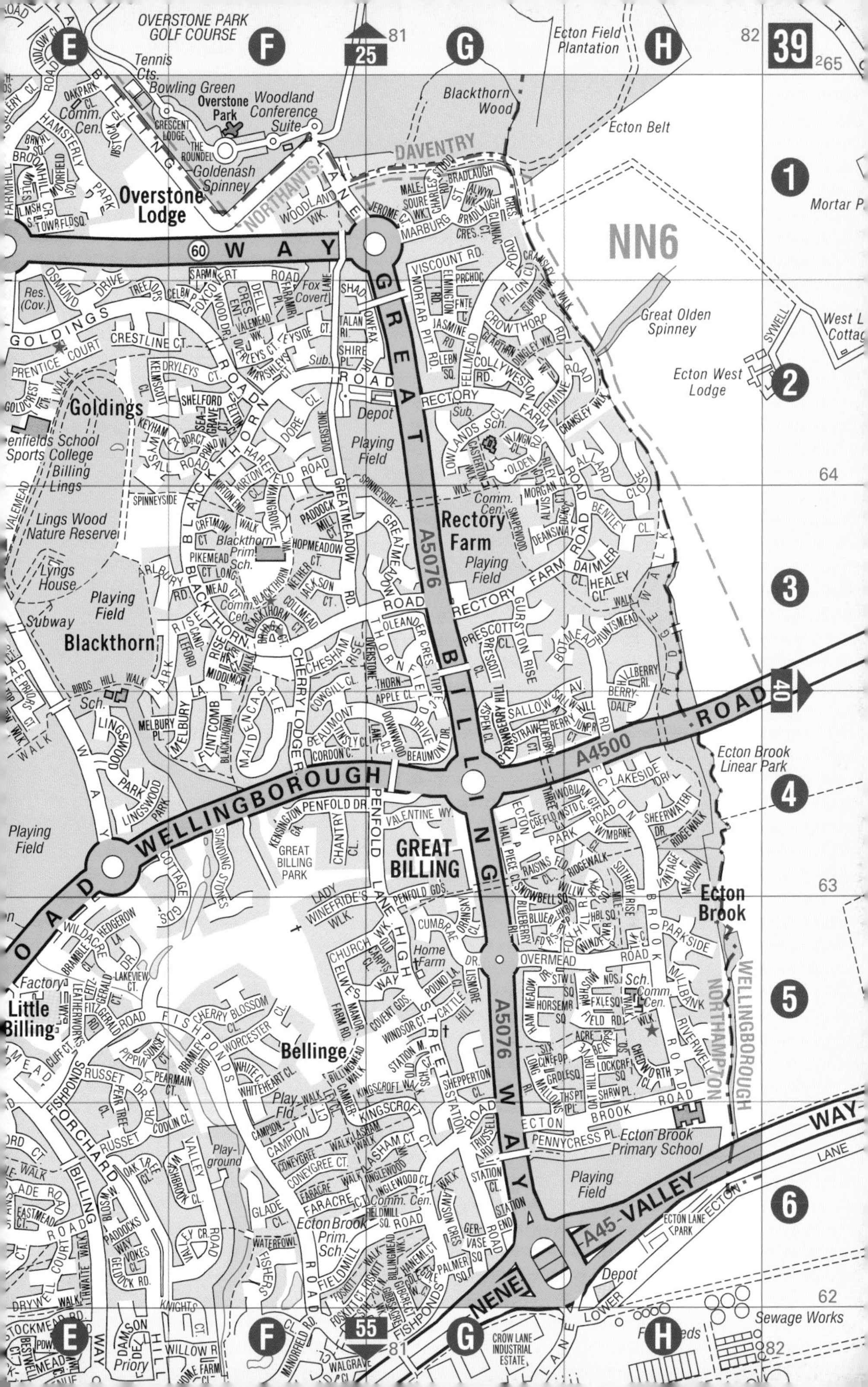

39
25
55
40
E
F
G
H
1
2
3
4
5
6
81
82
265
64
63
62
OVERSTONE PARK GOLF COURSE
Tennis Cts.
Bowling Green
Overstone Park
Woodland Conference Suite
Goldenash Spinney
Overstone Lodge
Ecton Field Plantation
Blackthorn Wood
Ecton Belt
DAVENTRY
NORTHANTS
LANE
NN6
Mortar P
Great Olden Spinney
Ecton West Lodge
West L Cottag
SYWELL
60
WAY
GREAT BILLING WAY
A5076
Goldings
Res. (Cov.)
GOLDINGS
CRESTLINE CT.
PRENTICE COURT
Weston Favell School Sports College
Billing Lings
Lings Wood Nature Reserve
Lyngs House
Playing Field
Subway
Blackthorn
Blackthorn Prim. Sch.
BLACKTHORN ROAD
Comm. Cen.
Depot
Playing Field
RECTORY ROAD
RECTORY FARM ROAD
Rectory Farm
Lowlands Sch.
Comm. Cen.
ERMINE ROAD
ALLARD CLOSE
BENTLEY CL.
DAIMLER CL.
HEALEY CL.
HUNTSMEAD
ROAD
A4500
Ecton Brook Linear Park
WELLINGBOROUGH
ROAD
GREAT BILLING
GREAT BILLING PARK
PENFOLD LANE
HIGH STREET
Home Farm
Bellinge
Little Billing
Factory
FISHPONDS ROAD
ORCHARD
BILLING
Play Fld.
Playground
Ecton Brook Prim. Sch.
Comm. Cen.
STATION ROAD
ECTON BROOK ROAD
Ecton Brook Primary School
Ecton Brook
Sch.
Comm. Cen.
Playing Field
WELLINGBOROUGH NORTHAMPTON
A45 VALLEY WAY
NENE
ECTON LANE PARK
LOWER ECTON LANE
Depot
Sewage Works
CROW LANE INDUSTRIAL ESTATE
Priory
WALGRAVE

Ecton North Lodge
Water Works Heritage Trail
Visitor Cen.
26
Sandwell Spinney
ECTON
LANE
Mortar Pits
Ecton East Lodge
Coppl Ba
Olden inney
SYWELL
West Lodge Cottages
LANE
WASHBROOK
Ecton W Lodg
Ash Spinney
Earls Barton Bridge
Football & Cricket Ground
Ecton Lodge
LANE
Dutch Walk
Nightingale Walk
BEECH
WELLINGBOROUGH
CHURCH VW.
WELLINGBOROUGH RD.
NORTHAMPTON RD.
The Clump
FRANKLINS CL.
Sch.
PARSONS CL.
AVENUE
A4500
SUNNYSIDE
THE COURTYARD
The Wilderness
CHURCH WY.
ECTON HALL
ECTON
HIGH
39
WEST
BARTON FLDS.
Ecton Brook Linear Park
THE LAURELS
Ryehill Spinney
Robersacks Spinney
Cricket Ground
STREET
RIDGEWALK
MEADOW
Blackthorn Spinney
Little Robersacks Spinney
PARKSIDE
Ecton Brook
MILLBANK
Crow Spinney
Long Ley Pond
RIVERWELL
ROAD
A45
NENE VALLEY WAY
LANE
Commander's Spinney
Brook School
ECTON
WELLINGBOROUGH
NORTHAMPTON
LOWER
ECTON LANE PARK
NN3
Beds

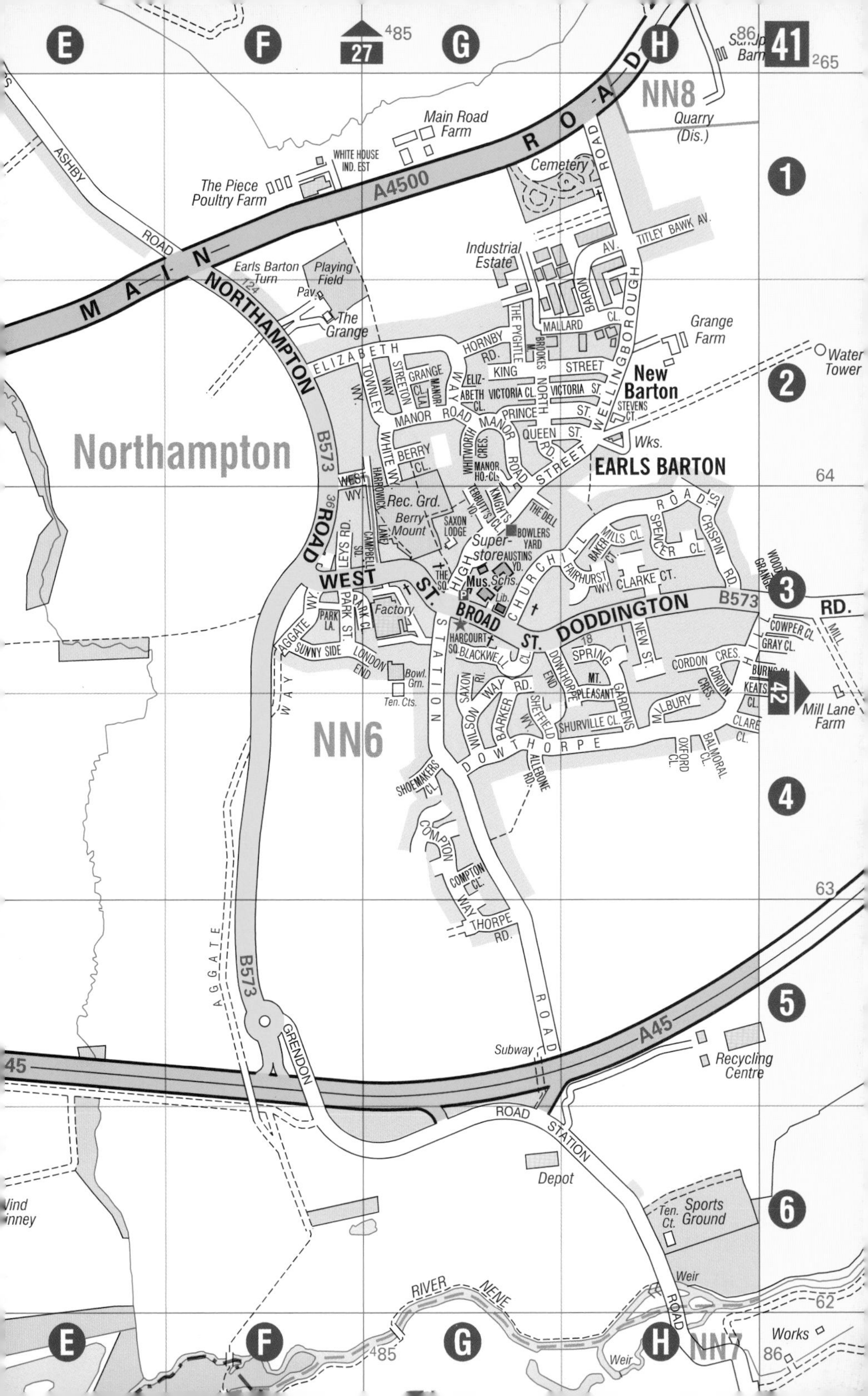

41
27
E
F
G
H
NN8
Main Road Farm
Quarry (Dis.)
WHITE HOUSE IND. EST
The Piece Poultry Farm
A4500
MAIN ROAD
Cemetery
ASHBY ROAD
Industrial Estate
TITLEY BAWK AV.
Earls Barton Turn
Playing Field
Pav.
The Grange
NORTHAMPTON ROAD
Grange Farm
Water Tower
New Barton
Northampton
B573
Wks.
EARLS BARTON
Rec. Grd.
Berry Mount
Super-store
Mus.
Schs.
Lib.
WEST ST.
BROAD ST.
DODDINGTON RD.
Factory
Bowl. Grn.
Ten. Cts.
Mill Lane Farm
42
NN6
STATION ROAD
AGGATE WAY
A45
Subway
Recycling Centre
GRENDON ROAD
Depot
Sports Ground
Ten. Ct.
Wind Spinney
Weir
RIVER NENE
NN7
Works

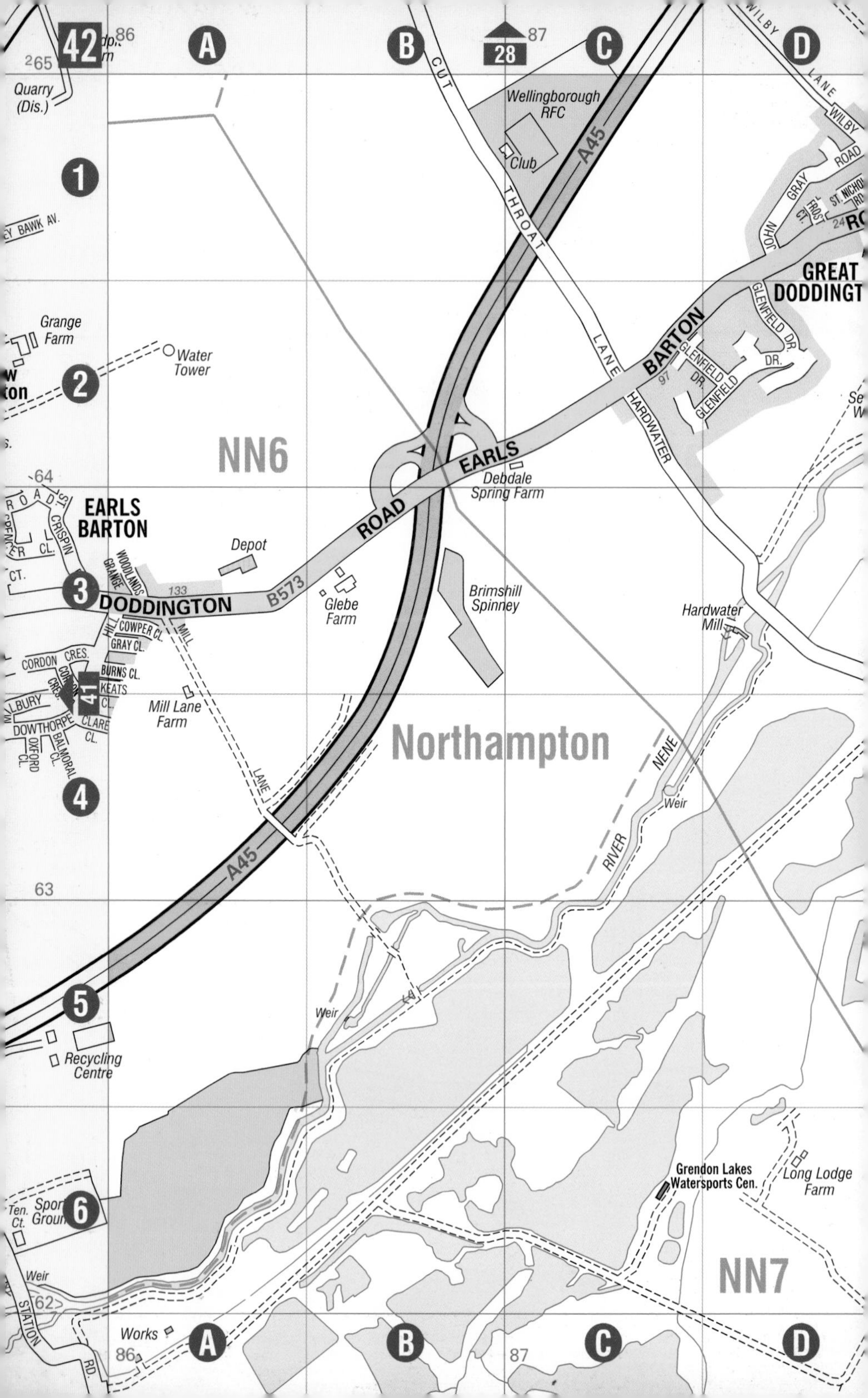

A
B
C
D
28
1
2
3
4
5
6
Quarry (Dis.)
Wellingborough RFC
Club
A45
CUT
THROAT
LANE
WILBY LANE
WILBY ROAD
GRAY
JOHN
FROST CT.
GREAT DODDINGTON
Grange Farm
Water Tower
BARTON
GLENFIELD DR.
GLENFIELD
HARDWATER
NN6
EARLS
ROAD
Debdale Spring Farm
EARLS BARTON
CRISPIN ST.
Depot
B573
DODDINGTON
Glebe Farm
Brimshill Spinney
Hardwater Mill
MILL
COWPER CL.
GRAY CL.
BURNS CL.
KEATS CL.
CLARE CL.
CORDON CRES.
DOWTHORPE
OXFORD CL.
BALMORAL CL.
Mill Lane Farm
Northampton
RIVER NENE
Weir
LANE
Recycling Centre
Grendon Lakes Watersports Cen.
Long Lodge Farm
Sports Ground
Ten. Ct.
NN7
STATION RD.
Works
86
87
63
64
62
133
97

E
F
G
H
29
89
490
265
GOODENS LANE
TOP FARM
THE
STREET
B573
Rec. Grd.
Top Fm.
Sch.
CHURCH LA.
50
12
Grove Farm
DOCTORS LA.
LOWER ST.
CHP. LA.
Wellingborough
Wollaston Mill
RIVER NENE
NN29
1
2
64
3
44
Summer Leys
Local Nature Reserve
Ryeholmes Bridge
Recycling Centre
4
Depots
DODDINGTON RD.
ROAD
63
Cringle House Farm
5
6
The Old Lodge
GRENDON
62
E
F
G
H
89
490

LONDON ROAD
30
Quarry (Disused)
WOLLASTON ROAD
B569
ROAD
Vicarage Farm
Abbey Farm
A509
Wellingborough
NN29
WELLINGBOROUGH ROAD
43
Fox Covert
Long Plantation
Recycling Centre
DODDINGTON ROAD
Depots
YORK
PRIORY RD.
LITTLE LA.
PROSPECT CL.
RED HILL CR.
LANCASTER CL.
NEALE CL.
UNITY CL.
ROSES CL.
FWS CL.
MANCHESTER
THE MALTINGS
DUCK END
ABBEY RI.
MONKS RD.
ORCHARD CL.
Cemy.
HICKMIRE
CHURCH VW.
CHURCH LA.
Wollaston Hall
Works
Water Tower
Tower Farm
TOWER CT.
COBB'S LANE
BELL END
FRANCIS DICKINS CL.
WOLLASTON
Mus.
IRCHESTER
SOUTH ST.
BACKWAY
EASTFIELD
GAP
Wks.
HOOKHAMS
Ten Ct.
Wollaston School
Ten Ct.
LONDON ROAD
COLLEGE STREET
Sch.
HOLYOAKE RD.
THE HTHS.
ROTTEN ROW
ST. MICHAEL'S LA.
QUEENS
THRIFT ST.
HIGH
NEWTON RD.
Lib.
HOWARD RD.
HOWARD'S CT.
STONE CL.
ROAD
PARK
WINDMILL CL.
MILL RI.
STREET
POPLAR PL.
PATH
GRANBY COURT
PEARSONS M.
HINWICK RD.
ST. MARYS RD.
GREEN ST.
THE GROVE
EAST FLD. CL.
ST. ALBANS PL.
HINWICK
RAYMOND CL.
WILLIAM'S WY.
WOLLASTON IND. EST.
Shepherds Hill Farm
SHEPHERDS HILL
DANDO CL.
PYGHTLES
BRIARWOOD WY.
HAZELDEN CL.
THE
B569 ROAD
176
Pavs.
Recreation Ground
Ten. Ct.
LONDON
Cottage Farm

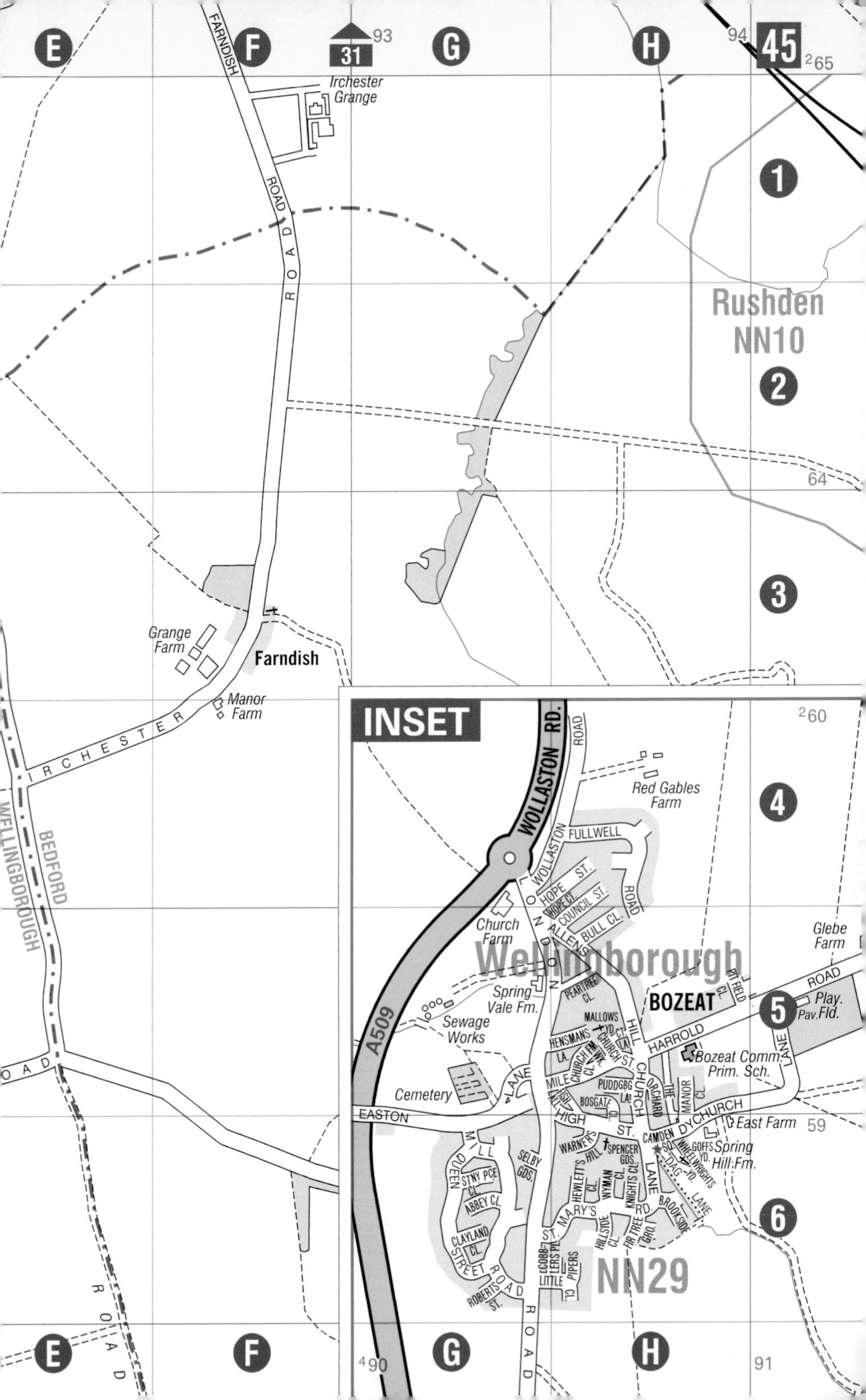

Irchester Grange
FARNDISH ROAD
Rushden NN10
Grange Farm
Farndish
Manor Farm
IRCHESTER ROAD
BEDFORD
WELLINGBOROUGH
INSET
WOLLASTON RD.
Red Gables Farm
FULLWELL
WOLLASTON ROAD
HOPE ST.
HOPE CT.
COUNCIL ST.
BULL CL.
ALLENS
LONDON ROAD
Church Farm
Wellingborough
Glebe Farm
Spring Vale Fm.
PEARTREE CL.
BOZEAT
PIT FIELD CL.
ROAD
Play. Fld.
Pav.
Sewage Works
A509
MALLOWS YD.
HENSMANS LA.
CHURCH ST.
CHURCH FM. WK.
HILL
HARROLD
Bozeat Comm. Prim. Sch.
LANE
Cemetery
MILE
PUDDGBG LA.
CHURCH
ORCHARD
THE
MANOR CL.
EASTON
BOSGATE
HIGH ST.
CAMDEN SQ.
DYCHURCH
East Farm
MILL
WARNERS HILL
SPENCER GDS.
GOFFS YD.
WHEELWRIGHTS
Spring Hill Fm.
QUEEN
STNY PCE CL.
SELBY GDS.
HEWLETT'S CL.
WYMAN CL.
KNIGHTS CL.
DAG YD.
ABBEY CL.
MARY'S RD.
BROOKSIDE
CLAYLAND CL.
STREET
ST.
COBBLERS PL.
HILLSIDE CL.
FIRTREE GRO.
LITTLE PIPERS CL.
NN29
ROBERTS ST.
ROAD
E
F
G
H
1
2
3
4
5
6
31
93
94
2 65
64
2 60
59
4 90
91

The Dial House
Canal Lower Belt
Skewbridge Spinney
Brooks's Plantation
Flore Fields Spinney
Greenway Spinney
M1 MOTORWAY
WATLING
Whilton Brook
Skew Bridge
Landing Spinney
Broamenthill Spinney
A5
Hobhill Spinney
Dodmoor Farm
Northampton
NN7
WEEDON LANE
Grand Union Canal
Reservoir
Hadland House Farm
HILLSIDE ROAD
Flore Hill Farm
Grange Farm
Globe Farm
A45
ORDNANCE ROAD
Dodford Wharf Farm
Weedon Junction
HIGH STREET
FLORE
Road Weedon
Depots
CAVALRY HILL IND. PK.
Depot
CAVALRY HILL
CAMPBELL CL.
CAVALRY FIELDS
EQUESTRIAN WY.
HARMANS WY.
REGENCY CL.
WINDSOR CL.
GLOUCESTER CL.
PRIEL RD.
LANCERS WY.
WEEDON BEC
FUSILIER WY.
TROOP WK.
THE OLD DEPOT
Dpt.
CHESTER TER.
THE CROFT CL.
ETON CL.
CROSSE CL.
BULL INN CL.
BRIDGE ST.
A5 STREET
River Nene
RIVERSIDE DR.
RIVERSIDE CT.
NENESIDE CL.
BROOKSIDE
WEST STREET
ROAD
KINGS PK.
Comm. Cen.
Sch.
MARTYNS WY.
MANOR RD.
Rec. Grd.
ST. PETER'S WY.
ST. MARY'S WY.
BUSWELL CL.
CHURCH ST.
SOUTH ST.
BILLING SCHOOL PL.
The Vicarage
Cemy.
Weedon Wharf
Sewage Works
QUEEN'S PK.
Upper Weedon
Lower Weedon
DUKELANDS
PRINCES CL.
TITHE RD.
NEW STREET
CROFT WAY
NEW CROFT
FARTHINGSTONE RD.
HOME FM. CL.
HOLM CL.
QUEEN
OAKLANDS
PRIORY CT.
A B C D
1 2 3 4 5 6
59 60 61 62 63

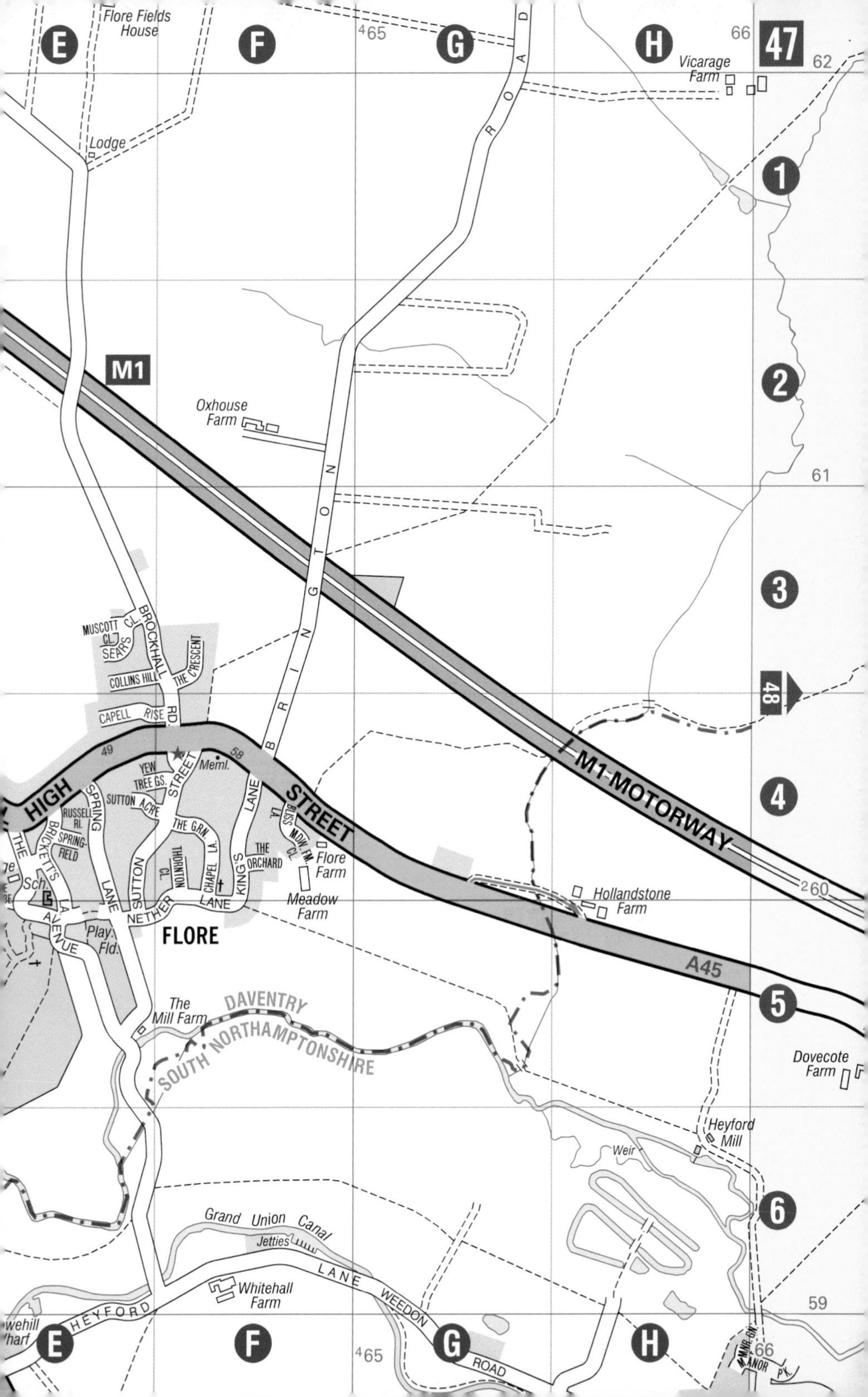
Flore Fields House
E
F
G
H
465
66
62
Vicarage Farm
Lodge
ROAD
1
2
3
4
5
6
M1
Oxhouse Farm
BRINGTON
61
48
MUSCOTT CL.
SEARS CL.
BROCKHALL
COLLINS HILL
THE CRESCENT
CAPELL RISE
RD.
HIGH STREET
49
58
Meml.
YEW TREE GS.
SUTTON ACRE
STREET
SPRING
RUSSELL RI.
SPRINGFIELD
BRICKETT'S LA.
THE GRN.
THORNTON CL.
CHAPEL LA.
KING'S LANE
THE ORCHARD
BLISS LA.
MDW. FM. CL.
Flore Farm
Meadow Farm
M1 MOTORWAY
260
Hollandstone Farm
Sch.
SUTTON LANE
NETHER LANE
AVENUE
Play. Fld.
FLORE
A45
The Mill Farm
DAVENTRY
SOUTH NORTHAMPTONSHIRE
Dovecote Farm
Heyford Mill
Weir
Grand Union Canal
Jetties
LANE
WEEDON
ROAD
Whitehall Farm
HEYFORD
wehill harf
59
MNR. GN.
MANOR PK.

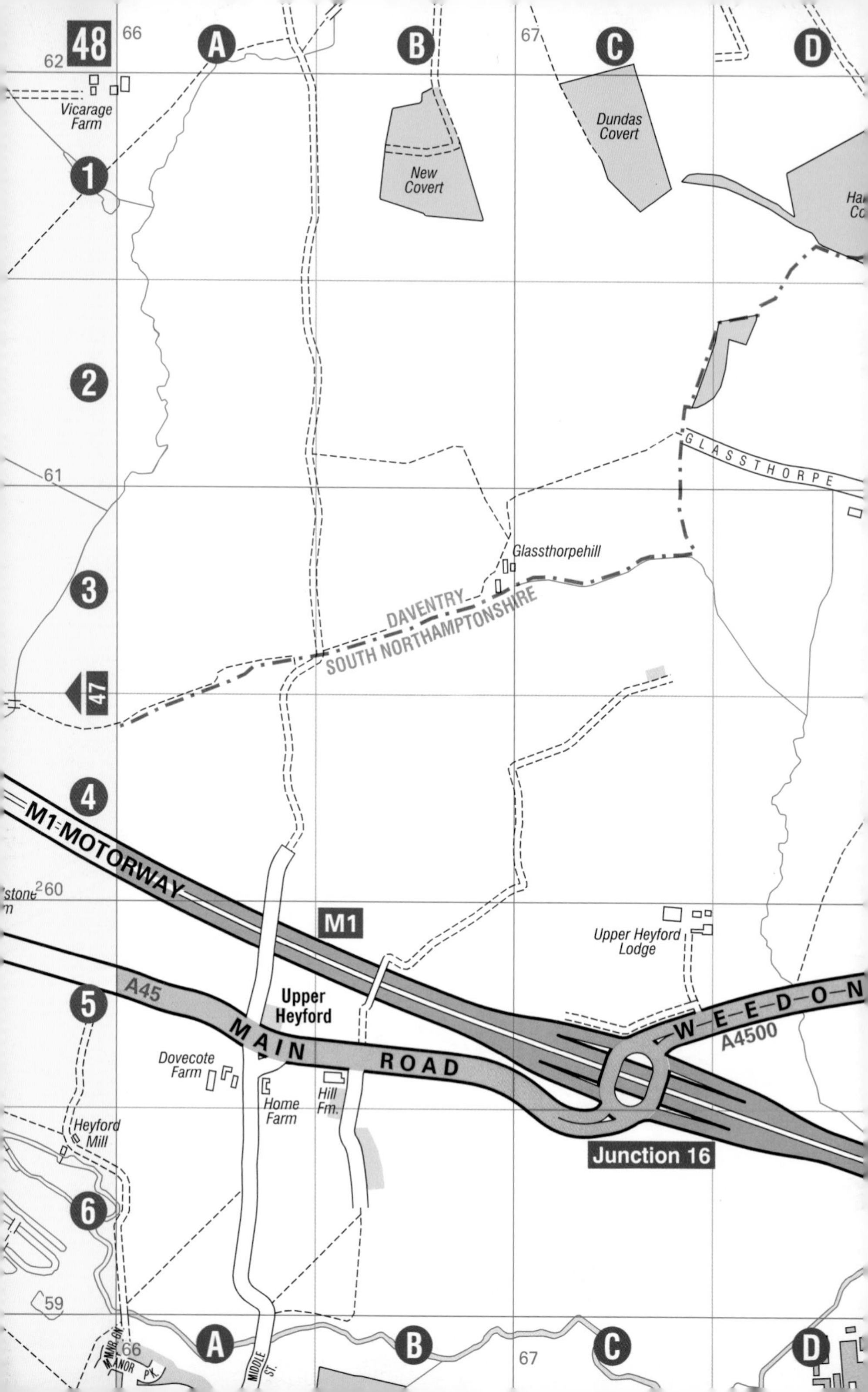
A
B
C
D
1
2
3
4
5
6
66
67
62
61
60
59
Vicarage Farm
New Covert
Dundas Covert
GLASSTHORPE
Glassthorpehill
DAVENTRY
SOUTH NORTHAMPTONSHIRE
47
M1 MOTORWAY
M1
Upper Heyford Lodge
A45
Upper Heyford
MAIN ROAD
WEEDON
A4500
Dovecote Farm
Home Farm
Hill Fm.
Heyford Mill
Junction 16
MIDDLE ST.
MANOR PK.

E
F
G
H
69
570
62
Roman Road
NOBOTT
Brices Spinney
Wood Farm
1
2
Northampton
NN7
Grange Farm
HIGH STREET
MOUNT PLEASANT
GARNERS
LARKHALL WY.
Church Farm
Hall
CORY GDS.
61
Recreation Ground
Tennis Cts.
Riding Hill Farm
SCHOOL LANE
UPPER HIGH ST.
LARKHALL WAY
CHESTER AV.
THE MOTTS
MANOR
ORCHARD WY.
CLOSE
LANE
SANDY LANE
Harpole Prim. School
Bowl. Green
Nursery
3
HALL CL.
Hall Farm
DUCK LA.
HIGH STREET
PARK LA.
CARR'S
SHEPHERDS WLK.
HARPOLE
The Lake
CARR'S WY.
NORTHAMPTON RD.
50
4
ROAD
SOUTH
W
A4500
BANBURY ROAD
260
RIVERSIDE CT.
ST.
5
KISLINGBURY
HIGH
HODGES LA.
Kislingbury Prim. Sch.
HALL CL.
BEECH LANE
CHURCH
STARMERS LA.
HIGH ST.
SCHOOL LA.
Club
THE ORCHARD
CHAPEL LA.
THE GREEN
LICHFIELD CL.
ROAD
MILL ROAD
WILLOW VW.
MILL LANE
Hall
CAMP LA.
CAMP
Hall Farm
6
WILLOW VIEW
NENE WAY
ROAD
LANE
WATTS CL.
ROTHERSTHORPE ROAD
DUKES GREEN RD.
ASHBY CT.
M1 MOTORWAY
M1
TWIGDEN RD.
Hall
59
BUGBROOKE
Wks.
MILLER'S CL.
570

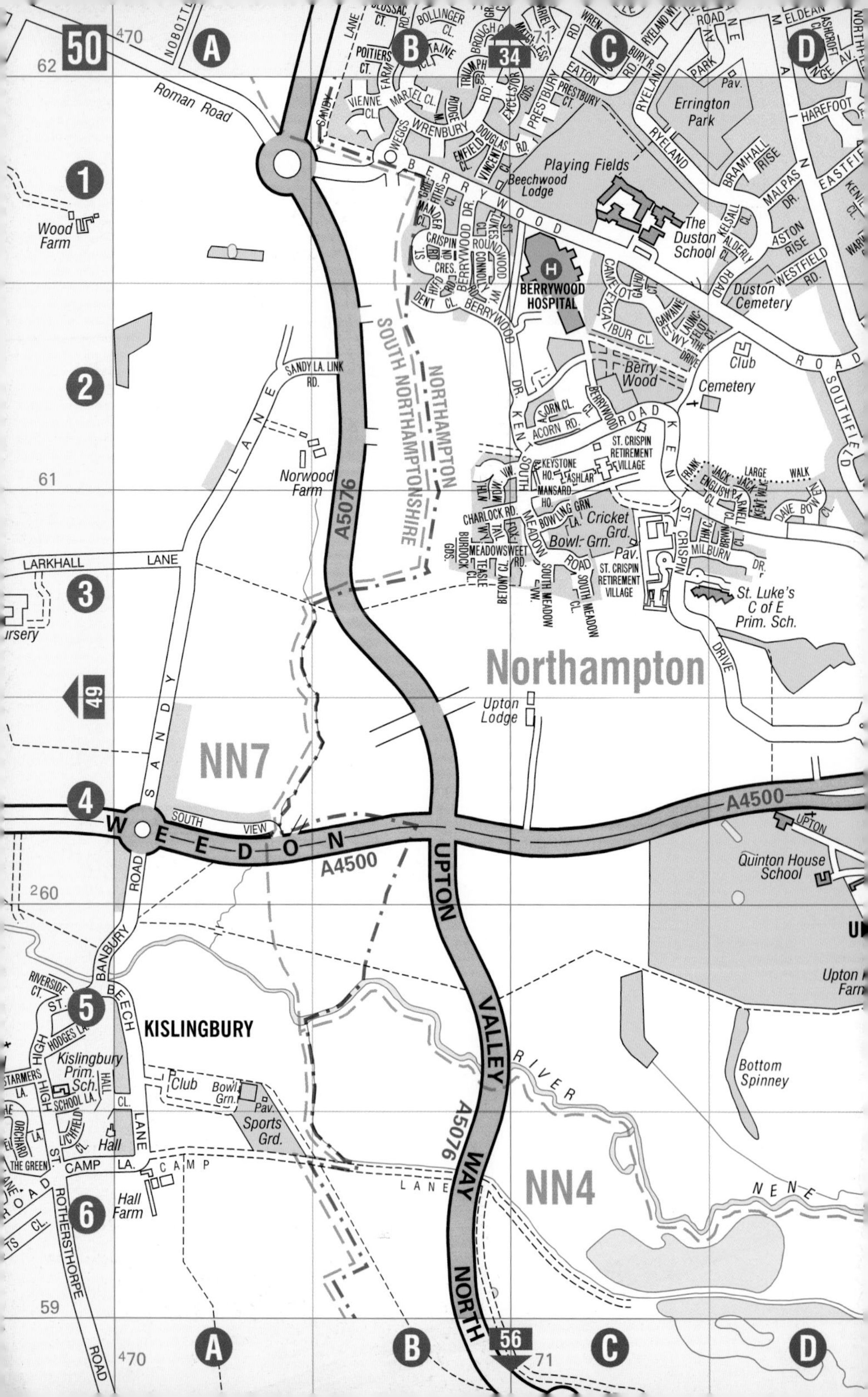

A
B
C
D
1
2
3
4
5
6
34
49
56
Roman Road
Wood Farm
Norwood Farm
LARKHALL LANE
SANDY LANE
SANDY LA. LINK RD.
A5076
SOUTH NORTHAMPTONSHIRE
NORTHAMPTON
BERRYWOOD ROAD
Beechwood Lodge
Playing Fields
The Duston School
BERRYWOOD HOSPITAL
Errington Park
Duston Cemetery
Berry Wood
Cemetery
Club
ST. CRISPIN RETIREMENT VILLAGE
Cricket Grd.
Bowl. Grn.
Pav.
St. Luke's C of E Prim. Sch.
Northampton
Upton Lodge
NN7
WEEDON
A4500
SOUTH VIEW
UPTON VALLEY WAY NORTH
Quinton House School
Upton Farm
KISLINGBURY
Kislingbury Prim. Sch.
Sports Grd.
Hall
Hall Farm
CAMP LANE
Bottom Spinney
RIVER NENE
NN4
BANBURY ROAD
ROTHERSTHORPE ROAD

DALLINGTON
HARLESTONE ROAD
A428
NN5
Cemetery
St.Mary's Catholic Prim. Sch.
Tennis Courts
Chiltern Prim. Sch.
Duston Sports Centre
Playing Field
Bowling Green
Dallington Park
Temple
Warehouses
Millway Prim. Sch.
Superstore
WESTGATE INDUSTRIAL ESTATE
WEEDON ROAD
A4500
Nuffield Health Fitness & Wellbeing Centre
Tenpin
Cineworld Cinema
Sixfields Leisure
Northampton Town FC (Sixfields Stadium)
Sixfields Athletics Stadium
WEEDON ROAD INDUSTRIAL ESTATE
Works
Bingo
Northampton Saints RFC
Sports Ground
ST. JAMES' END
Bus Depot
SILVANUS PARK
Northampton Indoor Karting
Storton's Pits Nature Reserve
RIVER NENE
ST. JAMES MILL BUSINESS PARK
Factory
Upton Meadows Prim. Sch.
UPTON WAY
A5076
Grand Union Canal
BRIAR HILL
Briar Hill Prim. Sch.
NN4
CAMP WAY
DANES
Mill Stream
SPENCER RD.
USTON
35
57
52
73
74
62
61
59
E
F
G
H
1
2
3
4
5
6

A
B
C
D
1
2
3
4
5
6
36
51
58
4
30
NORTHAMPTON
NN2
NN4
NN5
KINGSTHORPE HOLLOW
Semilong
Spencer
St. James'
ST. JAMES' END
BRIAR HILL
COTTON END
Northampton
University of Northampton (Avenue Campus)
Racecourse Park (Recreation Ground)
Dallington Park
Northampton Saints RFC
Northampton Indoor Karting
Victoria Park
Foot Meadow
Grand Union Canal
Duston Junc. West
Bridge Junc.
Delapre Abbey
The Lodge
Park Cottage
ST. ANDREW'S ROAD
BRIDGE RD.
GRAFTON ST.
BARRACK RD.
KINGSTHORPE ROAD
SPENCER RD.
HARLESTONE RD.
WEEDON RD.
ST. JAMES' RD.
ST. PETER'S WAY
VICTORIA PROM.
HORSE MKT.
BROAD ST.
MARE FAIR
UP. MOUNTS
LONDON ROAD
COTTON END
BRIDGE ST.
TOWCESTER ROAD
ST. LEONARD'S RD.
RANSOME ROAD
SOUTHFIELD AV.
ST. JAMES' MILL RD.
HARVEY REEVES RD.
EDGAR MOBBS WAY
RING WAY
ROTHERSTHORPE RD.
A5095
A4500
A428
A508
A5123
ST. JAMES RETAIL PARK
NENE VALLEY RETAIL PARK
DW Fitness
Superstore
Sorting Office
Government Offices

37
Phippsville
ABINGTON
Boating Lakes
The Spinney
Pigeonry
ABINGTON PARK
Playground
NN3
Northants. CCC (The County Grd.)
Abington Pk. Mus.
WELLINGBOROUGH ROAD
A4500
ABINGTON AV.
ABINGTON GRO.
KETTERING ROAD
A5123
B5346
PARK AVENUE
PARK AVENUE SOUTH
Sports Ground
Northampton
Cemetery
BILLING ROAD
St. Christopher's
NORTHAMPTON GENERAL HOSP.
Barratt Maternity Hosp.
Cliftonville Cen.
Northampton Sch. of Podiatry
Cripps Cen.
NN1
ST. ANDREW'S HEALTHCARE
THREE SHIRES BMI HOSPITAL
Northampton Sch. for Boys
Playing Field
Northampton Old Scouts RFC
Sports Field
Hospital Golf Course
Cliftonville House
THE NENE CENTRE
Works
CLIFTONVILLE RD.
A4501
BEDFORD ROAD
A428
RUSHMERE ROAD
A5095
NENE VALLEY WAY
A45
RIVER NENE
Picnic Area
Midsummer Meadow
Barnes Meadow Interchange
Delapre Works Factory
Electricity Generating Station
Nene Whitewater Centre
Rush Mills Ho.
St. Peters Bri.
Refuse Transfer Station
REDBOURNE PARK
Foundry
Industrial Estate
Northampton Water Ski Club
Factory
Depot
54
5
59
E
F
G
H
1
2
3
4
5
6

A
B
C
D
38
WELLINGBOROUGH
ROAD
A4500
ABINGTON
WESTON FAVELL
The Spinney
ABINGTON PARK
NN3
Bridgewater Prim. Sch.
Abington Vale
Play. Fld.
Pav.
Ten. Cts.
HIGH
WESTON WAY
RIDGEWAY
GRASPIN LANE
PARK
CRESCENT
HOLMFIELD WAY
GREENWAY
MEADWAY
PARKWAY
CHURCH WAY
THORBURN ROAD
EDGEMONT ROAD
LUMBERTUBS WAY
A43
VALLEY
BRIDGEWATER DRIVE
MILVERTON CRESCENT
DULVERTON RD.
EAST BEWICK
WESTCOTT WAY
ABINGTON
LANDCROSS
TAUNTON
LYNMOUTH AV.
CHULMLEIGH
PARRACOMBE
MESHAW
ROAD
SOUTH
BILLING
DRIVE
KNOWLE CL.
WISTERIA
CAVENDISH DRIVE
ANNESLEY CL.
BOWTHORPE CL.
Rushmere
WESTON MILL LANE
RIVERSIDE BUSINESS PARK
FAIRGROUND
FORTUNE CL.
MUSEUM WY.
MARQUEE DR.
CAROUSEL WY.
FERRIS RW.
Virgin Active Health Club
Northampton Boat Club
A45
NN1
53
A5095
30
Sports Field
NENE
RIVER
Reservoir
Council Offs. (John Dryden Ho.)
THE LAKES
BEDFORD ROAD
A428
NN4
LILIPUT RD.
Industrial Estate
FORD LA.
Cattle Market
Martins Farm
Depot
Playing Field
Great Houghton Preparatory School
HIGH ST.
Cemetery
War Mem.
CHERRY TREE LA.
Broadacres
Hardingstone
60
GREAT HOUGHTON
1
2
3
4
5
6

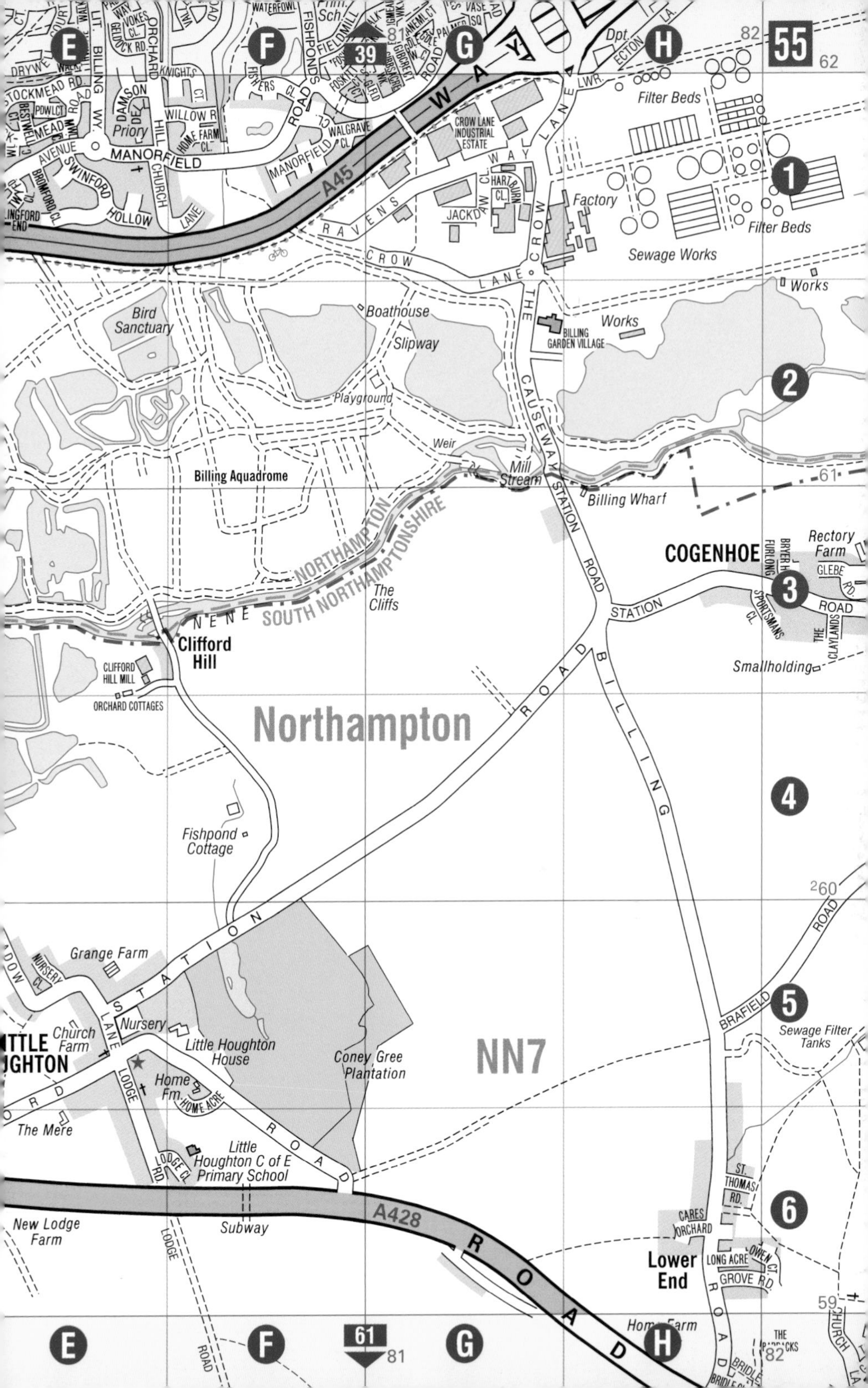

E
F
G
H
39
81
82
62
1
2
3
4
5
6
61
260
59
Filter Beds
Sewage Works
Factory
Works
CROW LANE INDUSTRIAL ESTATE
A45
MANORFIELD
Priory
Bird Sanctuary
Boathouse
Slipway
Playground
BILLING GARDEN VILLAGE
Weir
Mill Stream
Billing Aquadrome
Billing Wharf
NORTHAMPTON
SOUTH NORTHAMPTONSHIRE
NENE
The Cliffs
Clifford Hill
CLIFFORD HILL MILL
ORCHARD COTTAGES
COGENHOE
Rectory Farm
Smallholding
Northampton
Fishpond Cottage
Grange Farm
Nursery
Church Farm
Little Houghton House
Coney Gree Plantation
NN7
Sewage Filter Tanks
Home Fm.
The Mere
Little Houghton C of E Primary School
New Lodge Farm
Subway
A428
Lower End
Home Farm
STATION ROAD
BILLING ROAD
THE CAUSEWAY
CROW LANE
RAVENS WAY
BRAFIELD ROAD

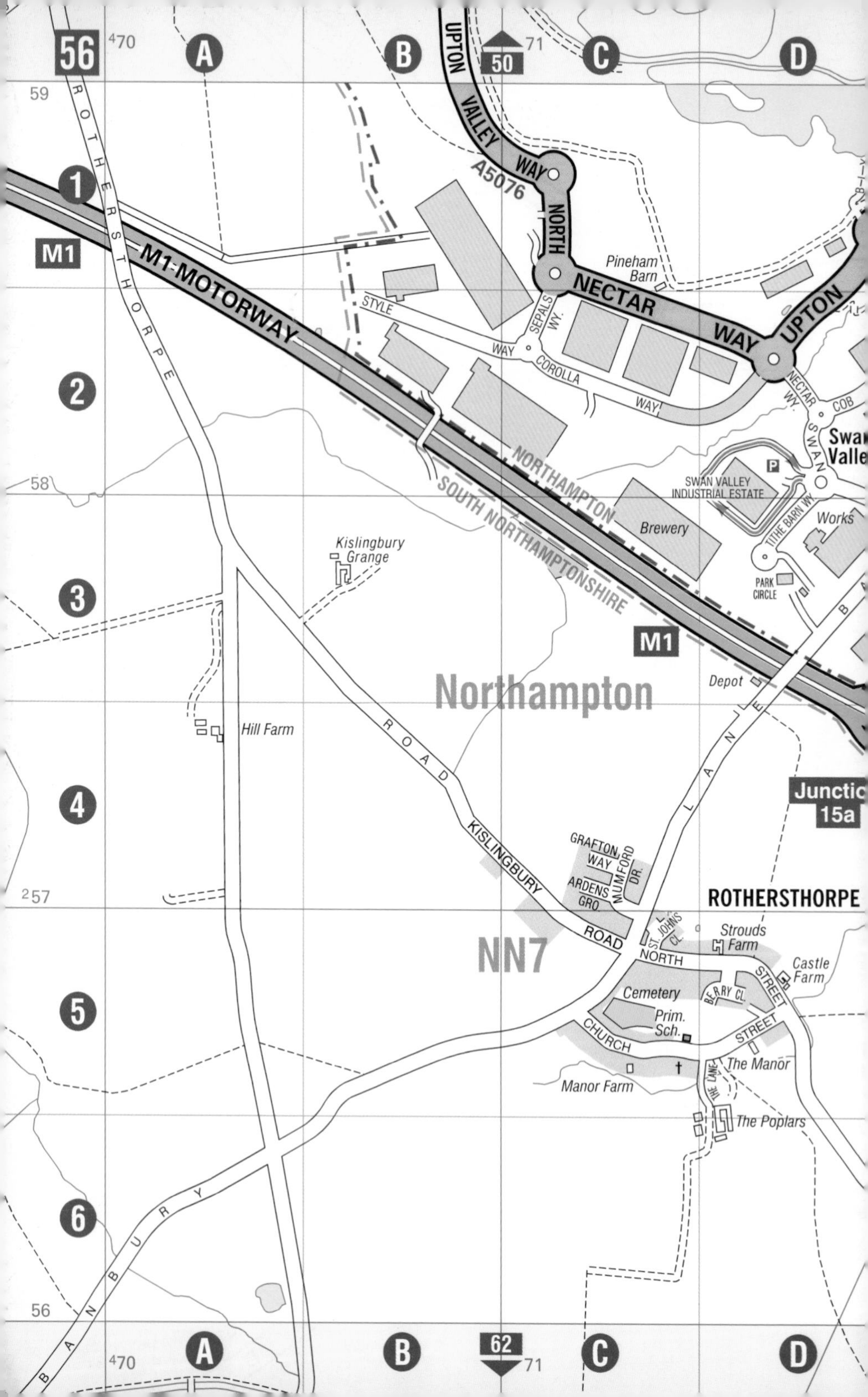

A
B
C
D
50
71
470
59
58
257
56
1
2
3
4
5
6
M1
M1-MOTORWAY
ROTHERSTHORPE
UPTON VALLEY WAY
A5076
NORTH WAY
NECTAR WAY
UPTON
Pineham Barn
STYLE WAY
SEPALS WY.
COROLLA WAY
NECTAR WY.
COB
SWAN
Swan Valle
SWAN VALLEY INDUSTRIAL ESTATE
P
TITHE BARN WY.
Works
PARK CIRCLE
Brewery
NORTHAMPTON
SOUTH NORTHAMPTONSHIRE
Kislingbury Grange
M1
Northampton
Depot
LANE
Junctio
15a
Hill Farm
ROAD
KISLINGBURY ROAD
GRAFTON WAY
MUMFORD DR.
ARDENS GRO
ROTHERSTHORPE
ST. JOHNS CL.
Strouds Farm
NN7
NORTH STREET
Castle Farm
Cemetery
BERRY CL
Prim. Sch.
CHURCH STREET
The Manor
Manor Farm
THE LANE
The Poplars
BANBURY
62

E
F
G
H
51
73
74
A5076
EAST
DANES
CAMP
WAY
Hunsbury Hill Country Park (Nature Reserve)
CAMP HILL
Comm. Cen.
Hunsbury Park Prim. Sch.
Northamptonshire Ironstone Railway Trust
Playing Fields
Hunsbury Hill Fort
HUNSBURY HILL
Northamptonshire Ironstone Railway
Hunsbury Tunnel
Shelfleys
NN4
SWAN VALLEY OFFICE VILLAGE
Grand Union Canal
BLISWORTH AND MILTON MALSOR BY-PASS
A5123
A43
Milton Ham
Lady Bridge
Northampton Service Area
The Counties Crematorium
Drawbridge
Subway
Shepherd's Lodge
M1 MOTORWAY
M1
TOWCESTER RD
LOWER RD
Spring Farm
Sand Pit
LADYBRIDGE DRIVE
HUNSBURY HILL ROAD
ROWTREE RD
DAYRELL RD
HUNSLET LANE
SOUTHCREST
ICKNIELD
AVIEMORE GDS.
REEDHILL
BANBURY CL.
WOODHALL CL.
WHITEGATES
HERONSFORD
TEAL CL.
FOXFORD CL.
STUART CL.
YEOMAN
WOODPECKER WY.
HAWKSNEST
KITES CL.
TITHE BARN WY.
SAMWELL WY.
CAULDECOTT CL.
KEYSTONE
SPINNEY
58
59
1
2
3
4
5
6
63
257
56

58
A
B
C
D
1
2
3
4
5
6
52
57
64
M1
NN4
FAR COTTON
MEREFIELD
Blacky More
Collingtree Park
DELAPRE
CRESCENT
ROAD
LONDON ROAD
A508
A45
A5123
A5076
TOWCESTER ROAD
DANES CAMP WAY
MERE WAY
NEWPORT PAGNELL RD. W.
M1-MOTORWAY
ROWTREE ROAD
CLANNELL RD.
HILLDROP ROAD
GRANARY ROAD
WOOTTON HALL PK.
QUEEN ELEANOR RD.
GLOUCESTER AVENUE
FRIAR'S AVENUE
BRIAR HILL RD.
BRIAR HILL WALK
BLENHEIM RD.
PLEYDELL RD.
PARKFIELD AVENUE
DELAMERE RD.
WINCHESTER RD.
FOREST RD.
EASTFIELD RD.
SALCEY ST.
STEVENSON ST.
PILGRIMS PL.
ROCKINGHAM RD.
FAWSLEY RD.
HEREWARD RD.
LAUDERDALE AV.
CHELMSFORD CL.
CLEVELAND PL.
LEAH BANK
RADLEIGH CL.
MERSEY CL.
HEXHAM CT.
HEDGELEY CT.
LANCASTER WAY
MORTIMER CL.
BARNET CL.
BOSWORTH CL.
TEWKESBURY CL.
CAMBORNE CL.
COVERACK CL.
REDRUTH CL.
FRIAR'S CRES.
FRIAR'S CL.
FRIAR'S CT.
FOX HILL
GLASNBY RD.
OVERSLADE CL.
YEOMAN
WOOTTON HILL FARM
AMBRIDGE CL.
FARM HILL RISE
KITES CL.
HAWKSNEST
RAVENS CT.
FALCONERS RI.
PEREGRINE PL.
BARN OWL CL.
HOBBY CL.
MERLIN GRO.
HARRIER PARK
KIMBLE CL.
OSPREY RI.
OLYMPIA CL.
CLAREGATE
AVEBURY WY.
SPRINGBANKS WY.
BRAEMAR CR.
HARDWICK RD.
MELDON CL.
STAMFORD WAY
THAMES RD.
HIDCOTE RD.
MANNINGTN GS.
TAPELEY GDS.
BRESSINGHAM GS.
COTTESBROOKE GDNS.
MUNCASTER GDS.
HODNET CL.
ROSEMOOR DR.
WISLEY CL.
WEST RISING
EAST RISING
WAKEHURST DR.
FLEETWIND DR.
TIFFANY GDS.
STOURHEAD DR.
LAMBROOK DR.
TRENTHAM CL.
THE WEAVERS
HEDGEWAY
HEDGE END
BUTTS RD.
BUTTS CROFT CL.
KING RICHARD CT.
WOOTTON BROOK CL.
SHEDFIELD WY.
SANDOVER
OAKGROVE PL.
LIMEFIELDS
BRASHLAND DR.
SHAFTSBURY
VERDANT VALE
PEPPERCORN WY.
CINNAMON WY.
TARRAGON WY.
BASIL CL.
MARJORAM CL.
SAFFRON CL.
BLACKYMORE LA.
CHESTNUT AV.
LANGFORD
GRANGE WOOD
SKIPTON CL.
LICHFIELD DR.
BUCKINGHAM CL.
KELBURN CL.
MARLOWE CL.
CARDINAL CL.
COPSE
BANK VW.
PENVALE RD.
CROFTERS
REA CL.
COLLINGCROFT CL.
SPYGLASS HILL
DOWNSWAY
RUSHY END
FROSTY HOLLOW
AUGUSTA
HOLLOW
LAKESIDE
AVENUE
WILDERN LA.
OAKMONT CL.
COLONIAL DRIVE
WINDINGBROOK LANE
TURNBERRY LANE
BELFRY LANE
SHOAL CREEK
MEDINAH CL.
LAUREL VALLEY
TANGLEWOOD
SPINNEY DR.
SWALLOW CL.
PYGHTLE WY.
KINGFISHER CL.
CHAFFINCH CL.
LAPWING CL.
THE HAYRIDE
PENN GDNS.
Delapre Abbey
Delapre Prim. Sch.
Queen Eleanor Prim. Sch.
Rec. Grd.
Bowl. Grn.
Club
Sch.
Eleanor Lodge
Playground
Cemetery
The Abbey Prim. Sch.
Abbeyfield Sch.
Tennis Courts
Queen Eleanor's Cross
Hunsbury Park Prim. Sch.
Hunsbury Hill Country Park (Nature Reserve)
Hunsbury Hill Fort
Hunsbury Hill Tunnel
Northamptonshire Ironstone Railway
Subways
Sub.
Super-store
HUNSBURY DISTRICT CENTRE
Lib.
Danes Camp Leisure Cen.
Simon de Senlis Prim. Sch.
Wootton Grange
Ten. Ct.
Council Offices
Wootton Hall Park (Sports Grd.)
Wootton Hall
Wootton Hall (Northamptonshire Police HQ)
Grange Wood Park
Golf Course
East Hunsbury Prim. Sch.
Shop. Cen.
Comm. Cen.
Garden Cen.
Virgin Active
COLLINGTREE PARK GOLF COURSE
Club House
56
57
74
475

59
53
65
60
E
F
G
H
1
2
3
4
5
6
77
78
59
58
57
56
Northampton Water Ski Club
Brackmills
Factory
Foundry
LILIPUT
Works
Depot
Warehouse
MERCURY DR.
SALTHOUSE
BURRYPORT
RHOSILI ROAD
OSYTH CL.
PENNARD CL.
BRACKMILLS BUS. PK.
KILVEY ROAD
HARROWDEN RD.
CORNWELL BUSINESS PARK
STERLING BUSINESS PARK
REYNOLDSTON CL.
SKETTY
GALLOWHILL RD.
LYVEDEN RD.
OXWICH CL.
CASWELL
GOWERTON
COMPASS BUSINESS PARK
EAGLE DRIVE
Home Farm
Driving Range
Club Ho.
A45
VALLEY WAY
Sub.
PAVILION DRIVE
PAVILION DR.
PAVILION CT.
Criminal Justice Cen.
Golf Course
HOUGHTON HILL
ILEX CL.
HARDINGSTONE
Blue Barns Farm
Hall
BACK LA.
HIGH STREET
Ivy House
BAXTER CT.
War Meml.
BOUVERIE R.
COLDSTREAM LA.
GLEBE AV.
GLEBE CL.
GLEBE WAY
MASSEY CL.
Rec. Grd.
FIRS CT.
CONEY GREE
WINDRUSH RD.
HERITAGE FARM CL.
THE GREEN
THE WARREN
Northampton
LANE
Hardingstone Prim. Sch.
Play. Field
Water Twr.
HARDY DR.
B526
CASTERBRIDGE CT.
TATE GRO.
PAGNELL
LANDIMORE ROAD
PAGNELL CT.
NORTHAMPTON
SOUTH NORTHANTS.
ROAD
VETERAN CL.
EDWARDIAN CL.
SPRINGFIELD
WATER LA.
HARRIS
HOLCUTT CL.
WOOLLON
BALLAND
TUDELY
LEXDEN CL.
MUSGRAVE WY.
KIRBY CL.
ALDWELL CL.
FLINTERS CL.
BROWNLEE PL.
CURLBROOK CL.
MILITIA CL.
BLANCHARD
PIONEER
TOULOUSE CL.
DRIVE
NEW RD.
STOKE FIRS CL.
BREEZEHILL
CROSSBROOKS
CROSS WATERS
HOCKNELL CL.
WRAY CL.
WOOTTON TRAD. EST.
BEDDOES CL.
BUSH
EARLSFIELD CL.
MIDDLE GREEVE
HIGH GREEVE
GREEVE DRIVE
LOW GREEVE
ORCHARD CL.
JARRETTS YARD
GRAFTON
WATER
ROAD
FOSBERRY CL.
NETTLE GAP CL.
HOPE
HILL
DITCHFORD CL.
COPYMOOR CL.
MORTONS
LORDS WD.
LADY
HOLLOWS
THE CHOAKLES
THE ASHES
LONGMEADOW
Prim. Sch.
FARMCLOSE
Spts. Grd.
Comm. Cen.
Cemy.
GATEWAY CL.
WOOTTON FLDS. CEN.
TUDOR CT.
BANCROFT CL.
BANCROFT WY.
ELM GRO.
WHITTLES CROSS
WICKERY DENE
TRUPP BRI.
MILTON BRI.
Little Gap Spinney
SUNNYSIDE
CHURCH STREET
CHURCHILL VW.
THE MULLIONS
CHISHOLM CL.
WOODGATE
FIELDGATE CL.
BROOKS CL.
ROBINSON WY.
WOOTTON
VILLA WAY
ROMAN CL.
SPARTAN CL.
CHARIOT RD.
NN7
BURHAM CL.
SORREL CL.
CURTLEE
QUINTON
MARTLET CL.
CENTURION
GLADIATOR
ROMULUS CL.
BROOKEND
GREEN FLDS.
STRADLERS CL.
COWBECK CL.
Caroline Chisholm School (The Wooldale Centre for Learning)
Sports Pitches
Sewage Works (Disused)
Grange
Estate
SCOTIA CL.

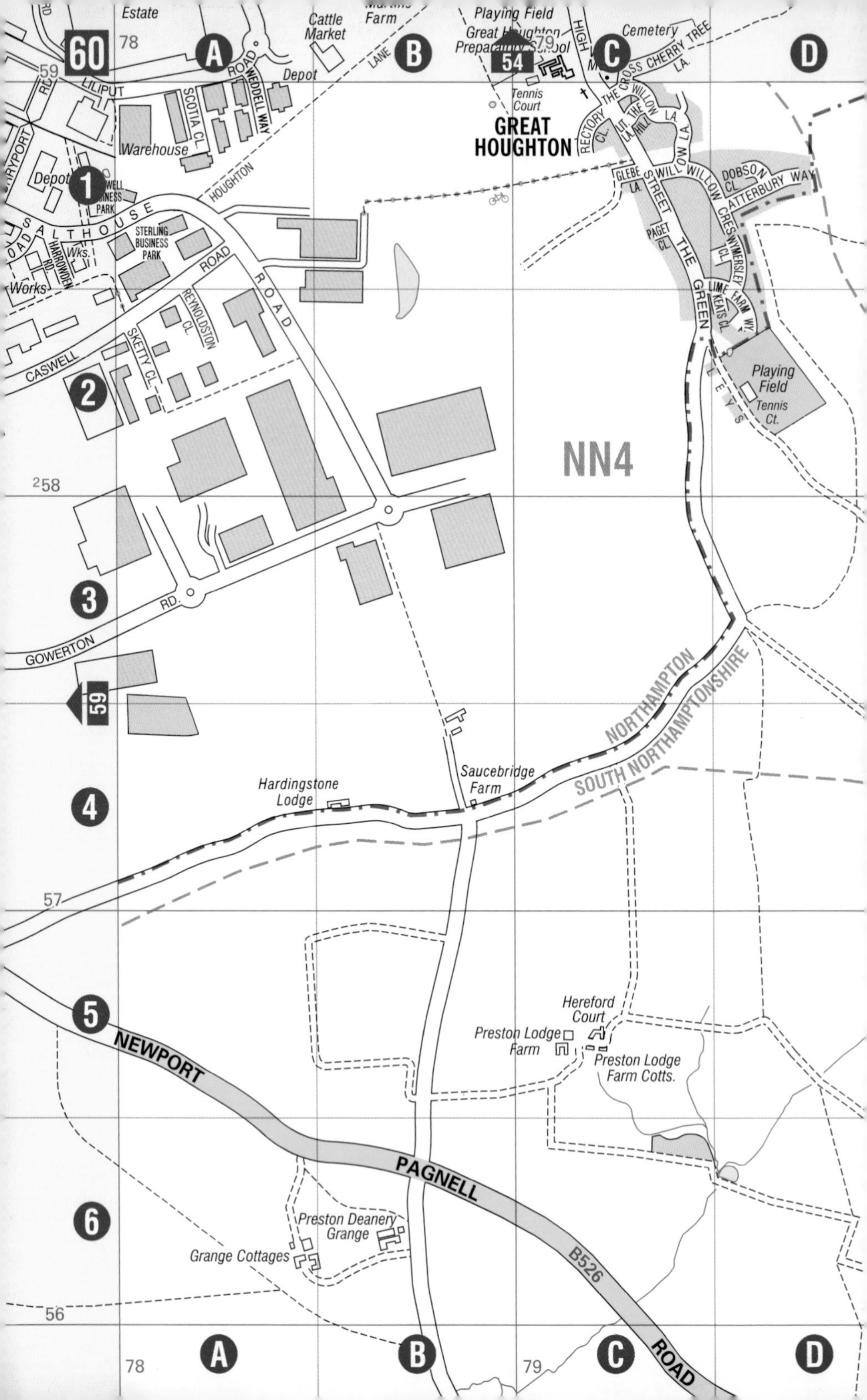
Estate
Cattle Market
Farm
Playing Field
Great Houghton Preparatory School
54
Cemetery
CHERRY TREE LA.
THE CROSS
HIGH
A
B
C
D
78
79
59
LILIPUT
RD.
ROAD
WEDDELL WAY
SCOTIA CL.
Depot
LANE
Tennis Court
GREAT HOUGHTON
RECTORY CL.
WILLOW LA.
LIT. THE LA.
THE HILL
Warehouse
HOUGHTON
Depot
1
BUSINESS PARK
SALTHOUSE
STERLING BUSINESS PARK
ROAD
HARROWDEN RD.
Wks.
Works
GLEBE LA.
STREET
WILLOW
DOBSON CL.
ATTERBURY WAY
PAGET CL.
THE GREEN
WILLOW CRES.
WYMERSLEY CL.
LIME
KEATS CL.
FARM WY.
REYNOLDSTON CL.
SKETTY CL.
CASWELL
2
LEYS
Playing Field
Tennis Ct.
NN4
258
3
RD.
GOWERTON
59
NORTHAMPTON
SOUTH NORTHAMPTONSHIRE
Saucebridge Farm
Hardingstone Lodge
4
57
5
NEWPORT
Hereford Court
Preston Lodge Farm
Preston Lodge Farm Cotts.
PAGNELL
6
Preston Deanery Grange
Grange Cottages
B526
56
ROAD

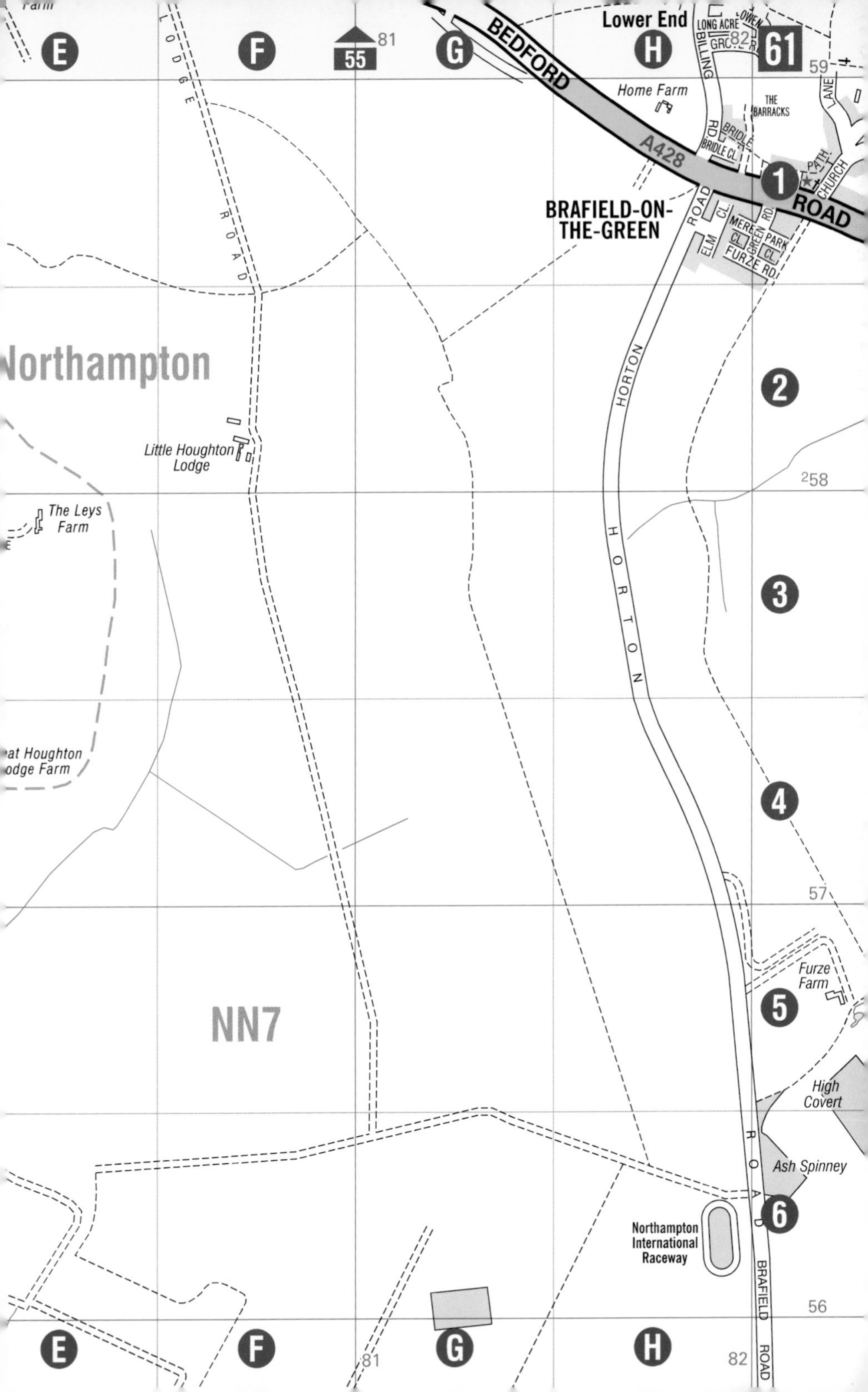
E
F
55
81
G
H
Lower End
BEDFORD
LONG ACRE
BILLING
82
59
Home Farm
THE BARRACKS
A428
BRIDLE CL.
1
CHURCH
ROAD
BRAFIELD-ON-
THE-GREEN
ELM
MERE
GREEN
PARK
FURZE RD.
Northampton
HORTON
2
258
Little Houghton
Lodge
The Leys
Farm
3
4
57
Furze
Farm
5
NN7
High
Covert
Ash Spinney
6
Northampton
International
Raceway
BRAFIELD
ROAD
56
82

A
B
C
D
56
470
71
1
2
3
4
5
6
255
54
53
BANBURY LA.
WRIGHTS LANE
Grand Union Canal
Sewage Works
MILTON ROAD
GAYTON
PARK LA.
DEANS ROW
STREET
ST. MARYS CT.
BLISWORTH
HIGH ST.
BAKER
BACK LANE
BUGBROOKE ROAD
Glebe Farm
Sch.
HILLCREST RD.
ROAD
TIFFIELD ROAD
Ckt. Grd.
EASTCOTE
The Old Wilds
GAYTON ROAD
BLISWORTH AND MILTON
A43
STATION RD.
Fox Cove
Gayton Wood Farm
Rectory

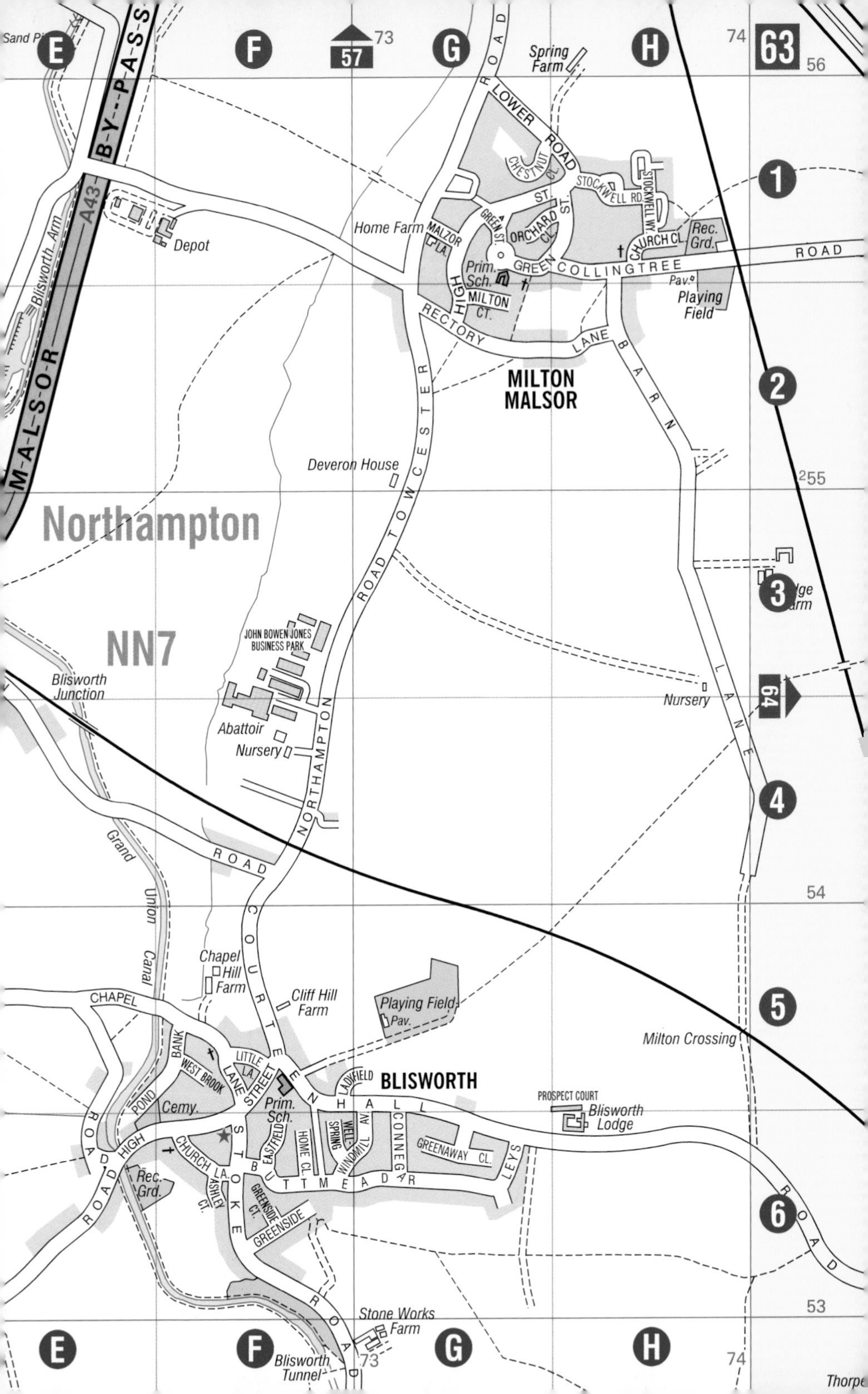
63
57
64
E
F
G
H
1
2
3
4
5
6
73
74
56
55
54
53
Northampton
NN7
MILTON
MALSOR
BLISWORTH
MALSOR BY-PASS
A43
Blisworth Arm
Depot
Home Farm
Spring Farm
LOWER ROAD
CHESTNUT CL.
STOCKWELL RD.
STOCKWELL WY.
ORCHARD CL.
GREEN ST.
MALZOR LA.
Prim. Sch.
MILTON CT.
HIGH ST.
GREEN
COLLINGTREE ROAD
CHURCH CL.
Rec. Grd.
Pav.
Playing Field
RECTORY LANE
BARN LANE
TOWCESTER ROAD
NORTHAMPTON ROAD
Deveron House
JOHN BOWEN JONES BUSINESS PARK
Abattoir
Nursery
Blisworth Junction
Grand Union Canal
ROAD
COURTEENHALL ROAD
Chapel Hill Farm
Cliff Hill Farm
Playing Field
Pav.
Milton Crossing
CHAPEL
BANK
LITTLE LA.
LANE
WEST BROOK
STREET
POND
Cemy.
LADYFIELD
PROSPECT COURT
Blisworth Lodge
HIGH
ROAD
CHURCH LA.
ASHLEY CT.
STOKE ROAD
EASTFIELD
HOME CL.
SPRING
WELL
WINDMILL AV.
CONNEGAR
GREENAWAY CL.
LEYS
BUTTMEADAR
GREENSIDE CT.
GREENSIDE
Rec. Grd.
Stone Works Farm
Blisworth Tunnel
Thorpe

Club House
58
Virgin Active
COLLINGTREE PARK
GOLF COURSE
M1
SPINNEY DR.
AVENUE
WINDINGBROOK
SHOAL CREEK
MEDINAH CL.
LAUREL VALLEY
TANGLEWOOD
LAKE WLK.
SARGEANTS LA.
Glebe Farm
Sch.
COLLINGTREE
BARN MS.
BARN CL.
GLEBE FARM CL.
WATERING LANE
HIGH STREET
TOMS CL.
Tennis Cts.
Playing Field
Golf Course
Cemetery
LANE
LivingWell Health Club
Hotel
LONDON ROAD
A45
MAPLE CT.
ASH ROAD
COLLINGTREE ROAD
COLLINGTREE CT.
Rec. Grd.
CHURCH CL.
STOCKWELL WY.
Pav.
Playing Field
SOUTH NORTHAMPTONSHIRE
NORTHAMPTON
M1 MOTORWAY
BARN LANE
Northampton
SAXON
LOAKE CT.
BASSET CT.
Junction 15
Lodge Farm
Churchill's
Nursery
63
Rectory Farm
A508
ROAD
Highgate
Miller's
Milton Crossing
NN7
The Moors
Watermill Spinney
Brickhill
West Lodge Cottages
60
COURTEENHALL ROAD
Courteenhall West Lodge
The Wake Knot
Windmill Spinney
Drive Spinney
LONDON
War Memorial
Lodge Spinney
Courteenhall Bridge
Bridge Cottage
Thorpewood Farm
Woodleys Farm

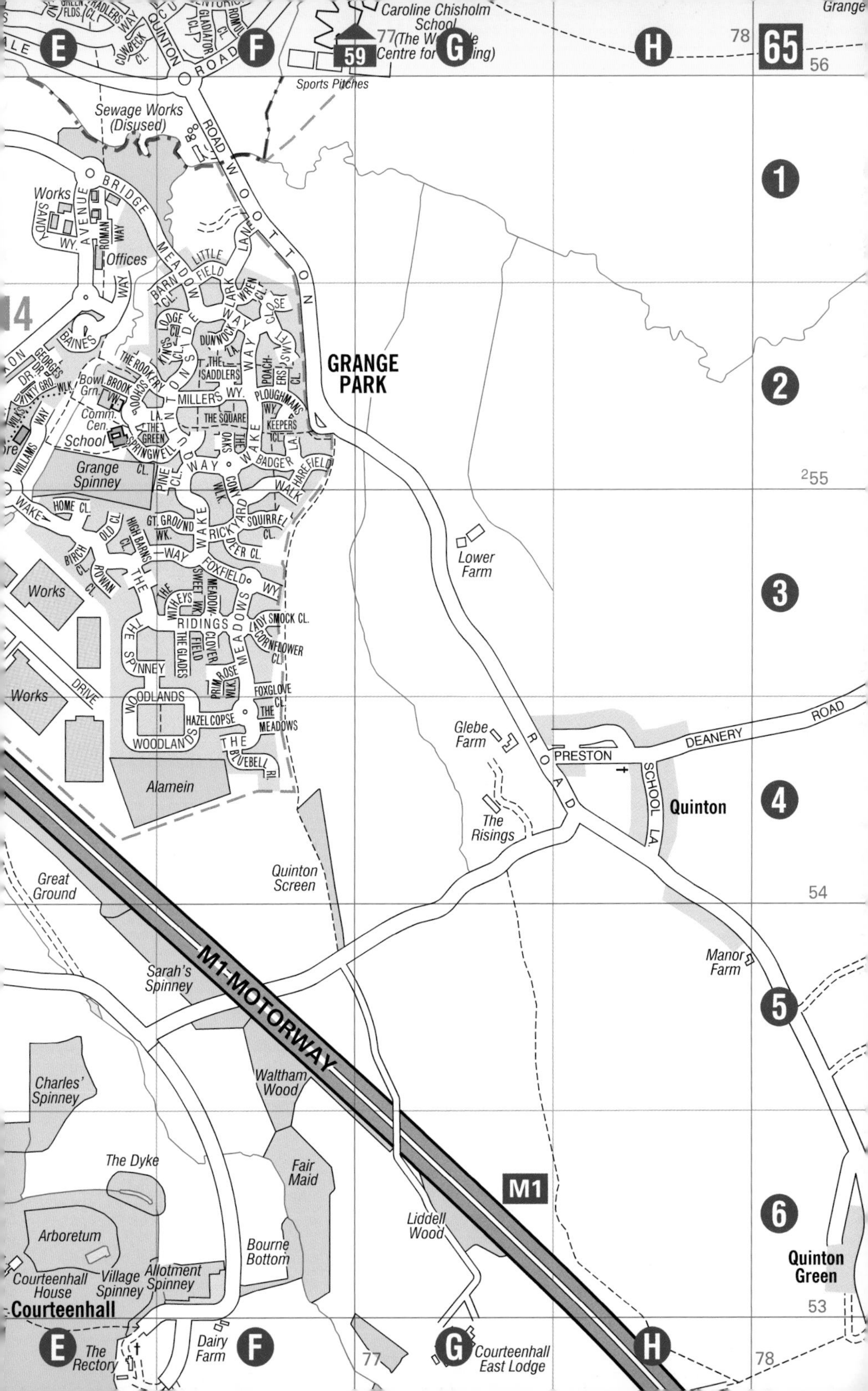

Caroline Chisholm School
59
GRANGE PARK
Sewage Works (Disused)
Sports Pitches
Works
Offices
School
Grange Spinney
Works
Works
Alamein
Lower Farm
Glebe Farm
The Risings
PRESTON
DEANERY ROAD
Quinton
Quinton Screen
Great Ground
Sarah's Spinney
M1-MOTORWAY
Manor Farm
Charles' Spinney
Waltham Wood
The Dyke
Fair Maid
Arboretum
Liddell Wood
M1
Bourne Bottom
Courteenhall House
Village Spinney
Allotment Spinney
Courteenhall
Quinton Green
The Rectory
Dairy Farm
Courteenhall East Lodge

INDEX

Including Streets, Places & Areas, Hospitals etc., Industrial Estates,
Selected Flats & Walkways, Service Areas, Stations, and Selected Places of Interest.

HOW TO USE THIS INDEX

1. Each street name is followed by its Postcode District, then by its Locality abbreviation(s) and then by its map reference;
   e.g. **Abbey St.** NN11: Dav . . . .5E **7** is in the NN11 Postcode District and the Daventry Locality and is to be found in square 5E on page **7**.
   The page number is shown in bold type.

2. A strict alphabetical order is followed in which Av., Rd., St., etc. (though abbreviated) are read in full and as part of the street name;
   e.g. **Ash Cl.** appears after **Ashby Wood M.** but before **Ashcroft Cl.**

3. Streets and a selection of flats and walkways that cannot be shown on the mapping, appear in the index with the thoroughfare to which they are
   connected shown in brackets; e.g. **Abbey Ho.** NN5: N'ton . . . .3A **52** (off Abbey St.)

4. Addresses that are in more than one part are referred to as not continuous.

5. Places and areas are shown in the index in BLUE TYPE and the map reference is to the actual map square in which the town centre or area is located and
   not to the place name shown on the map; e.g. ABINGTON 2G 53

6. An example of a selected place of interest is Abington Park Mus. 1G 53

7. An example of a station is Northampton Station (Rail) 4A 4 (4B 52)

8. Service Areas are shown in the index in BOLD CAPITAL TYPE; e.g. **NORTHAMPTON SERVICE AREA** 4E 57

9. An example of a Hospital, Hospice or selected Healthcare Facility is BERRYWOOD HOSPITAL 2C 50

10. Map references for entries that appear on large scale pages **4** & **5** are shown first, with small scale map references shown in brackets;
    e.g. **Abington Pl.** NN1: N'ton 3E **5** (3E **53**)

GENERAL ABBREVIATIONS

All. : Alley	**Est.** : Estate	**Mans.** : Mansions	**Sth.** : South
App. : Approach	**Fld.** : Field	**Mkt.** : Market	**Sq.** : Square
Av. : Avenue	**Flds.** : Fields	**Mdw.** : Meadow	**Sta.** : Station
Bri. : Bridge	**Gdn.** : Garden	**Mdws.** : Meadows	**St.** : Street
Bldgs. : Buildings	**Gdns.** : Gardens	**M.** : Mews	**Ter.** : Terrace
Bus. : Business	**Ga.** : Gate	**Mt.** : Mount	**Twr.** : Tower
Cen. : Centre	**Gt.** : Great	**Mus.** : Museum	**Trad.** : Trading
Circ. : Circle	**Grn.** : Green	**Nth.** : North	**Up.** : Upper
Cl. : Close	**Gro.** : Grove	**Pde.** : Parade	**Va.** : Vale
Cnr. : Corner	**Hgts.** : Heights	**Pk.** : Park	**Vw.** : View
Cotts. : Cottages	**Ho.** : House	**Pas.** : Passage	**Vis.** : Visitors
Ct. : Court	**Ind.** : Industrial	**Pl.** : Place	**Wlk.** : Walk
Cres. : Crescent	**Info.** : Information	**Prom.** : Promenade	**W.** : West
Cft. : Croft	**La.** : Lane	**Res.** : Residential	**Yd.** : Yard
Dr. : Drive	**Lit.** : Little	**Ri.** : Rise	
E. : East	**Lwr.** : Lower	**Rd.** : Road	
Ent. : Enterprise	**Mnr.** : Manor	**Shop.** : Shopping	

LOCALITY ABBREVIATIONS

Badby : **Badby**	Far C : **Far Cotton**	Knus : **Knuston**	Rother : **Rothersthorpe**
Blis : **Blisworth**	Farn : **Farndish**	Lit A : **Little Addington**	Rushd : **Rushden**
Bou : **Boughton**	Fine : **Finedon**	Lit B : **Little Billing**	Stanw : **Stanwick**
Boz : **Bozeat**	Flore : **Flore**	Lit Harr : **Little Harrowden**	Stav : **Staverton**
Brack : **Brackmills**	G'ton : **Gayton**	Lit Hou : **Little Houghton**	Strix : **Strixton**
Braf G : **Brafield on the Green**	Gra P : **Grange Park**	Lit I : **Little Irchester**	Swan H : **Swan Valley**
Brix : **Brixworth**	Gt Bil : **Great Billing**	Lwr H : **Lower Harlestone**	Syw : **Sywell**
Broc : **Brockhall**	Gt Dod : **Great Doddington**	Mears A : **Mears Ashby**	Up Harl : **Upper Harlestone**
Bur L : **Burton Latimer**	Gt Har : **Great Harrowden**	Mil M : **Milton Malsor**	Up Hey : **Upper Heyford**
Chap B : **Chapel Brampton**	Gt Hou : **Great Houghton**	Moul : **Moulton**	Upton : **Upton**
Cog : **Cogenhoe**	Gren : **Grendon**	Neth H : **Nether Heyford**	Weed : **Weedon**
Col : **Collingtree**	H'stone : **Hardingstone**	New D : **New Duston**	Well : **Wellingborough**
Court : **Courteenhall**	H'wick : **Hardwick**	Newn : **Newnham**	Welt : **Welton**
Dav : **Daventry**	Harp : **Harpole**	N'ton : **Northampton**	West F : **Weston Favell**
Del : **Delapre**	High F : **Higham Ferrers**	Over : **Overstone**	Wilby : **Wilby**
Dod : **Dodford**	Hort : **Horton**	Pits : **Pitsford**	Woll : **Wollaston**
Dus : **Duston**	Irch : **Irchester**	Pres D : **Preston Deanery**	Woot : **Wootton**
E Bart : **Earls Barton**	Irth : **Irthlingborough**	Quin : **Quinton**	Wym : **Wymington**
Ect : **Ecton**	K'thpe : **Kingsthorpe**	Raun : **Raunds**	
Ect B : **Ecton Brook**	Kisl : **Kislingbury**	Roa : **Roade**	

---

78 Derngate 4E 5

A

Abbey Cl. NN29: Boz 6G 45
Abbey Ho. NN5: N'ton 3A 52
          (off Abbey St.)
Abbey Lodge NN3: N'ton 2A 54
Abbey Retail Pk.
  NN11: Dav 5F 7
Abbey Ri. NN29: Woll 4B 44
Abbey Rd. NN4: Far C 6B 52
  NN8: Well 2F 29
Abbey St. NN5: N'ton 3A 52
  NN11: Dav 5E 7
Abbey Way NN10: Rushd 5C 32
Abbot Cl. NN11: Dav 1F 9

Abbots Way NN5: N'ton 3H 51
  NN8: Well 1F 29
Abbotts Way NN10: Rushd 4B 32
Aberdare Rd. NN5: N'ton 1A 52
Aberdeen Ter. NN5: N'ton 3A 52
          (off Harlestone Rd.)
ABINGTON 2G 53
Abington Av. NN1: N'ton 1F 53
  NN3: N'ton 1F 53
Abington Cotts. NN1: N'ton 1G 53
Abington Ct. NN3: N'ton 6H 37
  NN5: Upton 5F 51
          (off Black Cat Dr.)
Abington Gro. NN1: N'ton 1F 53
Abington Pk. Cres.
  NN3: N'ton 2H 53
Abington Park Mus. 1G 53
Abington Pl.
  NN1: N'ton 3E 5 (3E 53)
Abington Sq.
  NN1: N'ton 2E 5 (3D 52)

Abington St.
  NN1: N'ton 3D 4 (3D 52)
ABINGTON VALE 2A 54
Abthorpe Av. NN2: K'thpe 2D 36
Accurate Boot, The
  NN1: N'ton 2E 53
          (off Hood St.)
Acorn Cl. NN5: Dus 2C 50
Acorn Rd. NN5: Dus 2C 50
Acre Cl. NN11: Dav 1E 7
Acre La. NN2: K'thpe 2A 36
Adams Av.
  NN1: N'ton 1H 5 (2F 53)
Adams Cl. NN8: Well 6H 17
  NN9: Stanw 4A 14
Addington Pk. Ind. Est.
  NN14: Lit A 2E 13
Addington Rd. NN9: Irth 1B 20
          (not continuous)
Addison Rd. NN3: N'ton 5G 37
Addlecroft Cl. NN2: K'thpe 4B 36

Adelaide Ho. NN2: N'ton 2C 5
          (off Lwr. Adelaide S
Adelaide Pl.
  NN1: N'ton 4B 4 (4C 5
Adelaide St. NN2: N'ton 2C 5
Adelaide Ter. NN2: N'ton 1C
          (off Barrack Rc
Adit Vw. NN9: Irth 3A
Admirals Way NN11: Dav 4G
Adnitt Rd. NN1: N'ton 2F 5
  NN10: Rushd 3C 3
Affleck Bri. NN9: Fine 5D 1
Aggate Way NN6: E Bart 5F 4
Agnes Rd. NN2: N'ton 1C 5
Ainsdale Cl. NN2: N'ton 4F 3
Aintree Dr. NN10: Rushd 5F 3
Aintree Rd. NN3: N'ton 3F 3
Alastor NN8: Well . . . . .6B •
Albany, The NN11: Dav 5E
          (off Primrose H
Albany Rd. NN1: N'ton 2G 5

Albert Pl.—Belgrave Ho.

Albert Pl. NN1: N'ton 3D 4 (3D 52)
Albert Rd. NN8: Well 5H 17
NN9: Fine 4D 10
NN10: Rushd 3D 32
Albion Ct. NN1: N'ton 4E 5
Albion Pl. NN1: N'ton 4D 4 (4D 52)
NN10: Rushd 4D 32
Alcombe Rd.
NN1: N'ton 2E 5 (2D 52)
Alcombe Ter.
NN1: N'ton 1F 5 (2E 53)
Aldbury Ct. NN1: N'ton 1B 4
Alder Ct. NN3: N'ton 2D 38
Alderley Cl. NN5: Dus 1D 50
Aldsworth Cl. NN8: Well 5E 29
Aldwell Cl. NN4: Woot 4F 59
Alexander Cl. NN9: Fine 5D 10
Alexander Ct. NN3: N'ton 4C 38
NN29: Irch 5F 31
Alexander Pl. NN9: Irth 5C 12
Alexander Rd. NN9: Irth 5C 12
Alexandra Rd.
NN1: N'ton 3F 5 (3E 53)
NN8: Well 5H 17
NN10: Rushd 2F 33
Alexandra Ter. NN2: K'thpe 4C 36
Alfoxden NN8: Well 2B 28
Alfred Knight Cl. NN5: Dus 2E 51
Alfred St. NN1: N'ton 3H 5 (3F 53)
NN9: Stanw 5H 13
NN10: Rushd 3D 32
NN29: Irch 5E 31
Alibone Cl. NN3: Moul 4B 24
Alington Cl. NN9: Fine 4E 11
Alken Cl. NN8: Well 3F 17
Allan Bank NN8: Well 2B 28
Allard Cl. NN3: N'ton 2H 39
Allebone Rd. NN6: E Bart 4G 41
Allen Ct. NN9: Fine 4E 11
Allen Rd. NN1: N'ton 2F 53
NN9: Fine 4E 11
NN9: Irth 2A 20
NN10: Rushd 2E 33
Allens Hill NN29: Boz 5H 45
Alley Yd. NN1: N'ton 3C 4 (3C 52)
Alliance Ter. NN8: Well 6G 17
Alliston Gdns. NN2: N'ton 2C 52
Alma St. NN5: N'ton 3A 52
NN8: Well 6G 17
Almond Gro. NN3: N'ton 6A 38
Alpha Ho. NN1: N'ton 2B 4
Alpine Rd. NN10: Rushd 3B 32
Alpine Way NN5: Dus 4C 34
Alsace Cl. NN5: Dus 6B 34
Althorp Cl. NN8: Well 4C 16
NN11: Dav 1C 6
Althorp Rd. NN5: N'ton 3A 52
Althorp St. NN1: N'ton . . .2B 4 (3C 52)
Alton St. NN4: Far C 6B 52
Alvis Ct. NN3: N'ton 3G 39
Alvis Way NN11: Dav 4B 6
Alwyn Wlk. NN3: N'ton 1G 39
Ambidge Ct. NN1: N'ton 2H 5
Ambleside Cl. NN3: N'ton 3A 38
NN8: Well 6C 16
Ambridge Cl. NN4: N'ton 3H 57
Ambush St. NN5: N'ton 3B 52
Amen Corner NN14: Lit A 1E 13
Amen Pl. NN14: Lit A 1E 13
AMF Bowling
Wellingborough 3H 29
Amundsen Cl. NN11: Dav 2D 6
Anchor Dr. NN2: K'thpe 1B 36
Anderson Grn. NN8: Well 1C 28
Andrew Cl. NN10: High F 4E 21
Andrews Ct. NN6: Brix 1A 22
Andrews Way NN9: Raun 4B 14
Angel La. NN8: Well 1G 29
Angel St. NN1: N'ton 4C 4 (4C 52)
Anglian Rd. NN11: Dav 6D 6
Anglia Way NN3: N'ton 2F 37
Anjou Ct. NN5: New D 5B 34
Anne Cl. NN10: High F 4E 21
Anne Rd. NN8: Well 3E 29
Annesley Cl. NN3: N'ton 3B 54
Ansell Way NN4: H'stone 3E 59
Anson Cl. NN11: Dav 6F 7
Antona Cl. NN9: Raun 5B 14
Antona Dr. NN9: Raun 5B 14
Antona Gdns. NN9: Raun 5B 14
Apollo Cl. NN11: Dav 4D 6
Applebarn Cl. NN4: Col 1C 64
Appleby Cl. NN9: Well 2F 17
Appleby Wlk. NN3: N'ton 3A 38
Appledore Cl. NN2: K'thpe 2C 36
Appletree Ct. NN9: Fine 4D 10
Approach, The NN5: N'ton 3H 51
Aquitaine Cl. NN5: Dus 6B 34
Arbour Ct. NN3: N'ton 3C 38
ARBOURS, THE 4H 37
Arbour Vw. Ct. NN3: N'ton 2C 38
Arbour Wlk. NN3: N'ton 2C 38
Archangel Rd. NN4: N'ton 1G 57
Archangel Sq. NN4: N'ton 1H 57
Archers Cl. NN2: K'thpe 2A 36
Archfield NN8: Well 1F 29
Archfield Ter. *NN9: Irth 1B 20*
(off Lilley Ter.)
Arden Cl. NN11: Dav 3D 6
Ardens Gro. NN7: Rother 4C 56
Ardington Rd. NN1: N'ton 2G 53
Argyle St. NN5: N'ton 3A 52
Ariel Cl. NN5: Dus 6C 34
Arkwright Rd. NN29: Irch 5F 31
Arlbury Rd. NN3: N'ton 3E 39
Arndale NN2: K'thpe 2H 35
Arnold Rd. NN2: N'ton 1C 52
Arnsby Cres. NN3: Moul 4H 23
Arnull Cres. NN11: Dav 3D 6
Arrow Head Rd. NN4: N'ton 6H 51
Arthur St. NN2: N'ton 6C 36
NN8: Well 1E 29
Arthur Ter. NN2: N'ton 6C 36
Artizan Rd. NN1: N'ton . . .1H 5 (2F 53)
Arum Cl. NN10: Rushd 6E 33
Arundel Ct. NN10: Rushd 5C 32
Arundel St. NN1: N'ton . . .1B 4 (2C 52)
Ascot Rd. NN10: Rushd 5F 33
Ashbrow Rd. NN4: N'ton 6H 51
Ashburnham Rd. NN1: N'ton 1F 53
Ashby Cl. NN8: Well 4D 16
Ashby Ct. NN3: Moul 4A 24
NN5: Upton 5F 51
(off Clickers M.)
NN7: Kisl 6H 49
Ashby Dr. NN10: Rushd 5C 32
Ashby Gdns. *NN3: Moul 4A 24*
(off Ashby Ct.)
Ashby Pk. NN11: Dav 3E 7
Ashby Rd. NN11: Dav 1D 6
(not continuous)
Ashby Wood Dr. NN5: Upton 5E 51
Ashby Wood M. NN5: Upton 5E 51
Ash Cl. NN11: Dav 3E 7
NN29: Irch 6E 31
Ashcroft Cl. NN5: Dus 6D 34
Ashcroft Gdns. NN3: N'ton 5G 37
Ashdale Cl. NN6: Syw 4H 25
Ashdown Rd. NN11: Dav 3E 7
Ash Dr. NN6: Syw 6H 25
Ashes, The NN4: Woot 5H 59
Ashfield Av. NN9: Raun 3C 14
Ashfield Ri. NN9: Raun 3C 14
Ashfield Rd. NN8: Well 1E 29
Ashford Cl. NN3: N'ton 3A 54
Ash Gro. NN2: K'thpe 1B 36
Ash La. NN4: Col 1B 64
Ashlar NN5: Upton 2C 50
Ashley Cl. NN3: Moul 4C 24
Ashley Ct. NN7: Blis 6F 63
Ashley La. NN3: Moul 4B 24
Ashley Way NN3: West F 5B 38
Ashmead NN3: Lit B 5E 39
Ashpole Spinney
NN4: N'ton 1E 57
Ashridge Cl. NN10: Rushd 5C 32
Ash Ri. NN2: K'thpe 6C 22
Ash St. NN1: N'ton 1C 4 (2C 52)
Ashton Cl. NN11: Dav 4C 6
Ashton Gro. NN8: Well 3D 16
Ashtree Way NN5: Dus 2E 51
Ashway, The NN6: Brix 1B 22
Ashwell Rd. NN10: Rushd 3F 33
Ashwood Rd. NN5: Dus 2E 51
Ashworth St. NN11: Dav 6E 7
Askham Av. NN8: Well 4E 29
Aspen Cl. NN3: N'ton 4G 39
NN10: Rushd 2D 32
Astbury Cl. NN11: Dav 1E 9
Astbury Ter. NN11: Dav 1F 9
Aster Cl. NN3: N'ton 3A 54
Aston Ri. NN5: Dus 1D 50
Atterbury Way
NN4: Gt Hou 1D 60
Attlee Cl. NN3: N'ton 3H 37
Attley Ct. NN8: Well 6C 16
Attley Way NN9: Irth 6C 12
Auckland Cl. NN2: K'thpe 5D 36
Auctioneers Ct.
NN1: N'ton 6D 4 (5D 52)
Auctioneers Way
NN1: N'ton 6D 4 (5D 52)
Augusta Av. NN4: N'ton 5B 58
Austin Cl. NN29: Irch 5G 31
Austin St. NN1: N'ton 2D 52
Austins Yd. NN6: E Bart 3G 41
Austin Way NN11: Dav 4B 6
Avebury Way NN4: N'ton 3B 58
Avenue, The
NN1: N'ton 4H 5 (4F 53)
NN2: K'thpe 1H 35
NN3: Moul 5C 24
NN3: N'ton 4G 37
NN5: N'ton 2H 51
NN6: Over 5C 24
NN7: Flore 4E 47
NN8: Well 5G 17
NN9: Stanw 6A 14
Avenue Cl. NN9: Fine 4C 10
Avenue Rd. NN8: Well 6G 17
NN9: Fine 4C 10
Aviemore Gdns. NN4: N'ton 2G 57
Avignon Cl. NN5: New D 5C 34
Avon Cl. NN8: Well 5C 16
NN11: Dav 1C 8
Avon Dr. NN5: N'ton 6G 35
Avon Rise NN10: Rushd 1E 33
Axe Head Rd. NN4: N'ton 5H 51
Aynho Cres. NN2: K'thpe 2C 36
Aynho Wlk. NN2: K'thpe 2D 36
Azalea Cl. NN3: N'ton 3B 54

B

Back La. NN4: H'stone 3F 59
NN7: G'ton 3A 62
NN14: Lit A 1D 12
Backway NN29: Woll 5B 44
Bacon Rd. NN8: Well 3F 17
BADBY .6B 8
Badby Cl. NN2: K'thpe 3E 37
Badby La. NN11: Stav 3A 8
Badby Pk. NN11: Dav 2C 6
Badby Rd. NN11: Dav 1D 8
NN11: Newn 5F 9
Badby Rd. W. NN11: Dav 2C 8
(not continuous)
Badger La. NN4: Gra P 2F 65
Badgers Wlk. NN2: K'thpe 2B 36
Bailey Ct. NN10: High F 6D 20
Bailey Wills Building, The
NN1: N'ton 1G 5
Bailiff St. NN1: N'ton 1C 4 (2C 52)
Baines Way NN4: Gra P 2E 65
Baird Av. NN5: Upton 5F 51
Baird Cl. NN11: Dav 2D 6
Baird Ct. NN8: Well 5B 16
Bakehouse Hill NN14: Lit A 1D 12
Bakehouse La. NN6: Mears A . . .3D 26
Baker Cres. NN29: Irch 5E 31
Baker's Ct. NN9: Raun 3D 14
Baker St. NN2: N'ton 1C 52
NN7: G'ton 3A 62
NN8: Well 6G 17
NN9: Irth 2A 20
Bakewell Cl. NN4: N'ton 3H 57
Baldwin Cl. NN3: N'ton 3H 37
Baler Cl. NN11: Dav 1E 7
Balfour Cl. NN2: N'ton 6C 36
Balfour Rd. NN2: N'ton 6C 36
Balham Cl. NN10: Rushd 5B 32
Balland Way NN4: Woot 4F 59
Ballantyne Rd. NN10: Rushd 4C 32
Balliol Rd. NN11: Dav 1D 8
Balmoral Av. NN10: Rushd 2E 33
Balmoral Cl. NN6: E Bart 4H 41
NN8: Well 4E 29
Balmoral Ho. *NN2: K'thpe 6C 36*
(off Queen's Pk. Pde.)
Balmoral Rd. NN2: K'thpe 6C 36
Banbury Cl. NN4: N'ton 1F 57
NN8: Well 4E 29
Banbury La. NN4: N'ton 3D 56
NN7: Rother 1A 62
Banbury Rd. NN7: Kisl 5H 49
Bancroft Cl. NN4: Woot 5F 59
Bancroft Way NN4: Woot 5G 59
Bank, The NN1: N'ton 3F 5
Banks, The NN9: Well 2F 17
Bankside NN2: N'ton 4F 37
NN10: High F 4D 20
Bank Vw. NN4: N'ton 4B 58
Bannatyne's Health Club
Wellingborough 1A 28
Banner Cl. NN10: Rushd 4C 32
Bants La. NN5: Dus, N'ton 2F 51
(not continuous)
Baring Rd. NN5: N'ton 2A 52
Barker Cl. NN10: Rushd 3D 32
Barker Rd. NN6: E Bart 4G 41
Barley Cl. NN11: Dav 1E 7
Barley Ct. NN10: Rushd 4E 33
Barley Hill Rd. NN3: N'ton 6D 24
Barley La. NN2: K'thpe 2B 36
Barlow La. NN3: Moul 4A 24
Barnard Cl. NN5: Dus 1D 50
Barn Cl. NN4: Gra P 2F 65
Barn Cnr. NN4: Col 1C 64
Barnes Cl. NN11: Dav 4D 6
Barneswell Cl. NN6: Brix 1A 22
Barnet Cl. NN4: N'ton 1A 58
Barnet's Stile NN2: K'thpe 4C 36
Barnfield Cl. NN2: K'thpe 3B 36
Barnhill Sq. NN3: N'ton 1E 39
Barn La. NN7: Mil M 2H 63
Barn M. NN4: Col 1C 64
Barn Owl Cl. NN4: N'ton 3A 58
Barnstaple Cl. NN3: West F 2C 54
Barn Way NN5: Dus 4D 34
Barnwell Dr. NN10: Rushd 5C 32
Barnwell Gdns. NN8: Well 4D 16
Barnwell Rd. NN2: K'thpe 3D 36
NN8: Well 4D 16
Baron Av. NN6: E Bart 2H 41
Baronson Gdns. NN1: N'ton 1F 53
Barons Way NN2: K'thpe 3A 36
Barrack Rd.
NN1: N'ton 1C 4 (2C 52)
NN2: N'ton 2C 52
Barracks, The NN7: Braf G 1H 61
Barret Cl. NN8: Well 1C 28
Barrett Cl. NN10: High F 6D 20
Barringers Ct. NN29: Irch 4F 31
Barringers Gdns. NN29: Irch 4F 31
Barring M. NN5: Upton 4E 51
Barring St. NN5: Upton 4E 51
Barrington Rd. NN10: Rushd 5E 33
Barry Rd. NN1: N'ton 2G 53
Barton Flds. NN6: Ect 4B 40
Bartons Close, The
NN5: N'ton 6H 35
Barwick Ho. NN10: Rushd 3C 32
Basil Cl. NN4: N'ton 5D 58
Bassett Ct. NN4: Gra P 3D 64
Bassett Lowke Dr.
NN5: Upton 5E 51
Bassett Lowke Hall
NN2: N'ton 1D 52
Bassett Lowke Ho. NN1: N'ton . . .4D 4
Bassett's Ct. NN8: Well 1F 29
Bates Cl. NN10: High F 6D 20
Batsmans Dr. NN10: Rushd 1C 32
Battalion Dr. NN4: Woot 4E 59
Battle Cl. NN4: Woot 4D 58
Baukewell Ct. NN3: N'ton 4C 38
Baulmsholme Cl. NN4: N'ton . . .5C 52
Baunhill Cl. NN3: N'ton 2B 54
Baxter Ct. NN4: H'stone 3F 59
Beacon Bingo
Northampton 3H 51
Beacon Ct. NN4: N'ton 6G 51
Beaconsfield Pl.
NN10: Rushd 2D 32
Beaconsfield Ter. NN1: N'ton . . .2D 52
NN10: Rushd 2D 32
Beatty Cl. NN11: Dav 6G 7
Beaufort Dr. NN5: Dus 6E 35
Beaumaris Cl. NN10: Rushd 4E 33
Beaumont Dr. NN3: N'ton 4F 39
Beaune Cl. NN5: Dus 6B 34
Beauvais Ct. NN5: Dus 5B 34
Beck Ct. NN8: Well 5D 16
Becket's Vw.
NN1: N'ton 5F 5 (4E 53)
Beckett Ho. NN1: N'ton . . .3F 5 (3E 53)
Becket Way NN3: N'ton 2H 37
Bective Rd. NN2: K'thpe 3C 36
Bective Vw. NN2: K'thpe 3D 36
Bedale Rd. NN8: Well 5G 17
Beddoes Cl. NN4: Woot 5G 59
Bede Cl. NN10: High F 6E 21
Bedford Mans. NN1: N'ton 4E 5
Bedford Pl. NN1: N'ton . . .4E 5 (4D 52)
Bedford Rd. NN1: N'ton . . .5F 5 (4E 53)
NN4: N'ton 5F 5 (5G 53)
NN7: Lit Hou, Braf G 6D 54
NN10: Rushd 4E 33
Beech Av. NN3: N'ton 5G 37
NN6: Ect 3B 40
Beech Cres. NN29: Irch 6E 31
Beechcroft Gdns. NN3: N'ton . . .5G 37
Beech Dr. NN8: Well 6E 17
Beech Gro. NN3: N'ton 2B 38
NN10: Rushd 2B 32
Beech La. NN7: Kisl 5A 50
Beech Rd. NN10: Rushd 1D 32
Beechwood Dr. NN3: West F 6C 38
Beechwood Rd. NN5: Dus 2E 51
Beeston Av. NN3: West F 1D 54
Belfield Cl. NN3: N'ton 4H 37
Belfry La. NN4: Col 6B 58
Belfry Way NN11: Dav 5G 7
Belgrade Cen. NN8: Well 3G 29
Belgrave Ho.
NN1: N'ton 3C 4 (3C 52)

A-Z Northampton 67

Bell Ct. NN8: Well .6G 17
Bell End NN29: Woll .5B 44
Bell Hill NN9: Fine .5C 10
BELLINGE .5F 39
Bellman Ga. NN6: Syw .1H 25
Bellropes Sq. NN3: Ect B .5H 39
Bell St. NN8: Well .6G 17
Belmont Ct. NN1: N'ton .1B 4
Belmont Gdns. NN9: Raun .3C 14
Belmont Rd. NN11: Dav .6D 6
Belstead Rd. NN3: N'ton .3B 54
Belton Cl. NN4: N'ton .3C 58
Belvedere Cl. NN5: N'ton .2H 51
Belvoir Cl. NN5: Dus .6D 34
NN10: Rushd .5E 33
Bembridge Dr. NN2: K'thpe .6B 36
Benbow Cl. NN11: Dav .5G 7
Benedict Cl. NN10: Rushd .5B 32
Bengeworth Ct. NN8: Well .6G 17
Benham Ct. NN3: N'ton .4D 38
Benham Sports Arena .1F 37
Benjamin Sq. NN4: N'ton .1H 57
Bennett Cl. NN11: Dav .3C 6
Bentley Cl. NN3: N'ton .3H 39
Bentley Ct. NN8: Well .2H 17
Bentley Way NN11: Dav .4B 6
Bergerac Cl. NN5: New D .5B 34
Berkeley Cl.
NN1: N'ton .3H 5 (3F 53)
Berkeley Ho. NN1: N'ton .3B 4
Bern Links NN4: N'ton .6A 52
Bern Side NN4: N'ton .6A 52
Berrill St. NN29: Irch .6E 31
Berrister Pl. NN9: Raun .2E 15
Berry Cl. NN6: E Bart .2G 41
NN7: Rother .5D 56
Berrydale NN3: N'ton .4H 39
Berry Grn. Rd. NN9: Fine .4C 10
Berry La. NN4: Woot .6D 58
Berrymoor Ct. NN8: Well .3E 29
Berrymoor Rd. NN8: Well .4E 29
Berrywood Cl. NN5: Dus .2C 50
Berrywood Dr. NN5: Dus .2B 50
BERRYWOOD HOSPITAL .2C 50
Berrywood Rd. NN5: Dus .1B 50
Berwick Ho. NN2: K'thpe .2D 36
Berzerk Leisure .1A 38
Bestwell Ct. NN3: Lit B .1E 55
Bethany Homestead
NN2: N'ton .6E 37
Betjeman Cl. NN10: High F .6C 20
NN11: Dav .4C 6
Betony Cl. NN5: Dus .3B 50
Betony Wlk. NN10: Rushd .5D 32
Better Bodies Gym .1C 52
(off Nene Ent. Cen.)
Bevan Cl. NN8: Well .4A 18
Bevan Ct. NN8: Well .3A 18
Beverley Cres. NN3: N'ton .5H 37
Bewick Rd. NN3: West F .2C 54
Bibury Cl. NN8: Well .4D 28
Bibury Cres. NN3: N'ton .2B 38
Bidders Cl. NN1: N'ton .6D 4 (5D 52)
Bideford Cl. NN3: West F .2B 54
Billing Aquadrome .2F 55
Billing Arbours Ho.
NN3: N'ton .3C 38
Billing Brook Rd.
NN3: N'ton, West F .2B 38
Billing Gdn. Village
NN3: Gt Bil .2H 55
Billing La. NN3: N'ton .1E 39
NN6: Over .5D 24
Billingmead Wlk. NN3: Gt Bil .5F 39
(Camberley Cl.)
NN3: Gt Bil .6G 39
(Gibbsacre Ct.)
Billing Rd. NN1: N'ton .3F 5 (3E 53)
NN7: Braf G .3H 55
Billing Rd. E. NN3: N'ton .3H 53
Billing School Pl. NN7: Weed .6C 46
Billington St.
NN1: N'ton .1H 5 (2F 53)
Bilsdon Cl. NN10: Rushd .5B 32
Bilton Ct. NN8: Well .6D 16
Binder Cl. NN10: High F .4C 20
Birchall Rd. NN10: Rushd .3B 32
Birch Barn La. NN2: K'thpe .2A 36
Birch Barn Way NN2: K'thpe .2B 36
Birch Cl. NN4: Gra P .3E 65
Birchfield Ct. NN3: N'ton .6H 37
Birchfield Cres. NN3: N'ton .5A 38
Birchfield Rd. NN1: N'ton .1F 53
NN8: Well .1D 28
Birchfield Rd. E. NN3: N'ton .6G 37
Birch Rd. NN10: Rushd .3E 33
Birds Hill Rd. NN3: N'ton .4D 38
Birds Hill Wlk. NN3: West F .5D 38
(not continuous)
Birkdale Cl. NN2: N'ton .4F 37
NN11: Dav .5G 7
Birkdale Dr. NN10: Rushd .4F 33
Biscay Cl. NN29: Irch .5F 31
Bishops Ct. NN10: High F .5E 21
NN11: Dav .5E 7
Bishops Dr. NN2: K'thpe .4B 36
Bitten Ct. NN3: N'ton .4C 38
Bittern St. NN4: N'ton .3G 57
Blackberry La. NN4: N'ton .6H 51
Blackbird Ct. NN8: Well .5H 17
Black Cat Dr. NN5: Upton .5F 51
Black Cat St. NN5: Upton .5F 51
Blackfriars NN10: Rushd .4B 32
Black Lion Hill
NN1: N'ton .4A 4 (4B 52)
Blacksmith's Yd. NN6: Ect .3B 40
(off High St.)
BLACKTHORN .3F 39
Blackthorn Bri. Ct. NN3: N'ton .3F 39
Blackthorn Local Cen.
NN3: N'ton .3F 39
(off Blackthorn Bri. Ct.)
Blackthorn Rd. NN3: N'ton .3F 39
Blackthorn Wlk. NN3: N'ton .4F 39
(not continuous)
Blackwall Cl. NN4: N'ton .1A 58
Blackwell Cl. NN6: E Bart .3G 41
NN10: High F .3D 20
Blackwell Hill NN4: N'ton .3H 57
BLACKY MORE .5D 58
Blackymore La. NN4: N'ton .6D 58
Bladon Cl. NN3: N'ton .2A 38
Blake Cl. NN11: Dav .1G 9
Blakesley Cl. NN2: K'thpe .2C 36
Blake Wlk. NN10: High F .6C 20
Blanchard Cl. NN4: Woot .4E 59
Blaydon Wlk. NN8: Well .4E 17
Bledlow Ri. NN4: N'ton .3H 57
Blenheim Cl. NN10: Rushd .4C 32
Blenheim Rd. NN4: Far C .1B 58
NN8: Well .4D 16
Blinco Rd. NN10: Rushd .3E 33
Bliss La. NN7: Flore .4F 47
BLISWORTH .6F 63
Blisworth & Milton Malsor By-Pass
NN4: N'ton .1F 57
NN7: Blis, G'ton, Rother .6C 62
Blisworth Cl. NN4: N'ton .1A 58
Blisworth Pk. NN7: Blis .4D 62
Blisworth Rd. NN7: G'ton .3B 62
Bloomfield Cl. NN10: Rushd .3C 32
Bloomsbury Ho. NN1: N'ton .4D 4
Blossac Ct. NN5: Dus .6B 34
Blossom Way NN3: Lit B .6E 39
Blott's Gdns. NN9: Raun .2D 14
Bluebell Cl. NN8: Well .5H 17
Bluebell Ct. NN3: N'ton .3A 54
Bluebell Pk. (Mobile Home Pk.)
NN3: Moul .4A 24
Bluebell Ri. NN4: Gra P .4F 65
NN10: Rushd .5E 33
Blueberry Ri. NN3: Ect B .5G 39
Bly La. NN4: Upton .1D 56
NN5: Upton .4D 50
Boarden Cl. NN3: N'ton .6G 23
Board St. NN9: Irth .1B 20
Bobtail Ct. NN5: Dus .6E 35
Bodleian Cl. NN11: Dav .1D 8
Bolingbroke Pl. NN10: High F .3E 21
Bollinger Cl. NN5: Dus .6B 34
Bondfield Av. NN2: K'thpe .4D 36
Booth Dr. NN8: Well .6A 16
Booth La. Nth. NN3: N'ton .2A 38
Booth La. Sth. NN3: West F .4B 38
Booth Mdw. Ct. NN3: N'ton .2C 38
Booth Mdw. Wlk. NN3: N'ton .2B 38
Booth Ri. NN3: N'ton .1A 38
BOOTHVILLE .2A 38
Boothville Grn. NN3: N'ton .2B 38
Bordeaux Cl. NN5: Dus .6B 34
Borough Ct. NN10: High F .6D 20
BOROUGH HILL .6H 7
Borough Hill Country Pk. .5H 7
Borrowdale Wlk. NN3: N'ton .3A 38
Bosgate Cl. NN29: Boz .5H 45
Bostock Av. NN1: N'ton .1H 5 (2F 53)
Bostock M. NN1: N'ton .1H 5 (2F 53)
Bosworth Cl. NN4: N'ton .2A 58
Botmead Rd. NN3: N'ton .3G 39
Bougainvillea Dr. NN3: N'ton .3A 54
BOUGHTON .5C 22
Boughton Dr. NN10: Rushd .5B 32
Boughton Fair La. NN3: Moul .2H 23
BOUGHTON GREEN .1C 36
Boughton Grn. NN2: N'ton .6E 23
Boughton Grn. Rd.
NN2: K'thpe .3C 36
Boughton House & Gardens .5B 22
Boughton La. NN3: Moul .6F 23
Boughton Park .4C 22
Boughton Rd. NN2: Moul .5F 23
NN3: Moul .5F 23
Boulevard, The NN3: West F .5C 38
Boundary Av. NN10: Rushd .3A 32
Bourne Cl. NN8: Well .5C 16
Bourne Cres. NN5: N'ton .6G 35
Bourton Cl. NN4: N'ton .3H 57
Bourton Way NN8: Well .5E 29
Bouverie Rd. NN4: H'stone .3F 59
Bouverie St.
NN1: N'ton .2H 5 (3F 53)
Bouverie Wlk.
NN1: N'ton .2H 5 (3F 53)
Bow Ct. NN4: N'ton .6G 51
Bowden Rd. NN5: N'ton .3A 52
Bowen Sq. NN11: Dav .6E 7
Bower Wlk. NN3: N'ton .1C 38
(East Bank)
NN3: N'ton .2C 38
(Farm Fld. Ct.)
Bowlers Yd. NN6: E Bart .3G 41
Bowling Grn. La. NN5: Upton .3C 50
Bowmans Cl. NN4: N'ton .2F 57
Bowness NN8: Well .6C 16
Bowthorpe Cl. NN3: N'ton .3B 54
Box Gdns. NN8: Well .6G 17
BOZEAT .6H 45
Brackenborough NN6: Brix .2B 22
Brackenfield Sq. NN3: N'ton .6D 24
Brackenhill Cl. NN2: N'ton .4E 37
Brackley Cl. NN2: K'thpe .1D 36
BRACKMILLS .1G 59
Brackmills Bus. Pk.
NN4: Brack .1G 59
Bracknell NN8: Well .6C 16
Bradbury Rd. NN11: Newn .6F 9
Bradden Cl. NN2: K'thpe .2D 36
Bradfield Cl. NN8: Well .2G 17
NN10: Rushd .2F 33
Bradfield Rd. NN8: Well .2G 17
Bradgate Ho. NN1: N'ton .3G 5
Bradlaugh Cres. NN3: N'ton .1G 39
Bradmoor Ct. NN3: N'ton .2F 39
Bradshaw St.
NN1: N'ton .3C 4 (3C 52)
Bradshaw Way NN29: Irch .5D 30
Brad St. NN3: N'ton .2H 37
Braemar Cres. NN4: N'ton .3B 58
BRAFIELD-ON-THE-GREEN .1H 61
Brafield Rd. NN7: Cog .5H 55
NN7: Hort .6H 61
Braid Ct. NN8: Well .4D 16
Bramble Cl. NN3: West F .5E 39
Bramble End NN4: N'ton .3H 57
Bramcote Dr. NN3: West F .1D 54
Bramhall Ri. NN5: Dus .1D 50
Bramley Cl. NN10: Rushd .2B 32
Bramley Ct. NN29: Woll .4B 44
Bramley Gro. NN3: Lit B .5F 39
Bramley Ho. NN11: Dav .5E 7
(off Brook St.)
Brammar Ho. NN5: N'ton .2H 51
Brampton Apartments
NN6: Chap B .5A 22
Brampton Cl. NN8: Well .4D 16
Brampton Cotts. NN6: Chap B .5A 22
Brampton Heath Golf Course .1F 35
Brampton La. NN2: Chap B .6A 22
NN6: Chap B .6A 22
Brampton Valley La.
NN6: Chap B .6A 22
Brampton Wlk. NN3: N'ton .2F 37
Brampton Way NN6: Brix .2A 22
Branksome Av. NN2: K'thpe .6B 36
Brashland Dr. NN4: N'ton .5D 58
Braunston Cl. NN4: N'ton .1A 58
Braunston Rd. NN11: Dav .2A 6
Brawn Cl. NN9: Irth .3A 20
Brayford Cl. NN3: N'ton .2A 54
Breach Cl. NN6: Brix .1B 22
Brecon St. NN5: N'ton .1A 52
Breezehill NN4: Woot .5F 59
Breezehill Way NN8: Well .4G 17
Brembridge Cl. NN6: Syw .3H 25
Brendon Cl. NN3: West F .2A 54
Brentford NN8: Well .6B 16
Brer Ct. NN4: N'ton .4F 53
Bressingham Gdns.
NN4: N'ton .4C 58
Bretton Cl. NN5: Dus .6C 34
Briar Ct. NN9: Irth .1B 20
BRIAR HILL .6H 51
Briar Hill Rd. NN4: N'ton .1B 58
Briar Hill Wlk. NN4: N'ton .1B 58
Briars, The NN4: N'ton .6A 52
Briarwood Way NN29: Woll .6B 44
Brickett's La. NN7: Flore .4E 47
Brickhill Ct. NN8: Well .1E 29
Brickhill M. NN8: Well .1E 29
Brickhill Rd. NN8: Well .1C 28
Brick Kiln La. NN2: N'ton .1C 52
Brick Kiln Rd. NN9: Raun .1C 14
Brickwell Ct. NN3: West F .6E 39
Brickyard NN3: N'ton .1H 37
Bridge Mdw. Way NN4: Gra P .1E 65
Bridge St. NN1: N'ton .4C 4 (4C 52)
NN7: Weed .5C 46
NN9: Raun .2D 14
Bridgewater Dr.
NN3: West F, N'ton .2A 54
Bridle Cl. NN7: Braf G .1H 61
NN8: Well .2G 17
Bridle Path NN7: Braf G .1H 61
Brigadier Cl. NN4: Woot .4D 58
Brightwell Wlk. NN9: Irth .3H 19
Brindlestone Cl. NN4: N'ton .1F 57
Brindley Cl. NN10: Rushd .1B 32
NN11: Dav .2B 6
Brington Rd. NN7: Flore .4F 47
Briscoe Cl. NN2: K'thpe .1E 37
Bristle St. NN5: Upton .5E 51
Britannia Gdns. NN8: Well .1A 30
Britannia Trade Cen.
NN5: Dus .5F 35
Briton Gdns. NN3: N'ton .6H 37
Briton Rd. NN3: N'ton .1H 53
Briton Ter. NN3: N'ton .6H 37
Brittons Dr. NN3: N'ton .6D 24
BRIXWORTH .1A 22
Brixworth Country Park .3B 22
Brixworth Country Park Vis. Cen.
.3B 22
Brixworth Ct. NN5: Upton .5F 51
(off Clickers Dr.)
Brixworth Hall Pk. NN6: Brix .1A 22
Brixworth Ind. Est. NN6: Brix .1B 22
Broad Grn. NN8: Well .6F 17
Broadhurst Dr. NN3: West F .1D 54
Broadlands NN6: Brix .2A 22
NN6: Pits .1D 22
NN9: Raun .3E 15
NN10: Rushd .2D 32
Broad March NN11: Dav .1F 9
Broadmead Av. NN3: N'ton .5G 37
Broad St.
NN1: N'ton .2B 4 (3C 52)
NN6: Brix .2A 22
NN6: E Bart .3G 41
Broadway NN1: N'ton .6F 37
NN8: Well .2G 29
Broadway E. NN3: N'ton .6G 37
Brocade Cl. NN4: N'ton .1H 57
Brockhall Cl. NN2: K'thpe .3E 37
Brockhall Rd. NN2: K'thpe .3E 37
NN7: Flore .3E 47
Brockton St. NN2: N'ton .6D 36
Brockwood Cl. NN5: Dus .6C 34
Bromford Cl. NN3: Lit B .1E 55
Brooke Cl. NN8: Well .6B 16
NN10: Rushd .4D 32
Brooke Grn. NN8: Well .6B 16
Brooke M. NN8: Well .6B 16
Brookend NN4: Woot .6E 59
Brookes M. NN6: E Bart .2G 41
Brookfield Rd. NN2: N'ton .5E 37
NN10: Rushd .3C 32
Brookland Cres.
NN1: N'ton .6G 37
Brookland Rd. NN1: N'ton .6F 37
Brooklands Cl. NN11: Dav .6E 7
Brook La. NN5: N'ton .1H 51
Brooks Cl. NN4: Woot .5F 59
Brookside NN7: Weed .6B 46
NN9: Stanw .6A 14
NN29: Boz .6H 45
Brookside La. NN11: Badby .6C 8
Brookside Mdws.
NN5: N'ton .6G 35
Brooks Rd. NN9: Raun .2E 15
Brook St. NN1: N'ton .1A 4 (2B 52)
NN9: Raun .3D 14
NN11: Dav .5E 7
(not continuous)
Brook St. E. NN8: Well .1H 29
Brook St. W. NN8: Well .1F 29
Brook Ter. NN9: Irth .1B 20
Brook Va. NN8: Wilby .4C 28
Brook Vw. NN3: N'ton .4D 38
NN4: Gra P .2E 65
Broom Ct. NN4: N'ton .6H 51
Broomhill Cres. NN3: N'ton .1E 39
Brough Cl. NN5: Dus .6B 34
Broughton Pl. NN3: N'ton .4H 37
Brown Cl. NN5: Upton .3D 50
Browning Cl. NN10: Rushd .5F 33
NN11: Dav .3D 6

Browning Rd. NN8: Well 1C 28
Brownlee Pl. NN4: Woot 5G 59
Brownlow Ct. NN3: N'ton 3C 38
Browns Cl. NN3: Moul 3A 24
Browns Rd. NN11: Dav 6B 6
Browns Way
NN1: N'ton 5G 5 (4E 53)
Bruce St. NN5: N'ton 3H 51
Brundall Cl. NN3: N'ton 2B 54
Brunel Cl. NN8: Well 5B 16
NN11: Dav 3B 6
Brunel Dr. NN5: Upton 4E 51
Brunswick Pl.
NN1: N'ton 1G 5 (2E 53)
Brunswick Wlk. NN1: N'ton 1G 5
Brunting Rd. NN3: Moul 5A 24
Bryant Way NN10: High F 5D 20
Bryer Hill Furlong
NN7: Cog 3H 55
Buchanan Cl. NN4: N'ton 6A 52
Buckingham Cl. NN4: N'ton 4B 58
NN8: Well 4E 29
Buckle Ho. *NN5: N'ton 4B 52*
(off Byfield Rd.)
Buckwell Cl. NN8: Well 6F 17
Buckwell End NN8: Well 6F 17
Buckwell Pl. NN8: Well 1F 29
Bugbrooke Rd.
NN7: G'ton 3A 62
NN7: Kisl 6G 49
Bugby Dr. NN9: Irth 4D 12
Bugby Way NN9: Raun 2D 14
Bull Cl. NN29: Boz 5H 45
Bullfinch Way NN8: Well 4H 17
Bull Inn Cl. NN7: Weed 5C 46
Bullrush Wlk. *NN4: N'ton 3G 57*
(off Bitten St.)
Bunting Rd. NN2: N'ton 6C 36
Bunting Rd. Ind. Est.
NN2: N'ton 6C 36
Burdock Gdns. NN5: Dus 3B 50
Burford Av. NN3: N'ton 2B 38
Burford Way NN8: Well 3D 28
Burham Cl. NN4: Woot 6E 59
Burleigh Rd. NN2: N'ton 6C 36
Burleigh Ter. *NN29: Boz 5H 45*
(off Mile St.)
Burling Ho. NN1: N'ton 2G 53
Burlington Apartments
NN1: N'ton 2G 53
(off Roseholme Rd.)
Burns Cl. NN6: E Bart 3A 42
Burns Rd. NN8: Well 1B 28
NN11: Dav 3D 6
Burns St. NN1: N'ton 2E 53
BURROWS BUSH 4G 17
Burrows Bush *NN8: Well 5H 17*
(off Pym Cl.)
Burrows Ct. NN3: N'ton 3C 38
Burrows Farm La.
NN14: Lit A 1D 12
Burrows Va. NN6: Brix 1B 22
Burryport Rd. NN4: Brack 1H 59
Burton Cl. NN11: Dav 2D 6
Burton Rd. NN9: Fine 2C 10
Burton Ter. *NN29: Boz 5H 45*
(off Puddingbag La.)
Burtram Cl. NN3: West F 6C 38
Burwood Rd. NN3: N'ton 5H 37
BURY CLOSE 6E 21
Bury Cl. NN10: High F 5E 21
Burystead Pl. NN8: Well 1G 29
Burystead Ri. NN9: Raun 2E 15
Burywell Rd. NN8: Well 5H 17
Buscot Pk. Way
NN11: Dav 1D 6
Bush Cl. NN8: Well 6E 17
Bush Hill NN3: N'ton 6A 38
Bushland Rd. NN3: N'ton 5A 38
Business Centre, The
NN5: N'ton 3H 51
Buswell Cl. NN7: Weed 6B 46
Butchers Ct. NN8: Well 5H 17
Butcher's La. NN2: Bou 5C 22
Butlin Cl. NN11: Dav 4D 6
Butlin Ct. NN8: Lit I 4A 30
Butterfields NN8: Well 3F 29
Buttermere NN8: Well 6C 16
Buttermere Cl.
NN3: N'ton 4A 38
Buttmead NN7: Blis 6F 63
Butts Cft. Cl. NN4: N'ton 5C 58
Butts Rd. NN4: N'ton 5C 58
NN8: Well 4E 29
NN9: Raun 3E 15
Byfield Rd. NN5: N'ton 3A 52
Byron Cres. NN10: High F 6C 20
NN10: Rushd 3A 32
Byron Rd. NN8: Well 1D 28
Byron St. NN2: N'ton 6F 37
Byron Wlk. NN11: Dav 4D 6

C

Cabot Cl. NN11: Dav 2E 7
Cadnams La. NN9: Irth 6A 12
Caldbeck Wlk. NN3: N'ton 3A 38
Calder Grn. NN5: N'ton 6G 35
Caledonian Ho. *NN5: N'ton 3A 52*
(off Argyle St.)
Calstock Cl. NN3: West F 2B 54
Calvert Cl. NN8: Well 3F 17
Camberley Cl. NN3: Gt Bil 5F 39
Camborne Cl. NN4: Del 2B 58
Cambria Cres. NN3: N'ton 6A 38
Cambridge St. NN2: N'ton 1C 52
NN8: Well 6G 17
NN10: Wym 6C 32
Camden Sq. NN29: Boz 6H 45
Camelot Way NN5: Dus 1C 50
Cameron Cl. NN5: N'ton 2G 51
NN11: Dav 6D 6
Cameron Cres. NN5: N'ton 2G 51
Cameron Dr. NN5: N'ton 2G 51
Campaign Cl. NN4: Woot 4E 59
Campanula Cl. NN3: N'ton 3A 54
Campbell Cl. NN7: Weed 5A 46
NN10: Rushd 5F 33
Campbell Rd. NN8: Well 3G 29
Campbell Sq.
NN1: N'ton 2D 4 (3C 52)
NN6: E Bart 3G 41
Campbell St.
NN1: N'ton 1C 4 (2C 52)
CAMP HILL 1G 57
Campion Cl. NN10: Rushd 5D 32
Campion Ct. NN3: Gt Bil 6F 39
Campion Wlk. NN3: Gt Bil 6F 39
Camp La. NN4: Kisl 6A 50
NN7: Kisl 6H 49
Camrose Rd. NN5: N'ton 1A 52
Canal Way NN4: N'ton 2F 57
Candace Ct. NN5: N'ton 1G 51
Candleford NN3: N'ton 3F 39
Cannon St. NN8: Well 6G 17
Canonbury NN8: Well 1C 28
Canons Wlk. NN2: K'thpe 4A 36
Canterbury Ct. NN1: N'ton 5F 5
Capell Ri. NN7: Flore 4E 47
Cardigan Cl. NN5: N'ton 1H 51
Cardinal Cl. NN4: N'ton 4B 58
Cares Orchard NN7: Braf G 6H 55
Carey Cl. NN3: Moul 4H 23
Carey Ct. NN3: Moul 4H 23
Carey St. NN1: N'ton 1F 5 (2E 53)
Carey Way NN10: Rushd 2F 33
Carline Ct. NN3: N'ton 3B 38
Carlton Cl. NN10: Rushd 6C 32
Carlton Gdns. NN2: N'ton 6E 37
Carlton M. NN10: High F 6E 21
Carlton Rd. NN2: N'ton 5E 37
Carlyle Av. NN5: N'ton 2G 51
Carmarthen Way
NN10: Rushd 5E 33
Carnegie St. NN10: Rushd 3C 32
Carol Trusler M. *NN2: N'ton 2B 52*
(off Mill La.)
Carousel Way NN3: N'ton 2D 54
Carrington Gdns.
NN3: West F 1D 54
Carr's Way NN7: Harp 3G 49
Carter Cl. NN8: Well 1H 29
Cartmel Pl. NN3: N'ton 4H 37
Cartmel Way NN10: Rushd 2F 33
Cartrill St. NN9: Raun 3C 14
Cartwright Rd. NN2: K'thpe 6C 36
Casterbridge Ct. NN4: H'stone . . .4E 59
Casterton Cl. NN9: Stanw 4A 14
Casterton Wlk. NN3: N'ton 2G 39
Castilian St.
NN1: N'ton 4D 4 (4D 52)
Castilian Ter.
NN1: N'ton 4E 5 (4D 52)
Castle, The
Wellingborough 1H 29
Castle Av. NN5: Dus 1E 51
Castle Bush NN5: Dus 1E 51
Castle Cl. NN5: Dus 1E 51
Castle Ct. NN8: Well 1H 29
NN10: Rushd 5C 32
Castlefields Cl. NN10: High F . . .5E 21
Castle Hill NN1: N'ton 3A 4 (3B 52)
NN11: Dav 6D 6
Castle La. NN8: Well 1G 29
Castle M. NN8: Well 1H 29
Castle Rd. NN8: Well 1H 29
Castle St. NN1: N'ton 3A 4 (3C 52)
NN8: Well 1H 29
Castle Ter. NN1: N'ton . . .3A 4 (3B 52)
Castle Vw. NN8: Well 1H 29
Castle Way NN8: Well 1G 29
Caswell Rd. NN4: Brack 2G 59
Catesby Cl. NN2: K'thpe 3E 37
Cathedral of Our Lady & St Thomas
Northampton 1C 52
Catlow Cl. NN9: Raun 1C 14
Cattle Hill NN3: Gt Bil 5G 39
Cattle Mkt. Rd.
NN1: N'ton 5C 4 (4C 52)
Catton Cres. NN2: K'thpe 2H 35
Cauldecott Cl. NN4: N'ton 2E 57
Causeway, The NN3: Gt Bil 2G 55
NN4: N'ton 6H 51
Cavalry Dr. NN11: Dav 6D 6
Cavalry Flds. NN7: Weed 5A 46
Cavalry Hill NN7: Weed 5A 46
Cavalry Hill Ind. Pk.
NN7: Weed 5A 46
Cavendish Dr. NN3: N'ton 3B 54
Caxton Cl. NN11: Dav 3C 6
Cecil Rd. NN2: K'thpe 6C 36
Cedar Cl. NN6: Syw 5H 25
NN10: Rushd 5C 32
NN11: Dav 2E 7
NN29: Irch 6E 31
Cedar Ct. NN3: Moul 6A 24
NN5: N'ton 1G 51
Cedar Rd. NN1: N'ton 6F 37
Cedar Rd. E. NN3: N'ton 6G 37
Cedar Way NN8: Well 4F 17
NN10: High F 5D 20
Cedrus Ct. NN2: K'thpe 1H 35
Celandine Cl. NN10: Rushd 6E 33
Celeborn Pl. NN3: N'ton 2F 39
Celtic Cl. NN10: High F 4D 20
Cemetery La. NN10: High F 5D 20
Centaine Rd. NN10: Rushd 4C 32
Central Av. NN2: K'thpe 1B 36
NN8: Well 3E 29
Centurion Way NN4: Woot 6F 59
Chace Rd. NN8: Well 1A 30
Chadstone Av. NN2: K'thpe 1D 36
Chadwick Gdns. NN5: Dus 6F 35
Chaffinch Cl. NN4: N'ton 4H 57
Chalcombe Av. NN2: K'thpe 2C 36
Chalcombe Rd. NN2: K'thpe 3C 36
Chalfont Ct. NN1: N'ton 1B 4
Chalk La. NN1: N'ton 4A 4 (4B 52)
Chalon Cl. NN8: Well 3F 17
Chamberlain Av. NN8: Well 4E 29
Chamberlain Way NN9: Raun 4C 14
NN10: High F 6E 21
Chambers, The NN1: N'ton 2G 5
Chantelle Ct. NN11: Dav 4D 6
Chantry Cl. NN3: Gt Bil 4F 39
Chapel Cl. NN10: Rushd 2E 33
Chapel Grn. NN5: N'ton 5A 36
Chapel Hill NN10: High F 4D 20
NN14: Lit A 2D 12
NN29: Irch 5F 31
Chapel La. NN7: Blis 5E 63
NN7: Flore 4F 47
NN7: Kisl 6H 49
NN9: Stanw 6A 14
NN11: Badby 6C 8
NN11: Dav 5E 7
NN29: Gt Dod 1E 43
Chapel Pl. NN1: N'ton 2F 5 (3E 53)
Chapel Row *NN3: Gt Bil 5G 39*
(off High St.)
Chapman Rd. NN8: Well 2A 30
Chapmans Cl. NN29: Irch 6F 31
Chappell Ho. NN3: Moul 5A 24
Chardonnay Cl. NN5: New D 5C 34
Chariot Rd. NN4: Woot 6F 59
Charlbury Cl. NN8: Well 5E 29
Charlecote Way NN11: Dav 1D 6
Charles Bradlaugh Hall
NN2: K'thpe 2E 37
Charles Cl. NN10: High F 4E 21
Charles Ho. NN1: N'ton 4E 5
Charles Parker Building, The
NN10: High F 5E 21
(off Midland Rd.)
Charles Partridge Ct.
NN8: Wilby 4C 28
Charles Robinson Ct.
NN8: Well 2E 29
Charles St. NN1: N'ton . . .1D 4 (2D 52)
NN8: Well 3E 29
Charles Studd Rd. NN3: N'ton . . .1G 39
Charles Ter. *NN11: Dav 6E 7*
(off Oxford St.)
Charlock Rd. NN5: Dus 3B 50
Charlotts Row NN10: Rushd 3C 32
Charlton Cl. NN2: K'thpe 2C 36
Charnwood Av. NN3: West F 5B 38
Charnwood Cl. NN11: Dav 3D 6
Charter Ga. NN3: N'ton 1H 37
Chartwell Av. NN3: N'ton 2A 38
Chartwell Cl. NN11: Dav 1D 6
Charwelton Rd. NN11: Badby 6B 8
Chase, The NN6: Pits 1D 22
Chater St. NN3: Moul 4B 24
Chatsworth Av. NN3: N'ton 2D 38
Chatsworth Dr. NN8: Well 4C 16
Chatsworth Wlk. *NN11: Dav 1C 6*
(off Althorp Cl.)
Chaucer Ct. NN2: N'ton 5F 37
Chaucer Rd. NN8: Well 1C 28
Chaucer St. NN2: N'ton 5F 37
Chaucer Way NN11: Dav 5D 6
Cheaney Dr. NN4: Gra P 3D 64
Cheddar Cl. NN5: Dus 2F 51
Chedworth Cl. NN3: Ect B 5H 39
Cheese La. *NN8: Well 1G 29*
(off Market St.)
Chelfham Cl. NN3: West F 2B 54
Chelmsford Cl. NN4: N'ton 1A 58
Cheltenham Cl. NN10: Rushd . . .5E 33
Chelveston Rd.
NN9: Raun, Stanw 4C 14
NN10: High F 5F 21
Chepstow Cl. NN5: N'ton 2A 52
Chepstow Dr. NN8: Well 4C 16
Chequers La. NN8: Well 6G 17
Cheriton Cl. NN11: Dav 1E 7
Cheriton Way NN1: N'ton 3A 54
Cherry Av. NN8: Well 4G 17
Cherry Blossom Cl.
NN3: Gt Bil 5F 39
Cherry Cl. NN3: N'ton 5A 38
Cherry Ct. NN9: Irth 2A 20
Cherry Lodge Rd. NN3: N'ton . . .3F 39
Cherry Orchard NN10: Rushd . . .4E 33
Cherry Orchard Pl.
NN3: N'ton 6A 38
Cherry St. NN9: Irth 2A 20
Cherry Tree La. NN4: Gt Hou 6C 54
Cherrytree Wlk. NN6: Syw 5H 25
Cherry Wlk. NN9: Raun 4B 14
Cherwell, The NN11: Dav 6B 6
Cherwell Grn. NN5: N'ton 6H 35
Chesham Ri. NN3: N'ton 3F 39
Chester Av. NN7: Harp 3F 49
Chester Rd. NN8: Well 1A 30
NN10: Rushd 3B 32
NN29: Irch 3E 31
Chester Ter. NN7: Weed 5C 46
Chestnut Av. NN4: Woot 6D 58
Chestnut Cl. NN7: Mil M 1G 63
NN10: Rushd 2B 32
Chestnut Ct. NN3: N'ton 5G 37
Chestnut Rd. NN3: N'ton 6G 37
Chestnut Ter. NN3: N'ton 5G 37
Cheviot Ct. NN4: N'ton 6G 51
Chewton Cl. NN5: Dus 2F 51
Cheyne Wlk.
NN1: N'ton 4E 5 (4D 52)
Chichele Cl. *NN10: High F 6D 20*
(off Hind Stile)
Chichele College 5D 20
Chichele Ct. *NN10: Rushd 2D 32*
(off North St.)
Chichele St. NN10: High F 5E 21
Chichester Cl. NN11: Dav 6F 7
Chieftan Bus. Pk.
NN8: Well 5A 16
Chiltern Av. NN5: Dus 1F 51
Chiltern Cl. NN5: Dus 1F 51
Chiltern Rd. NN11: Dav 2D 6
Chiltern Way NN5: Dus 1F 51
Chilwell Ct. NN3: West F 1D 54
Chipsey Av. NN1: N'ton 3H 53
Chisholm Cl. NN4: Woot 6E 59
Choakles, The NN4: Woot 5H 59
Chowns Mill Bus. Pk.
NN9: Irth 3D 20
Christchurch Dr. NN11: Dav 1D 8
Christchurch Rd. NN1: N'ton 2G 53
Christine Ct. NN9: Raun 3D 14
Chulmleigh Wlk.
NN3: N'ton 2A 54
(not continuous)
Church Cl. NN7: Mil M 1H 63
Church Farm Cl. NN29: Boz 5H 45
Churchfield Cl. NN2: K'thpe 3E 37
Church Grn. NN5: N'ton 5H 35
(not continuous)
NN11: Badby 6C 8
Church Hall Rd. NN10: Rushd . . .4B 32
Church Hill NN3: Moul 4A 24
NN4: Woot 6E 59
NN9: Fine 4C 10

Churchill Av. NN3: N'ton 3H 37
NN8: Well 4E 17
NN9: Irth 4D 12
Churchill Rd. NN6: E Bart 3G 41
Church La. NN1: N'ton 2C 4 (3C 52)
NN3: Lit B 1E 55
NN6: Pits 1D 22
NN6: Syw 2H 25
NN7: Blis 6F 63
NN7: Braf G 1H 61
NN7: Kisl 5H 49
NN7: Lwr H 1A 34
NN8: Wilby 4B 28
NN29: Boz 5H 45
NN29: Gt Dod 1E 43
NN29: Woll 4B 44
Church M. NN3: Moul 4A 24
Church of the Holy Sepulchre 2C 4
Church's Factory NN1: N'ton 1D 4
Church St. NN2: Bou 5C 22
NN3: Moul 4A 24
NN6: Brix 1A 22
NN6: Mears A 3D 26
NN7: Rother 5C 56
NN7: Weed 6C 46
NN8: Well 1G 29
NN9: Fine 5C 10
NN9: Irth 1B 20
NN9: Raun 2E 15
NN9: Stanw 6A 14
NN10: Rushd 3D 32
NN11: Newn 5G 9
Church Vw. NN2: K'thpe 4B 36
NN3: Moul 3A 24
NN4: Woot 6E 59
NN6: Ect 3B 40
NN9: Raun 2D 14
NN29: Woll 4B 44
Church Wlk. NN3: Gt Bil 5F 39
NN9: Irth 1B 20
NN11: Dav 5E 7
NN14: Lit A 1D 12
NN29: Boz 5H 45
Church Way NN3: West F 6B 38
NN6: Ect 3B 40
NN8: Well 1G 29
Church Way Ct. NN3: West F 1B 54
Cineworld Cinema Northampton 4F 51
Cinnamon Cl. NN4: N'ton 5D 58
Circus End NN5: Dus 6E 35
Cirrus Pk. NN3: N'ton 6G 23
Cissbury Rd. NN4: N'ton 5H 51
City Bldgs. NN1: N'ton 3D 4
Clannell Rd. NN4: N'ton 3A 58
Clare Av. NN11: Dav 5E 7
Clare Cl. NN6: E Bart 4H 41
Claregate NN4: N'ton 3B 58
Clarence Av. NN2: K'thpe 6C 36
Clarence Ct. NN10: Rushd 5C 32
Clare Rd. NN8: Well 2C 28
Clare St. NN1: N'ton 1E 5 (2D 52)
NN9: Raun 3D 14
Clare Wlk. NN10: High F 6D 20
Clarke Cl. NN9: Irth 5D 12
Clarke Ct. NN6: E Bart 3H 41
Clarke Ho. *NN1: N'ton 1G 53*
(off Roe Rd.)
Clarke Rd. NN1: N'ton 1G 53
Claudius Way NN8: Well 3A 30
NN29: Irch 3A 30
Claughton Rd. NN4: Far C 6D 52
Claydon Cl. NN8: Well 6E 17
Claydon Rd. NN11: Dav 1C 6
Clayfield Cl. NN3: N'ton 1H 37
Clayland Cl. NN29: Boz 6G 45
Claylands, The NN7: Cog 3H 55
Claystones NN4: N'ton 1F 57
Cleburne Cl. NN9: Stanw 5A 14
Clee Ri. NN5: Dus 1F 51
Cleeve Way NN8: Well 4D 28
Clevedon Ct. *NN11: Dav 1D 6*
(off Hidcote Way)
Cleveland Pl. NN4: N'ton 1A 58
Clickers Dr. NN5: Upton 5F 51
Clickers M. NN5: Upton 5F 51
Clickers Pl. NN5: Upton 5F 51
Cliff Ct. NN3: Lit B 5E 39
CLIFFORD HILL 3F 55
Clifford Hill Mill NN7: Lit Hou 3E 55
Cliftonville NN1: N'ton 4G 5 (4E 53)
Cliftonville Ct. NN1: N'ton 3H 5 (3F 53)
Cliftonville Rd. NN1: N'ton 3H 5 (4F 53)
Clinton Rd. NN4: Far C 6B 52
Clipston Fld. Pl. NN3: Ect B 5G 39
Clipston Way NN5: Dus 6E 35
Clock Twr. Ct. NN3: N'ton 1C 38
Cloisters, The NN8: Well 2H 29
NN11: Dav 5F 7
Close, The NN2: K'thpe 3C 36
NN9: Irth 2B 20
Cloutsham St. NN1: N'ton 1E 5 (2D 52)
Clover Dr. NN10: Rushd 5E 33
Clover Fld. NN4: Gra P 3F 65
Clover La. NN2: K'thpe 2A 36
Clover St. NN5: Upton 4E 51
Clumber Dr. NN3: West F 2C 54
Cluniac Ct. NN3: N'ton 1G 39
Coaching Wlk. NN3: West F 5B 38
Cobblers Pl. NN29: Boz 6G 45
Cobblestone Ct. NN4: N'ton 1F 57
Cobb's La. NN29: Woll 4A 44
Cob Dr. NN4: Swan H 2D 56
Codlin Cl. NN3: Lit B 6E 39
Coffee Tavern Ct. *NN10: Rushd 3D 32*
(off High St.)
Coffee Tavern La. NN10: Rushd 3D 32
COGENHOE 3H 55
Coggins Cl. NN9: Raun 3C 14
Coldstream Cl. NN11: Dav 6D 6
Coldstream La. NN4: H'stone 3E 59
Cole Ct. NN9: Raun 4C 14
Coleman St. NN9: Raun 3D 14
Coleraine Cl. NN2: K'thpe 3A 36
Coleridge Wlk. NN11: Dav 3D 6
Cole St. NN10: Rushd 1A 32
College Fld. Cl. NN3: Ect B 4G 39
College St. NN1: N'ton 3C 4 (3C 52)
NN8: Well 1E 29
NN9: Irth 1A 20
NN10: High F 5E 21
NN10: Rushd 3D 32
NN29: Woll 5B 44
College St. M. NN1: N'ton 3C 4
Collingcroft Cl. NN4: N'ton 4A 58
Collingdale Rd. NN3: N'ton 4B 38
Collingham Cl. NN9: Stanw 4A 14
COLLINGTREE 1C 64
Collingtree Ct. NN4: Col 1B 64
COLLINGTREE PARK 5C 58
Collingtree Park Golf Course 6C 58
Collingtree Rd. NN7: Mil M 1H 63
Collingwood Rd. NN1: N'ton 6F 37
Collingwood Way NN11: Dav 5G 7
Collins Hill NN7: Flore 3E 47
Collins St. NN1: N'ton 2F 53
Collmead Ct. NN3: N'ton 3F 39
Collyweston Rd. NN3: N'ton 2G 39
Colmar Cl. NN11: Dav 3C 6
Colne Way NN5: N'ton 6G 35
Colonial Dr. NN4: N'ton 6C 58
Coltsfoot Rd. NN10: Rushd 6E 33
Columbus Ct. NN11: Dav 2D 6
Colwell Rd. NN8: Well 1A 30
Colwyn Rd. NN1: N'ton 2E 53
Comfrey Cl. NN10: Rushd 6D 32
Commercial St. NN1: N'ton 5C 4 (4C 52)
NN10: High F 6D 20
Commercial Way NN8: Well 1G 29
Compass Bus. Pk. NN4: Brack 2H 59
Compton Cl. NN6: E Bart 4G 41
Compton Ho. NN1: N'ton 3A 4
Compton Rd. NN8: Well 6A 18
Compton St. NN1: N'ton 2A 4 (3C 52)
Compton Way NN6: E Bart 4G 41
Concourse NN1: N'ton 3C 4
Conduit La. NN1: N'ton 3C 4 (3C 52)
Coneygree NN4: H'stone 3F 59
Coneygree Ct. NN3: Gt Bil 6F 39
Coneygree Wlk. NN3: Gt Bil 6F 39
Coneywell Ct. NN3: West F 6D 38
Conifer Ri. NN3: West F 5C 38
Coniston Av. NN3: N'ton 4H 37
Coniston Cl. NN8: Well 6C 16
NN10: High F 3D 20
NN11: Dav 5C 6
Connaught St. NN1: N'ton 1D 4 (2D 52)
Connegar Leys NN7: Blis 6G 63
Connolly Rd. NN5: Dus 1B 50
Constable Dr. NN8: Well 4E 17
Conway Cl. NN5: N'ton 5G 35
NN8: Well 5C 16
NN10: Rushd 5C 32
Conyngham Rd. NN3: West F 5D 38
Cony Wlk. NN4: Gra P 2F 65
Cook Cl. NN11: Dav 2E 7
Co-operative Row NN10: Rushd 4D 32
Cooper Dr. NN8: Well 3F 17
Copper Leaf Cl. NN3: Moul 1A 38
Coppice Cl. NN11: Dav 1E 9
Coppice Dr. NN3: N'ton 2G 37
Copse Cl. NN2: K'thpe 2H 35
Copymoor Cl. NN4: Woot 5G 59
Corbieres Cl. NN5: New D 5C 34
Cordon Cl. NN3: N'ton 4F 39
Cordon Cres. NN6: E Bart 3H 41
Cordwainer Ho. *NN5: N'ton 4A 52*
(off Byfield Rd.)
Cordwainers NN10: Rushd 4E 33
Cornfield Cl. NN2: K'thpe 2B 36
Cornflower Cl. NN4: Gra P 3F 65
Cornhill Cl. NN5: Dus 4E 35
Corn La. NN8: Well 1G 29
Corn Mill Cl. NN8: Well 2B 30
Cornwell Bus. Pk. NN4: Brack 1H 59
Corolla Way NN4: Upton 2C 56
Coronation Av. NN10: Rushd 4A 32
Coronation Ct. NN4: N'ton 6A 52
Coronation Rd. NN11: Newn 5F 9
Corran Cl. NN5: N'ton 1G 51
Cory Gdns. NN7: Harp 2G 49
Cosgrove Rd. NN2: K'thpe 2C 36
Cosgrove Way NN2: K'thpe 2C 36
Cotswold Av. NN5: Dus 1E 51
Cotswold Cl. NN11: Dav 2D 6
Cotswold Ct. NN5: Dus 1E 51
Cotswold Dr. NN8: Well 4D 28
Cottage Cl. NN2: K'thpe 3A 36
Cottage Gdns. NN3: Gt Bil 4F 39
NN10: Rushd 6E 33
Cottagewell Ct. NN3: West F 6D 38
COTTARVILLE 6B 38
Cottarville NN3: West F 6B 38
Cottesbrooke Gdns. NN4: N'ton 4D 58
Cottesbrooke Pk. NN11: Dav 2C 6
Cottesmore Cl. NN5: Dus 6D 34
Cottesmore Way NN8: Well 1D 28
Cottingham Dr. NN3: Moul 6H 23
Cotton Ct. *NN4: N'ton 5C 52*
(off Pomfret Arms Cl.)
COTTON END 6B 52
Cotton End NN4: N'ton 6C 4 (5C 52)
Cotton La. NN9: Stanw 6G 13
Cotton Mdw. NN5: N'ton 2G 51
Cottons, The NN8: Well 4D 16
Coughton Cl. NN11: Dav 1D 6
Coulon Cl. NN29: Irch 6E 31
Council St. NN29: Boz 5H 45
NN29: Woll 5B 44
Countess Ct. NN5: N'ton 2A 52
Countess Rd. NN5: N'ton 2A 52
Counties Crematorium, The NN4: Mil M 5G 57
County Court Northampton 2D 4 (3D 52)
County Court Bulk Cen. Northampton 4B 4 (4C 52)
County Ground, The 1G 53
COURTEENHALL 6E 65
Courteenhall Cl. NN2: K'thpe 2D 36
Courteenhall Rd. NN7: Blis, Court 5F 63
Court La. NN29: Boz 5H 45
Courtman Rd. NN9: Stanw 5A 14
Court M. NN8: Well 2H 29
Courtney Rd. NN10: Rushd 4C 32
Court Rd. NN1: N'ton 4B 4 (4C 52)
Courtwood NN9: Stanw 6A 14
Courtyard, The NN3: N'ton 6A 38
NN6: Ect 3B 40
Court Yd. La. NN11: Badby 6C 8
Covallen Ct. NN10: Rushd 2E 33
Covent Gdns. NN3: Gt Bil 5G 39
Coverack Cl. NN4: Del 2B 58
Coverdale NN2: K'thpe 2H 35
Covert Cl. NN2: K'thpe 1A 36
Covington Gro. NN8: Well 5G 17
Covington St. NN1: N'ton 2G 53
Cowbeck Cl. NN4: Woot 6E 59
Cowgill Cl. NN3: N'ton 4F 39
Cowley Cl. NN4: Woot 4D 58
Cowley Rd. NN11: Dav 4D 6
Cowper Cl. NN6: E Bart 3A 42
NN9: Irth 2H 19
Cowper Rd. NN8: Well 1C 28
NN11: Dav 5D 6
Cowper St. NN1: N'ton 2E 53
Cowper Ter. NN2: N'ton 6E 37
Cowslip Cl. NN10: Rushd 5E 33
Cow Yd. NN2: K'thpe 4B 36
Crabb St. NN10: Rushd 4D 32
Crabb Tree Dr. NN3: N'ton 6D 24
Crabtree Cl. NN8: Well 3F 29
Crabtree Ho. *NN11: Dav 5E 7*
(off Brook St.)
Craddock Ct. NN29: Irch 5F 31
Cragside NN8: Well 5C 16
Craigie NN8: Well 1C 28
Cranbrook Rd. NN2: N'ton 6C 36
Crane Cl. NN8: Well 3G 29
NN10: Rushd 1D 32
Crane Wlk. NN3: N'ton 1C 38
Cranford Ho. *NN2: K'thpe 4C 36*
(off Kingsland Av.)
Cranford Rd. NN2: K'thpe 4C 36
Cranmere Av. NN1: N'ton 3H 53
Cransley Wlk. NN3: N'ton 1G 39
Cranstoun St. NN1: N'ton 1D 4 (2D 52)
Craven St. NN1: N'ton 1D 4 (2D 52)
Crawford Av. NN5: N'ton 2G 51
Crawley Av. NN8: Well 4D 16
Crediton Cl. NN3: West F 2B 54
Crescent, The NN1: N'ton 1F 53
NN3: Moul 4B 24
NN7: Flore 3F 47
NN8: Well 4D 16
NN10: Rushd 3A 32
Crescent Lodge NN6: Over 1E 39
Cresswell Rd. NN10: Rushd 3B 32
Crestline Ct. NN3: N'ton 2E 39
Crestwood Gdns. NN3: N'ton 2D 38
Crestwood Rd. NN3: N'ton 1C 38
Cricklade Cl. NN3: N'ton 3B 54
Crickley Cres. NN4: N'ton 6G 51
Crimea Cl. NN4: Woot 4E 59
Crispian Ct. NN10: Rushd 3C 32
Crispin Ct. NN9: Irth 2A 20
Crispin Ho. NN1: N'ton 3A 4
Crispin St. NN1: N'ton 2B 4 (3C 52)
Crocket Cl. NN2: N'ton 5E 37
Crocus Way NN10: Rushd 6D 32
Croft, The NN5: N'ton 6H 35
NN6: Brix 1A 22
NN7: Weed 5C 46
NN11: Dav 1E 9
Croft Cl. NN8: Well 6C 16
Crofters Cl. NN4: N'ton 4B 58
Croftmeadow Ct. NN3: N'ton 3F 39
Crofton Ct. NN3: N'ton 6F 23
Croft Way NN7: Weed 6A 46
NN10: Rushd 2F 33
Crome Cl. NN8: Well 3F 17
Cromer Rd. NN9: Fine 5D 10
Cromwell Ct. NN8: Well 6H 17
Cromwell Rd. NN10: Rushd 2E 33
Cromwell St. NN1: N'ton 1B 4 (3C 52)
Cropedy Wlk. NN11: Dav 1C 6
Cross, The NN4: Gt Hou 1C 60
Crossbrooks NN4: Woot 5F 59
Crosse Cl. NN7: Weed 5C 46
Cross Hill NN6: Brix 1A 22
Cross Rd. NN8: Well 5H 17
Cross St. NN3: Moul 4A 24
NN11: Dav 5D 6
Cross Waters Cl. NN4: Woot 5F 59
Cross Way NN9: Irth 3H 19
Crouch Rd. NN9: Irth 2B 20
Croughton Cl. NN2: K'thpe 2C 36
Crowberry Av. NN3: Moul 6A 24
Crow La. NN3: Lit B 1G 55
Crow La. Ind. Est. NN3: Gt Bil 1G 55
Crown Court Northampton 2D 4 (3D 52)
Crown Ct. NN10: Rushd 2A 32
Crown Pk. NN10: Rushd 1A 32
Crownsmead NN4: N'ton 2F 57
Crown Way NN10: Rushd 1A 32
Crowthorp Rd. NN3: N'ton 2G 39
Croxdale Cl. NN2: K'thpe 2H 35
Croyland Rd. NN8: Well 1E 29
Cube, The NN1: N'ton 4E 5
Cubleigh Cl. NN3: Moul 1A 38
Cullahill Ct. NN4: N'ton 1G 57
Culworth Cres. NN2: K'thpe 2D 36
Cumberland Av. NN9: Stanw 5A 14
Cumberland Cl. NN3: N'ton 4G 37
Cumbrae Dr. NN3: Gt Bil 5G 39
Cunningham Cl. NN10: High F 6D 20
NN11: Dav 5G 7
Curlbrook Cl. NN4: Woot 5G 59
Curlew Way NN11: Dav 4E 7
Currie Rd. NN2: K'thpe 6C 36
Curtis M. NN8: Well 4C 16
Curtlee Hill NN4: Woot 6F 59
Cut Throat La. NN29: Gt Dod 6B 28
Cyclamen Cl. NN3: N'ton 3A 54
Cygnet Dr. NN4: Swan H 3E 57
CYNTHIA SPENCER HOSPICE 3H 37

Cypress Ct.—Embankment Golf Course

Cypress Ct. NN3: N'ton 4C **38**
Cyril St. NN1: N'ton 2G **5** (3E **53**)

D

Daffodil Dr. NN10: Rushd 6D **32**
Dag La. NN29: Boz 6H **45**
Daimler Cl. NN3: N'ton 3H **39**
NN11: Dav 4C **6**
Dainty Gro. NN4: Gra P 2E **65**
Dairy Cl. NN6: Brix 2A **22**
Dairymeadow Ct. NN3: N'ton . . .1D **38**
Dairy Way NN9: Irth 3A **20**
Daisy Cft. NN10: Rushd 5E **33**
Dale, The NN8: Well 6C **16**
Dale Av. NN8: Well 6C **16**
Dale Cl. NN6: Mears A 3E **27**
NN8: Well 6C **16**
NN11: Dav 2D **6**
Dale Ho. *NN8: Well 1F 29*
(off Hill St.)
Dalestones NN4: N'ton 1F **57**
Dale St. NN8: Well 1F **29**
Dalkeith Rd. NN8: Well 4F **29**
DALLINGTON 6H **35**
Dallington Ct. NN5: N'ton 1H **51**
Dallington Grn. NN5: N'ton 1H **51**
Dallington Haven NN5: N'ton . . .1H **51**
Dallington Pk. Rd.
NN5: N'ton 1H **51**
Dallington Rd. NN5: N'ton 1H **51**
Dalston Wlk. NN3: N'ton 3A **38**
Damherst Piece NN6: Brix 2B **22**
Damson Dell NN3: Lit B 1E **55**
Dance Way NN8: Well 3F **17**
Dando Cl. NN29: Woll 6B **44**
Danefield Rd. NN3: N'ton 5H **37**
Daneholme Av. NN11: Dav 3E **7**
Daneholme Cl. NN11: Dav 3E **7**
Dane Ridge NN5: Dus 3E **51**
Danes Backside NN2: K'thpe 4B **36**
Danes Camp Leisure Cen. 3B **58**
Danes Camp Way NN4: N'ton . . .1F **57**
Danetre Dr. NN11: Dav 5F **7**
Danetree Gdns. NN3: N'ton 5H **37**
DANETRE HOSPITAL 1E **9**
Danewood Gdns. NN3: N'ton 5H **37**
Daniels Rd. NN8: Lit I 4A **30**
Dapplestone Cl. NN4: N'ton 1F **57**
Darby Cl. NN8: Well 6A **16**
Dardis Cl. NN2: N'ton 6E **37**
Darenth Ct. NN1: N'ton 1C **4**
Dark La. NN9: Gt Har 1D **16**
Darnell Way NN3: N'ton 2H **37**
Dartford Cl. NN4: N'ton 1A **58**
Dartmouth Row NN11: Dav 6F **7**
Darwin Wlk. NN5: Dus 6E **35**
Dave Bowen Cl. NN5: Upton 3D **50**
DAVENTRY 6E **7**
Daventry & District Golf Course
. . . . .4G **7**
Daventry & District Sports Club
. . . . .2F **9**
Daventry Country Park 3F **7**
Daventry Country Park Vis. Cen.
. . . . .2F **7**
Daventry Indoor Bowling Club . . .6A **6**
Daventry Interchange
NN11: Dav 2D **6**
Daventry Leisure Cen. 5E **7**
Daventry Mus. (Moot Hall) *5E 7*
(off Market Sq.)
Daventry Retail Pk. NN11: Dav . . .2C **6**
Daventry Rd. NN11: Newn 5F **9**
Daventry Sports Pk. 6A **6**
Da Vinci Cl. NN5: Upton 4E **51**
Davy Cl. NN8: Well 5A **16**
Dayrell Rd. NN4: N'ton 1G **57**
Dayrell Sq. NN4: N'ton 1H **57**
Dayrell Wlk. NN4: N'ton 1H **57**
Dayton St. NN10: Rushd 3C **32**
Deacon Cl. NN10: Rushd 2F **33**
Deacons Ct. NN3: N'ton 3G **39**
Deal Ct. NN1: N'ton 1D **4** (2D **52**)
Deal St. NN1: N'ton 1C **4** (2C **52**)
Dean Cl. NN9: Raun 2D **14**
NN10: Rushd 5C **32**
Deancourt Dr. NN5: Dus 6C **34**
Deans Row NN7: G'ton 3A **62**
Deansway NN3: N'ton 3G **39**
Dean Wlk. NN11: Dav 3D **6**
Dearlove Ct. *NN1: N'ton 2B 4*
(off Regent St.)
Debdale Rd. NN3: N'ton 4A **38**
NN8: Well 6E **17**
Deer Cl. NN4: Gra P 3F **65**
Deer Pk. Rd. NN3: N'ton 1G **37**
Dee Wlk. NN11: Dav 6B **6**
De Ferneus Dr. NN9: Raun 2D **14**
Delamere Rd. NN4: Del 2C **58**
Delapre Abbey Gdns. 6E **53**
Delapre Ct. NN4: Del 1C **58**
Delapre Cres. NN4: Del 6C **52**
Delapre Cres. Rd. NN4: Del 6B **52**
Delapre Park Golf Course 1E **59**
Delapre St. NN4: Far C 6B **52**
Delf La. NN7: Lwr H 1A **34**
Dell, The NN6: E Bart 3G **41**
Dell Cres. NN3: N'ton 2F **39**
Dell Pl. NN10: Rushd 3D **32**
Delta Ho. NN1: N'ton 2B **4**
Delta Way NN2: K'thpe 2H **35**
Delves, The NN9: Raun 3C **14**
Demswell NN6: Brix 1B **22**
Denbigh Rd. NN3: N'ton 3B **54**
Denby Dale NN8: Well 4D **16**
Dencora Bus. Pk. NN8: Well 1A **28**
Dene Cl. NN8: Well 5C **16**
Denford Way NN8: Well 4D **16**
Denington Ct. NN8: Well 3G **29**
Denington Ind. Est. NN8: Well . . .3G **29**
(not continuous)
Denington Rd. NN8: Well 3G **29**
Denmark Ct. NN10: Rushd 4E **33**
Denmark Rd.
NN1: N'ton 3F **5** (3E **53**)
NN10: Rushd 4E **33**
Dennetts Cl. NN11: Dav 2D **6**
Denney Cres. NN11: Dav 5D **6**
Denston Cl. NN4: N'ton 3B **58**
Dent Cl. NN5: Dus 2B **50**
Denton Cl. NN10: Rushd 2E **33**
NN29: Irch 5F **31**
Derby Rd. NN1: N'ton 2E **53**
Derling Dr. NN9: Raun 3E **15**
Derngate NN1: N'ton 4D **4** (4D **52**)
Derngate Gym 4D **4**
Derngate Theatre, The
. . . . .4D **4** (4D **52**)
Derwent Cl. NN5: N'ton 6H **35**
NN8: Well 5C **16**
NN11: Dav 6C **6**
Derwent Dr. NN5: N'ton 6H **35**
Devonshire Cl. NN2: Bou 5C **22**
NN8: Well 5E **17**
Devonshire Ho. *NN5: N'ton 3A 52*
(off Alma St.)
Devon Wlk. NN10: Rushd 4E **33**
Devon Way NN3: N'ton 2G **37**
Dewar Dr. NN11: Dav 3C **6**
Diamond Centre, The
Irthlingborough 1D **20**
Diamond Dr. NN9: Irth 3H **19**
Diamonds Bus. Cen.
NN9: Irth 6C **12**
Diamond Way NN9: Irth 1C **20**
Diana Ho. NN8: Well 6D **16**
Diana's Health & Fitness
Wellingborough Squash Club
. . . . .4A **18**
Dickson Cl. NN4: N'ton 6H **51**
Digby Cl. NN5: Dus 2E **51**
Dimock Sq. NN4: N'ton 1H **57**
Dingle, The NN11: Dav 1E **9**
Dingle Rd. NN10: Rushd 3H **31**
Dingley Wlk. NN3: N'ton 2G **39**
Ditchford Cl. NN4: Woot 5F **59**
Ditchford La.
NN8: Irth, Rushd 6G **19**
Ditchford Rd. NN8: Well 4F **19**
Dixon Rd. NN2: K'thpe 1E **37**
Dobson Cl. NN4: Gt Hou 1D **60**
Doctors La. NN29: Gt Dod 1E **43**
Doddington Rd. NN6: E Bart 3H **41**
NN8: Well 5F **29**
NN8: Wilby 5B **28**
NN29: Woll 4H **43**
Doddridge Ho. NN1: N'ton 3B **4**
Doddridge St.
NN1: N'ton 3B **4** (4C **52**)
(not continuous)
Dolben Av. NN9: Stanw 6H **13**
Dolben Cl. NN9: Fine 5C **10**
Dolben Sq. NN9: Fine 5D **10**
Donellan Grn. NN3: N'ton 1D **38**
Donne Cl. NN10: High F 6C **20**
Donovan Ct. NN3: West F 1C **54**
Don White Rd. NN8: Well 1H **17**
Dorchester Ct. *NN5: Dus 5D 34*
(off Port Rd.)
Dore Cl. NN3: N'ton 2F **39**
Dorman Cl. NN3: N'ton 3H **37**
Dorset Gdns. NN2: K'thpe 4D **36**
Dorset Rd. NN2: K'thpe 4D **36**
Doubles, The NN11: Dav 6D **6**
Douglas Rd. NN5: Dus 1B **50**
Dovecote Cl. NN9: Raun 2E **15**
Dovecote Dr. NN14: Lit A 2D **12**
Dover Cl. NN10: Rushd 4F **33**
Dover Ct. NN5: N'ton 4B **52**
Dove's La. NN3: Moul 4B **24**
Downing Way NN11: Dav 2E **9**
Downs, The NN9: Well 2E **17**
Downsway NN4: N'ton 5B **58**
Downwood Cl. NN3: N'ton 4G **39**
Dowthorpe End NN6: E Bart 3G **41**
Dowthorpe Hill NN6: E Bart 4G **41**
Drake Cl. NN11: Dav 6G **7**
Drapery NN1: N'ton 3C **4** (3C **52**)
Draycott Cl. NN3: West F 2B **54**
DRAYTON 5C **6**
Drayton Cl. NN10: Rushd 5C **32**
Drayton Flds. Ind. Est.
NN11: Dav 2B **6**
Drayton Pk. NN11: Dav 1D **6**
Drayton Pl. NN9: Irth 6B **12**
Drayton Rd. NN9: Irth 6B **12**
Drayton Wlk. NN2: K'thpe 3D **36**
Drayton Way NN11: Dav 3B **6**
Drive, The NN1: N'ton 6F **37**
NN5: Dus 2C **50**
NN8: Well 2G **29**
NN10: Rushd 4D **32**
Drovers Wlk. NN2: K'thpe 2A **36**
Druids Way NN3: N'ton 2F **37**
Drum La. NN1: N'ton 3C **4** (3C **52**)
Drummond Cl. NN6: Pits 1D **22**
Drydale Av. NN3: N'ton 4H **37**
Dryden Av. NN11: Dav 5D **6**
Dryden Rd. NN5: N'ton 2H **51**
NN8: Well 6A **18**
Dryden St. NN9: Raun 3C **14**
Dryden Way NN10: High F 6C **20**
Dryfield Wlk. *NN3: West F 6E 39*
(off Brickwell Ct.)
Dryland Rd. NN3: N'ton 5A **38**
Dryleys Ct. NN3: N'ton 2F **39**
Drywell Ct. NN3: West F 6E **39**
Duchess End NN6: Mears A 3E **27**
Duchy Cl. NN10: High F 6E **21**
Duck End NN29: Woll 4B **44**
Duck La. NN7: Harp 3F **49**
Duck St. NN10: Rushd 3D **32**
Duckworth Dell NN3: N'ton 1D **38**
Dukelands NN7: Weed 6A **46**
Dukes Grn. Rd. NN7: Kisl 6G **49**
Duke St. NN1: N'ton 1D **4** (2D **52**)
NN8: Well 3D **28**
Dulce Rd. NN5: Dus 1E **51**
Dulley Av. NN8: Well 4F **29**
Dulverton Rd. NN3: West F 2B **54**
Duncan Cl. NN3: N'ton 6F **23**
Duncan Ct. NN8: Well 3D **28**
Dundee St. NN5: N'ton 3H **51**
Dunnock La. NN4: Gra P 2F **65**
Dunster St. NN1: N'ton . . .2E **5** (3D **52**)
DUSTON 1E **51**
Duston Cl. NN11: Dav 4C **6**
Duston Mill La. NN5: N'ton 5F **51**
Duston Rd. NN5: N'ton 2F **51**
Duston Sports Cen. 1E **51**
Duston Wildes NN5: Dus 5C **34**
DW Fitness
Northampton 5A **4** (4B **52**)
Dybdale Cres. NN8: Well 6E **17**
Dychurch La.
NN1: N'ton 3D **4** (3D **52**)
NN29: Boz 6H **45**

E

Eady Cl. NN3: Moul 4B **24**
Eagle Dr. NN4: Del 1E **59**
Eaglehurst NN6: Brix 1B **22**
Ealing Ter. NN10: Rushd 2C **32**
EARLS BARTON 3G **41**
Earls Barton Mus. 3G **41**
Earls Barton Rd.
NN6: Mears A 3D **26**
NN29: Gt Dod 2B **42**
Earlsfield Cl. NN4: Woot 5G **59**
Earl St. NN1: N'ton 2D **4** (3D **52**)
East Bank NN3: N'ton 1C **38**
E. Butterfield Ct. NN3: N'ton 2D **38**
Eastcote Rd. NN7: G'ton 5A **62**
East Cres. NN10: Rushd 3B **32**
Eastern Av. Nth. NN2: K'thpe 2D **36**
Eastern Av. Sth. NN2: K'thpe 5D **36**
Eastern Cl. NN2: K'thpe 2D **36**
Eastern Way NN11: Dav 5E **7**
Eastfield NN7: Blis 6F **63**
Eastfield Cl. NN5: Dus 6E **35**
Eastfield Cres. NN9: Fine 4E **11**
Eastfield Rd. NN4: Del 6C **52**
NN5: Dus 1D **50**
Eastfield Rd. NN6: Brix 2A **22**
NN8: Well 5H **17**
NN9: Irth 1B **20**
NN29: Woll 5B **44**
East Gro. NN10: Rushd 2D **32**
Eastlands Rd. NN9: Fine 4E **11**
E. Langham Rd. NN9: Raun 2D **14**
E. Leys Ct. NN3: Moul 6A **24**
Eastmead Ct. NN3: West F 6E **39**
Easton La. NN29: Boz 5G **45**
East Oval NN5: N'ton 5H **35**
E. Paddock Ct. NN3: N'ton 3E **39**
East Pk. Pde. NN1: N'ton 1F **53**
E. Priors Ct. NN3: N'ton 3E **39**
East Rising NN4: N'ton 4D **58**
East St. NN1: N'ton 2H **5** (3F **53**)
NN9: Stanw 6A **14**
NN29: Irch 5F **31**
Eaton Ho. NN1: N'ton 1G **5**
Eaton Rd. NN5: Dus 6C **34**
Eaton Wlk. NN10: Rushd 3D **32**
Ebbw Va. Rd. NN9: Irth 2H **19**
ECTON 3B **40**
ECTON BROOK 5H **39**
Ecton Brook Rd. NN3: Ect B 4H **39**
Ecton Hall NN6: Ect 3B **40**
Ecton La. NN6: Syw, Ect 2H **25**
Ecton La. Pk. NN3: Gt Bil 6H **39**
Ecton Pk. Rd. NN3: Ect B 4G **39**
Ecton St. NN1: N'ton 3F **5** (3E **53**)
Eden Cl. NN3: N'ton 3H **37**
NN11: Dav 6C **6**
Eden M. *NN9: Irth 2A 20*
(off Hayway)
Edgar Mobbs Way NN5: N'ton . . .4F **51**
Edgehill Dr. NN11: Dav 1E **7**
Edgehill Rd. NN5: Dus 6F **35**
Edgemead Cl. NN3: N'ton 6C **24**
Edgemont Rd. NN3: West F 6C **38**
Edges Ct. NN3: Moul 6A **24**
Edinburgh M. NN2: K'thpe 5C **36**
Edinburgh Rd. NN2: K'thpe 5C **36**
NN8: Well 4E **29**
Edinburgh Sq. NN11: Dav 4D **6**
Edison Cl. NN8: Well 5A **16**
Edison Ct. NN8: Well 5A **16**
Edison Dr. NN5: Upton 5F **51**
Edith St. NN1: N'ton 2G **5** (3E **53**)
Edmonds Cl. NN8: Well 3G **29**
Edward Cl. NN10: High F 4E **21**
Edwardian Cl. NN4: Woot 4E **59**
Edward Rd. NN29: Irch 6F **31**
Edwards Dr. NN8: Well 6D **16**
Edward Watson Cl.
NN2: K'thpe 2B **36**
Edwinstowe Cl. NN3: West F 2C **54**
Egerton Cl. NN11: Dav 3C **6**
Eider Cl. NN11: Dav 4E **7**
Einstein Cres. NN5: Dus 2E **51**
Einstein Wlk. NN5: Dus 2E **51**
Ekins Cl. NN3: West F 5B **38**
Eldean Rd. NN5: Dus 6D **34**
Elderberry Ct. NN3: N'ton 4G **39**
Elder Dr. NN11: Dav 3E **7**
Eleonore Ho. NN3: N'ton 4A **38**
Elgin St. NN5: N'ton 3H **51**
Eliot Way NN10: High F 6C **20**
Elizabeth Cl. NN6: E Bart 2G **41**
NN8: Well 3D **28**
Elizabeth Ct. NN10: High F 4E **21**
Elizabeth Rd. NN11: Dav 4D **6**
Elizabeth St.
NN1: N'ton 2H **5** (3F **53**)
Elizabeth Wlk.
NN1: N'ton 2H **5** (3F **53**)
Elizabeth Way NN6: E Bart 2F **41**
NN9: Irth 3A **20**
NN10: High F 3E **21**
Ellan Ct. NN10: Rushd 2A **32**
Ellesmere Av. NN5: N'ton 2G **51**
Ellfield Ct. NN3: N'ton 4D **38**
Ellis M. NN5: N'ton 5H **35**
Ellison Cl. NN9: Raun 2C **14**
Elm Cl. NN7: Braf G 1H **61**
Elm Gro. NN4: Woot 5G **59**
Elmhurst Av. NN3: N'ton 5G **37**
Elmhurst Ct. NN3: N'ton 5G **37**
Elmington Rd. NN3: N'ton 2G **39**
Elm St. NN1: N'ton 1D **4** (2D **52**)
NN8: Well 5F **17**
Elm Wlk. NN10: High F 5D **20**
Elmwood Wlk. NN5: Dus 6C **34**
Elsden Rd. NN8: Well 6A **18**
Elton Cl. NN3: N'ton 2F **39**
Elwes Way NN3: Gt Bil 5F **39**
Elysium Ter. NN2: N'ton 1C **52**
Embankment, The
NN8: Well 3A **30**
Embankment Golf Course 2A **30**

A-Z Northampton 71

Emerald Way
NN1: N'ton ... 4A 4 (4B 52)
Emley Cl. NN3: West F ... 6D 38
Emmanuel Cl. NN11: Dav ... 1E 9
Encon Ct. NN3: N'ton ... 6F 23
Enfield Cl. NN5: Dus ... 1B 50
Ennerdale Cl. NN3: N'ton ... 4G 37
NN11: Dav ... 5C 6
Ennerdale Rd. NN3: N'ton ... 4G 37
NN10: Rushd ... 2F 33
Enstone Ct. NN8: Well ... 4E 29
Enterprise Cl. NN8: Well ... 5A 16
Enterprise Rd. NN9: Raun ... 2D 14
Entwood Dr. NN3: N'ton ... 2F 39
Epping Wlk. NN11: Dav ... 3D 6
Epsom Cl. NN10: Rushd ... 5F 33
Equestrian Way
NN7: Weed ... 5B 46
Ericsson Cl. NN11: Dav ... 2E 7
Ermine Rd. NN3: N'ton ... 2G 39
Esher Ct. NN3: N'ton ... 3B 38
Eskdale Av. NN3: N'ton ... 4H 37
Eskdale Cl. NN8: Well ... 5C 16
Essex Rd. NN10: Rushd ... 4E 33
Essex St. NN2: N'ton ... 1C 52
Ethel St.
NN1: N'ton ... 2G 5 (3E 53)
Eton Cl. NN7: Weed ... 5C 46
Euston Rd. NN4: Far C ... 6C 52
Evans Cl. NN11: Dav ... 6G 7
Evelyn Wlk. NN9: Raun ... 3D 14
Evelyn Way NN29: Irch ... 6G 31
Evenley Rd. NN2: K'thpe ... 2C 36
Evensford Wlk. NN9: Irth ... 3H 19
Everdon Cl. NN2: K'thpe ... 3E 37
Everdon Pk. NN11: Dav ... 2C 6
Evergreen Dr. NN14: Lit A ... 2D 12
Everitt Cl. NN8: Well ... 3H 29
Evesham Cl. NN8: Well ... 4E 29
Evesham Ct. NN3: N'ton ... 6E 25
Ewenfield Rd. NN9: Fine ... 5D 10
Excalibur Cl. NN5: Dus ... 2C 50
Excelsior NN8: Well ... 1C 28
Excelsior Ct. NN9: Irth ... 1A 20
Excelsior Gdns. NN5: Dus ... 1C 50
Exeter Cl. NN11: Dav ... 1E 9
Exeter Pl. NN1: N'ton ... 1F 5 (2E 53)
Exmoor Cl. NN3: West F ... 2B 54
Express Bus. Pk.
NN10: Rushd ... 2H 31
Express Cl. NN9: Irth ... 3A 20
Eyeletter Ho. *NN5: N'ton ... 3A 52*
(off Greenwood Rd.)
Eynon Cl. NN3: Moul ... 4H 23

F

Fairfield NN7: Blis ... 3D 62
Fairfield Rd. NN2: N'ton ... 5F 37
Fairground Way NN3: N'ton ... 3C 54
Fairhurst Way NN6: E Bart ... 3H 41
Fairmead Cres. NN10: Rushd ... 5B 32
Fairmead Ri. NN2: K'thpe ... 1H 35
Fair Mile NN2: K'thpe ... 1A 36
Fairoaks, The NN3: West F ... 1D 54
Fairoaks Dr. NN9: Raun ... 2C 14
Fairway NN2: N'ton ... 5E 37
Fairway, The NN9: Well ... 2E 17
NN11: Dav ... 5G 7
Falconers Cl. NN11: Dav ... 4E 7
Falconers Ri. NN4: N'ton ... 3A 58
Falcutt Way NN2: K'thpe ... 2D 36
Fallowfield NN9: Well ... 3E 17
Fallow Wlk. NN2: K'thpe ... 1A 36
Faracre Ct. NN3: Gt Bil ... 6F 39
Faracre Wlk. NN3: Gt Bil ... 6F 39
Faraday Cl. NN5: Upton ... 4F 51
NN8: Well ... 5A 16
NN11: Dav ... 3C 6
Faraday Ct. NN8: Well ... 5A 16
Faramir Pl. NN3: N'ton ... 2F 39
Far Brook NN6: Brix ... 3A 22
FAR COTTON ... 1B 58
Far End NN5: N'ton ... 3H 51
Faringdon Ct. NN3: N'ton ... 6E 25
Farmbrook Ct. NN3: N'ton ... 2D 38
Farm Cl. NN2: K'thpe ... 3B 36
Farmclose Rd. NN4: Woot ... 5E 59
Far Mdw. Ct. NN3: N'ton ... 2C 38
Farmers Cl. NN4: Woot ... 6E 59
Farm Fld. Ct. NN3: N'ton ... 2C 38
Farmhill Rd. NN3: N'ton ... 1E 39
Farm Rd. NN8: Well ... 3E 17
Farnborough Dr. NN11: Dav ... 1C 6
FARNDISH ... 3F 45
Farndish Cl. NN10: Rushd ... 3B 32
Farndish Rd. NN29: Irch ... 5F 31
Farndon Cl. NN3: N'ton ... 1D 38
Farnham Dr. NN10: Rushd ... 5B 32
Farnworth Cl. NN5: Dus ... 6E 35
Farraxton Sq. NN4: N'ton ... 1G 57
Farthingstone Rd. NN7: Weed ... 6B 46
Favell Way NN3: West F ... 1B 54
Fawsley Dr. NN11: Dav ... 2C 6
Fawsley Rd. NN4: Far C ... 1C 58
Faxfield Wlk. NN3: West F ... 6D 38
Faxton Cl. NN2: K'thpe ... 3D 36
Feast Fld. Cl. NN29: Woll ... 6B 44
Fellmead Rd. NN3: N'ton ... 2G 39
Fellows Cl. NN29: Woll ... 4A 44
Fell Wlk. NN8: Well ... 5D 16
Fengate Cl. NN3: N'ton ... 2G 39
Fennel Ct. NN4: N'ton ... 6D 58
Fenners Cl. NN10: Rushd ... 3F 33
Ferndale Rd. NN3: N'ton ... 5B 38
Fernie Fld. NN3: Moul ... 1A 38
Fernie Way NN8: Well ... 1D 28
Fernmoor Dr. NN9: Irth ... 1B 20
Fern Rd. NN10: Rushd ... 2A 32
Ferrers Ct. NN10: High F ... 4E 21
Ferrestone Rd. NN8: Well ... 5G 17
Ferris Row NN3: N'ton ... 2D 54
Festival Cl. NN9: Irth ... 4D 12
Fetter St. NN1: N'ton ... 4D 4 (4D 52)
Fettledine Rd. NN9: Irth ... 4D 12
Fieldgate Cl. NN4: Woot ... 6F 59
Fieldmill Rd. NN3: Gt Bil ... 6F 39
Fieldmill Sq. NN3: Gt Bil ... 6G 39
Field Rose Sq. NN3: Ect B ... 5G 39
Fields Vw. NN8: Well ... 1H 29
Fieldway NN3: N'ton ... 6H 37
Fienesgate NN4: N'ton ... 2F 57
Fiennes Ct. NN11: Dav ... 1E 7
Fife St. NN5: N'ton ... 2H 51
Filleigh Way NN3: N'ton ... 2A 54
FINEDON ... 5D 10
Finedon Cally Banks Nature Reserve
... 6A 10
Finedon Community Sports &
Leisure Cen. ... 5D 10
Finedon Hall NN9: Fine ... 5C 10
Finedon Rd. NN8: Well ... 5H 17
NN9: Bur L, Fine ... 2A 10
NN9: Irth ... 6G 11
NN15: Bur L ... 2A 10
Finedon Rd. Ind. Est.
NN8: Well ... 2G 17
Finedon Sta. Rd. NN9: Fine ... 2A 10
Finney Dr. NN4: Gra P ... 2E 65
Firbank Cl. NN3: West F ... 1D 54
Firdale Av. NN10: Rushd ... 1D 32
Firecrest Wlk. *NN4: N'ton ... 3G 57*
(off Bittern St.)
Firs, The NN11: Dav ... 4E 7
Firs Ct. NN4: H'stone ... 3F 59
First Av. NN8: Well ... 2D 28
First La. NN5: N'ton ... 3H 51
Firsview Dr. NN5: Dus ... 6D 34
Fir Tree Gro. NN29: Boz ... 6H 45
Fir Tree Wlk. NN3: West F ... 5C 38
Fish All. NN29: Boz ... 5H 45
Fishers Cl. NN3: Lit B ... 6F 39
Fishmarket
Northampton ... 3C 4
Fishponds Rd. NN3: Lit B ... 5E 39
Fish St. NN1: N'ton ... 3D 4 (3D 52)
Fitness 4 Less
Northampton ... 4B 4
(off Sol Central)
Fitzgerald Ct. NN3: West F ... 5E 39
Fitzgerald Rd. NN3: West F ... 5E 39
Fitzroy Pl. NN1: N'ton ... 3A 4 (3B 52)
Fitzroy Ter. NN1: N'ton ... 1C 4 (2C 52)
Fitzwilliam Ct. *NN10: Rushd ... 3C 32*
(off Fitzwilliam St.)
Fitzwilliam Leys
NN10: High F ... 4D 20
Fitzwilliam Rd. NN9: Irth ... 6B 12
Fitzwilliam St.
NN10: Rushd ... 3C 32
Five Acres Fold NN4: N'ton ... 6H 51
Flaxlands Ct. NN3: N'ton ... 4D 38
Flaxwell Ct. NN3: West F ... 1D 54
Fleetwind Dr. NN4: N'ton ... 4D 58
Fleming Cl. NN8: Well ... 4B 16
Fletcher Rd. NN10: Rushd ... 2C 32
Flintcomb Ri. NN3: N'ton ... 4F 39
Flinters Cl. NN4: Woot ... 4F 59
Flint Jetty *NN4: N'ton ... 6H 51*
(off Pitstone Rd.)
FLORE ... 4F 47
Flore Hill NN7: Flore ... 5C 46
Florence Rd. NN1: N'ton ... 2F 53
Floribunda Dr. NN4: N'ton ... 6H 51
Flowerhill Dr. NN8: Well ... 5H 17
Flying Dutchman Way
NN11: Dav ... 4C 6
Ford La. NN4: Brack ... 6H 53
Forest Ct. NN10: Rushd ... 2F 33
Forest Rd. NN4: Del ... 6C 52
Forfar St. NN5: N'ton ... 2H 51
Forge, The *NN10: Rushd ... 4D 32*
(off Brooke Cl.)
Forresters, The *NN9: Raun ... 4D 14*
(off Thorpe St.)
Fort Pl. NN1: N'ton ... 3A 4 (3B 52)
Fortune Cl. NN3: N'ton ... 3C 54
Forum Cinema
Northampton ... 5D 38
Fosberry Cl. NN4: Woot ... 5F 59
Foskett Cl. NN10: Rushd ... 2C 32
Foskitt Ct. Nth. NN3: Gt Bil ... 6G 39
Foskitt Ct. Sth.
NN3: Gt Bil ... 1F 55
Foskitt Wlk. NN3: Gt Bil ... 6F 39
Fosse Cl. NN8: Well ... 4D 28
Fosse Grn. NN10: Rushd ... 2E 33
Foundry Ct. *NN11: Dav ... 6E 7*
(off Foundry Pl.)
Foundry Pl. NN11: Dav ... 6E 7
Foundry St.
NN1: N'ton ... 5C 4 (4C 52)
Foundry Wlk. NN11: Dav ... 6E 7
Fourth Av. NN8: Well ... 2D 28
Fowey Cl. NN8: Well ... 5C 16
Foxcovert Rd. NN3: N'ton ... 2F 39
Foxendale Sq. NN3: Ect B ... 5H 39
Foxfield Way NN4: Gra P ... 3F 65
Foxford Cl. NN4: N'ton ... 3H 57
Foxglove Cl. NN4: Gra P ... 3F 65
NN10: Rushd ... 5E 33
Foxgrove Av. NN2: K'thpe ... 3A 36
Fox Hill NN4: Del ... 2C 58
Foxhill Rd. NN3: Ect B ... 5H 39
Foxtail Way NN5: Dus ... 3B 50
Foxwell Sq. NN3: N'ton ... 6D 24
Foxwood Cl. NN10: Rushd ... 3A 32
Franciscan Cl. NN10: Rushd ... 5B 32
Francis Ct. NN10: Rushd ... 2A 32
Francis Dickins Cl.
NN29: Woll ... 4C 44
Francis Jetty
NN1: N'ton ... 4C 4 (4C 52)
Francis St. NN1: N'ton ... 1B 4 (2C 52)
NN9: Raun ... 5B 14
Francis Ter. *NN9: Raun ... 5B 14*
(off Stanwick Rd.)
Frank Large Wlk. NN5: Upton ... 2C 50
Franklin Cres. NN5: N'ton ... 2F 51
Franklin Point *NN5: N'ton ... 3A 52*
(off Weedon Rd.)
Franklin's Cl. NN6: Ect ... 3B 40
Franklin St. NN5: N'ton ... 3H 51
Franklin Way NN11: Dav ... 2D 6
Fraser Cl. NN11: Dav ... 5F 7
Fraser Rd. NN3: N'ton ... 1B 38
Freehold St. NN2: N'ton ... 1C 52
Freeman Ct. NN8: Well ... 6H 17
Freeman Way NN9: Fine ... 4F 11
Freeschool St.
NN1: N'ton ... 4B 4 (4C 52)
Fremeaux Ter. NN2: K'thpe ... 5B 36
Frencham Cl. NN4: N'ton ... 6H 51
Friar's Av. NN4: Del ... 2B 58
Friars Cl. NN4: Del ... 2B 58
NN8: Well ... 2G 29
Friar's Ct. NN4: Del ... 2B 58
Friar's Cres. NN4: Del ... 2C 58
Friary, The NN1: N'ton ... 3D 4
Friary Cl. NN11: Dav ... 5F 7
Frinton Cl. NN10: Rushd ... 5B 32
Frobisher Cl. NN11: Dav ... 5G 7
Frog Hall NN6: Brix ... 1A 22
Frontier Cen. ... 4D 12
Frost Ct. NN29: Gt Dod ... 1D 42
Frosty Hollow NN4: N'ton ... 5C 58
Froxhill Cres. NN6: Brix ... 2A 22
Froxhill Wlk. NN6: Brix ... 2A 22
Fuchsia Cl. NN3: N'ton ... 3A 54
Fuchsia Way
NN10: Rushd ... 6D 32
Fulford Dr. NN2: N'ton ... 4E 37
Fulleburn Ct. NN3: N'ton ... 4C 38
Fuller Rd. NN3: Moul ... 5A 24
Fullingdale Ct. NN3: N'ton ... 4A 38
Fullingdale Rd.
NN3: N'ton ... 5H 37
Fullwell Rd. NN29: Boz ... 4H 45
Fulmar La. NN8: Well ... 3G 17
Furber Ct. NN3: N'ton ... 3B 38
Furnace Dr. NN11: Dav ... 4C 6
Furnells Cl. NN9: Raun ... 2D 14
Furze Ct. NN4: N'ton ... 6A 52
Furze Rd. NN7: Braf G ... 1H 61
Furze Wlk. NN2: N'ton ... 5E 37
Fusilier Rd. NN11: Dav ... 6D 6
Fusilier Way NN7: Weed ... 5A 46
Fylingdale NN2: K'thpe ... 2H 35

G

Gable Cl. NN11: Dav ... 6D 6
Gable Ct. M. NN3: West F ... 6B 38
Gadesby Ct. NN3: N'ton ... 4C 38
Gainsborough Dr. NN8: Well ... 4F 17
Gainsborough Way NN11: Dav ... 1E 7
Gaiter & Spat
NN1: N'ton ... 3G 5 (3E 53)
Gala Casino
Northampton ... 1C 4
Galahad Ct. NN5: Dus ... 2C 50
Galane Cl. NN4: N'ton ... 2F 57
Galileo Cl. NN5: Dus ... 2E 51
Gallery Cl. NN3: N'ton ... 1E 39
Gallfield Ct. NN3: Gt Bil ... 1G 55
Galliard Ct. *NN1: N'ton ... 2F 53*
(off Stimpson Av.)
Gallowhill Rd. NN4: Brack ... 2H 59
Gambrel Rd. NN5: N'ton ... 3F 51
Gammidge Ct. *NN9: Fine ... 5D 10*
(off Milner Rd.)
Gannet La. NN8: Well ... 3G 17
Ganton Cl. NN11: Dav ... 5G 7
Gap, The NN29: Woll ... 5C 44
Gardenfield NN10: High F ... 6D 20
Gardenfields Cl. NN9: Irth ... 4D 12
Garden Flds. Ct. NN29: Irch ... 5F 31
Gardner Cl. NN9: Raun ... 2C 14
Garfield Cl. NN2: K'thpe ... 4C 36
Garfield St. NN2: K'thpe ... 4B 36
Garners Way NN7: Harp ... 2G 49
Garrick Rd. NN1: N'ton ... 2H 53
Garrow Cl. NN9: Irth ... 6A 12
Garsdale NN2: K'thpe ... 1H 35
Gas St. NN1: N'ton ... 4B 4 (4C 52)
Gatcombe Ho. *NN10: Rushd ... 3D 32*
(off Portland Rd.)
Gatelodge Cl. NN3: N'ton ... 1C 38
Gates Cl. NN9: Irth ... 6A 12
Gateway Cl. NN4: Woot ... 5F 59
Gawaine Ct. NN5: Dus ... 2C 50
Gayhurst Cl. NN3: Moul ... 6H 23
GAYTON ... 3A 62
Gayton Rd. NN7: Blis ... 5D 62
Gedling Cl. NN3: West F ... 1D 54
Geldock Rd. NN3: Lit B ... 6E 39
Gentian Cl. NN10: Rushd ... 5E 33
George Nutt Ct. NN4: Far C ... 1C 58
George Row
NN1: N'ton ... 4C 4 (4C 52)
Georges Dr. NN4: Gra P ... 2E 65
George St. NN8: Well ... 6G 17
NN9: Irth ... 2A 20
NN10: High F ... 4E 21
NN10: Rushd ... 3D 32
Gervase Sq. NN3: Gt Bil ... 6G 39
Gharana Nivas NN8: Well ... 6H 17
Gibbsacre Ct. NN3: Gt Bil ... 6G 39
Gibbsacre Wlk. NN3: Gt Bil ... 6G 39
Gibraltar Ct.
NN1: N'ton ... 1C 4 (2C 52)
Gibson La. NN5: N'ton ... 1H 51
Gifford Ct. NN5: Dus ... 1E 51
NN5: N'ton ... 4A 52
Gifford La. NN5: Upton ... 4E 51
Gilbey Cl. NN9: Well ... 2E 17
Gillitts Rd. NN8: Well ... 2E 29
Gillsway NN2: K'thpe ... 3A 36
Gipsy La. NN29: Irch ... 5A 30
Gisburne Rd. NN8: Well ... 5G 17
Glade, The NN9: Well ... 2E 17
Glade Cl. NN3: Lit B ... 6F 39
Glades, The NN4: Gra P ... 3F 65
Gladiator Cl. NN4: Woot ... 6F 59
Gladstone Cl. NN5: N'ton ... 1A 52
Gladstone Rd. NN5: N'ton ... 6A 36
Gladstone St. NN9: Raun ... 3D 14
Gladstone Ter. NN9: Raun ... 3D 14
Glaisdale Cl. NN2: K'thpe ... 2H 35
Glamis Cl. NN10: Rushd ... 4F 33
Glan y Mor Ter. NN2: K'thpe ... 2C 36
Glapthorn Wlk. NN3: N'ton ... 2G 39
Glasgow St. NN5: N'ton ... 2H 51
Glassbrook Rd. NN10: Rushd ... 3B 32
Glassthorpe La. NN7: Harp ... 2C 48
Glastonbury Rd. NN4: Del ... 2C 58
Glebe, The NN3: Moul ... 5A 24
NN7: Flore ... 4E 47
NN11: Badby ... 6C 8
NN11: Dav ... 1E 9
Glebe Av. NN4: H'stone ... 3E 59
Glebe Cl. NN4: H'stone ... 3E 59
Glebe Farm Cl. NN4: Col ... 1C 64
Glebe Farm Ct. NN29: Gt Dod ... 1E 43

Glebeland Cres. NN5: N'ton 1H **51**
Glebeland Gdns. NN5: N'ton 6H **35**
Glebeland Rd. NN5: N'ton 6H **35**
Glebeland Wlk. NN5: N'ton 6H **35**
Glebe La. NN4: Gt Hou 1C **60**
NN6: Pits 1C **22**
NN7: Lwr H 1A **34**
Glebe Rd. NN6: Mears A 3D **26**
NN7: Cog 3H **55**
Glebe Way NN4: H'stone 3E **59**
Glen Av. NN7: Blis 3D **62**
Glenbank NN8: Well 1G **29**
Glendale Ct. NN3: Gt Bil 6G **39**
Glendale Wlk. NN3: Gt Bil 6G **39**
Glendower Cl. NN11: Dav 3C **6**
Gleneagles Cl. NN11: Dav 4G **7**
Gleneagles Dr. NN8: Well 4D **16**
Glenfield Cl. NN10: Rushd 2B **32**
Glenfield Dr. NN29: Gt Dod 2D **42**
Glengary NN3: Moul 6B **24**
Glenville NN3: N'ton 3H **37**
Gloucester Av. NN4: Del 1B **58**
(not continuous)
Gloucester Cl. NN4: Del 1B **58**
NN7: Weed 5B **46**
Gloucester Cres. NN4: Del 1B **58**
NN10: Rushd 2E **33**
Gloucester Pl. NN8: Well 1G **29**
Glovers Cl. NN9: Irth 3A **20**
Glovers La. NN9: Raun 4C **14**
Godwin Wlk. NN5: Dus 5F **35**
Goffs Yd. NN29: Boz 6H **45**
Goldcrest Ct. NN3: N'ton 2E **39**
Goldenash Ct. NN3: N'ton 3D **38**
Golding Cl. NN11: Dav 5E **7**
GOLDINGS 2E **39**
Goldings Local Cen.
NN3: N'ton 2E ***39***
(off Goldings Rd.)
Goldings Rd. NN3: N'ton 2E **39**
Goldsmith Rd. NN8: Well 1C **28**
Gold St. NN1: N'ton 4B **4** (4C **52**)
NN8: Well 6F **17**
Gold St. M. NN1: N'ton 4B **4**
Goodens La. NN29: Gt Dod 6F **29**
Goodwin Cl. NN8: Well 3G **17**
Goodwood Av. NN3: N'ton 3F **37**
Goodwood Rd. NN10: Rushd 5F **33**
Gordon Rd. NN8: Well 6H **17**
Gordon St. NN2: N'ton 1B **52**
NN10: Rushd 3B **32**
Gorse Cl. NN2: K'thpe 1B **36**
Gorseholm Ct. NN9: Irth 2B **20**
Gosforth NN8: Well 1C **28**
Goslar, The NN8: Well 2B **28**
Goughs Cotts. NN5: Dus 2E **51**
Goulsbra Rd. NN10: Rushd 5F **33**
Gowerton Rd. NN4: Brack 2G **59**
Grafton Cl. NN8: Well 4D **16**
Grafton Ho. NN1: N'ton 2A **4**
Grafton Pl. NN1: N'ton . . .1B **4** (2C **52**)
Grafton Rd. NN10: Rushd 3F **33**
Grafton Sq. NN1: N'ton 1B **4**
Grafton St. NN1: N'ton . . .1A **4** (2C **52**)
Grafton St. Ind. Est.
NN1: N'ton 1A **4**
Grafton Vw. NN4: Woot 5E **59**
Grafton Way NN5: Dus 5D **34**
NN7: Rother 4C **56**
Granary Ct. NN4: N'ton 4C **58**
Granary Rd. NN4: N'ton 4C **58**
Granby Ct. NN29: Woll 5A **44**
Grandborough Cl. NN6: Brix 2B **22**
GRANGE, THE 6C **6**
Grange Av. NN5: Dus 6D **34**
Grange Cl. NN6: E Bart 2G **41**
NN29: Irch 6F **31**
Grange Ct. NN6: Brix 1A **22**
Grange La. NN6: Pits 1D **22**
GRANGE PARK 2F **65**
Grange Rd. NN3: N'ton 4A **38**
NN9: Stanw 6H **13**
NN9: Well 2E **17**
Grange Way NN29: Irch 6F **31**
Grangeway NN10: Rushd 5B **32**
Grangewood NN4: N'ton 4A **58**
Grant Rd. NN8: Well 6H **17**
Grasmere Grn. NN8: Well 2B **28**
Grasmere Way NN10: High F 3D **20**
Graspin La. NN3: West F 1B **54**
Grasscroft NN2: K'thpe 2A **36**
Grassmere Av. NN3: West F 5C **38**
Grass Slade NN6: Brix 1B **22**
Gravely St. NN10: Rushd 3B **32**
Gray Cl. NN6: E Bart 3A **42**
Gray St. NN1: N'ton 1E **5** (2E **53**)
NN29: Irch 6E **31**
GREAT BILLING 5G **39**
Gt. Billing Pk. NN3: Gt Bil 4F **39**
Gt. Billing Way NN3: N'ton 2G **39**
GREAT DODDINGTON 1D **42**
Great Fld. Ct. NN3: N'ton 2C **38**
Gt. Ground Wlk. NN4: Gra P 3F **65**
Gt. Gull Cres. NN3: N'ton 1D **38**
GREAT HARROWDEN 1D **16**
Gt. Holme Ct. NN3: N'ton 2C **38**
GREAT HOUGHTON 1C **60**
Greatmeadow NN3: N'ton 3G **39**
Greatmeadow Rd. NN3: N'ton . . .3F **39**
Great Pk. St. NN8: Well 6G **17**
Gt. Russell St.
NN1: N'ton 1E **5** (2D **52**)
Green, The NN1: N'ton . . .4B **4** (4B **52**)
NN2: K'thpe 4B **36**
NN4: Gra P 2E **65**
NN4: Gt Hou 1C **60**
NN4: H'stone 3F **59**
NN4: Woot 5E **59**
NN7: Flore 4F **47**
NN7: Kisl 6H **49**
NN7: Up Harl 3A **34**
NN11: Badby 6B **8**
NN11: Newn 5F **9**
NN14: Lit A 1D **12**
Greenacre Dr. NN10: Rushd 5D **32**
Greenaway Cl. NN7: Blis 6G **63**
Green Cl. NN8: Well 4C **16**
NN9: Irth 3H **19**
Greendale Sq. NN3: Ect B 5G **39**
Green End NN2: K'thpe 5B **36**
Greenfield Av. NN3: N'ton 4G **37**
Greenfield Rd. NN3: N'ton 4G **37**
Green Flds. NN4: Woot 6E **59**
Greenfield Way NN10: Rushd . . .4C **32**
Greenfinch Dr. NN3: Moul 1A **38**
Greenglades NN4: N'ton 2G **57**
Greenhill Cres. NN11: Dav 4D **6**
Greenhills Cl. NN2: K'thpe 1B **36**
Greenhills Rd. NN2: K'thpe 1B **36**
Green La. NN4: N'ton 2F **57**
NN4: Woot 6E **59**
NN9: Stanw 6H **13**
NN10: Wym 6B **32**
Greenlaw NN8: Well 1B **28**
Green Rd. NN7: Braf G 1H **61**
Greenside NN3: N'ton 4A **38**
NN7: Blis 6F **63**
Green St. NN1: N'ton 4A **4** (4B **52**)
NN7: Mil M 1G **63**
NN29: Woll 5C **44**
Greenview Dr. NN2: N'ton 5E **37**
Greenway NN3: West F 1A **54**
Greenway, The NN11: Dav 1E **9**
Greenway Av. NN3: N'ton 3B **38**
Greenwood Cl. NN3: Moul 5A **24**
Greenwood Rd. NN5: N'ton 3A **52**
(not continuous)
Greeves Cl. NN5: Dus 6B **34**
Gregory Gdns. NN3: N'ton 3A **38**
Gregory St. NN1: N'ton . . .4B **4** (4C **52**)
Grenadier Rd. NN11: Dav 6C **6**
Grendon Lakes Watersports Cen.
. . . . .6C **42**
Grendon Rd. NN6: E Bart 5F **41**
NN29: Woll 6F **43**
Grendon Wlk. NN3: N'ton 2F **37**
(not continuous)
Grenville Cl. NN11: Dav 6G **7**
Gresham Dr. NN4: N'ton 1G **57**
Gresley Cl. NN11: Dav 3C **6**
Gretton Ct. NN8: Well 4D **16**
Greville Av. NN3: N'ton 3G **37**
Greville Cl. NN2: Bou 5C **22**
Greyfriars NN1: N'ton 3C **4** (3C **52**)
Greyfriars Rd. NN11: Dav 1D **8**
Greys, The NN7: Weed 5B **46**
Griffiths Cl. NN5: Dus 1B **50**
Griffith St. NN10: Rushd 4D **32**
Grimmer Wlk. NN9: Irth 3H **19**
Grimston Jetty *NN4: N'ton 6H* ***51***
(off Pitstone Rd.)
Grombold Av. NN9: Raun 3C **14**
Grosvenor Cen.
NN1: N'ton 3D **4** (3C **52**)
Grosvenor Gdns. NN2: K'thpe . . .3D **36**
Groundwell Ct. NN3: West F 6D **38**
Grove, The NN3: Moul 2A **24**
NN29: Woll 5B **44**
Grovebury Dell NN2: K'thpe 3A **36**
Grove Farm La. NN3: Moul 3B **24**
Grovelands NN11: Dav 6C **6**
Grove Pl. NN9: Raun 4D **14**
Grove Rd. NN1: N'ton 1F **5** (2E **53**)
NN7: Braf G 6H **55**
NN10: Rushd 3E **33**
Grove St. NN8: Well 1E **29**
NN9: Raun 4C **14**
NN10: High F 5E **21**
Grove Way NN9: Fine 5C **10**
Grove Works
NN1: N'ton 1F **5** (2E **53**)
Guildhall Rd.
NN1: N'ton 4D **4** (4D **52**)
Guillemot La. NN8: Well 4G **17**
Gulliver Rd. NN9: Irth 6A **12**
Gurston Ri. NN3: N'ton 3G **39**

H

Hachenburg Pl. NN10: High F . . .6E **21**
Hackwood Rd. NN11: Dav 1G **9**
Haddon Cl. NN8: Well 3D **16**
NN10: Rushd 5C **32**
Haines Rd. NN4: Far C 6C **52**
Hallam Cl. NN3: Moul 6H **23**
Hall Av. NN10: Rushd 4C **32**
Hall Cl. NN5: Dus 3E **51**
NN7: Harp 3F **49**
NN7: Kisl 5H **49**
Hall Dr. NN9: Fine 5C **10**
Hall Farm Cl. NN6: Brix 1A **22**
Hall Piece Cl. NN3: Ect B 4G **39**
Halswell Ct. NN3: N'ton 3B **38**
Hambledon Ri. NN4: N'ton 6G **51**
Hamblin Ct. NN10: Rushd 3D **32**
Hamlet Grn. NN5: N'ton 1H **51**
Ham Mdw. Dr. NN3: Ect B 5G **39**
Hammerstone La. NN4: N'ton . . .6H **51**
Hampton Ho. *NN10: Rushd 3D* ***32***
(off Portland Rd.)
Hampton St.
NN1: N'ton 1A **4** (2B **52**)
Hamsterly Pk. NN3: N'ton 1E **39**
Hanbury Cl. NN11: Dav 1D **6**
Handcross Way
NN10: High F, Rushd 1E **33**
Handley Cl. NN5: Dus 6C **34**
Hanemill Ct. NN3: Gt Bil 6G **39**
Hanemill Wlk. *NN3: Gt Bil 6G* ***39***
(off Hanemill Ct.)
Hangerfield Ct. NN3: N'ton 4D **38**
Hanover Ct. NN3: N'ton 3F **39**
Harborough Rd. NN2: K'thpe 2C **36**
NN6: Brix 1A **22**
(Holcot Rd.)
NN6: Brix 3B **22**
(Highslade)
NN10: Rushd 4E **33**
Harborough Rd. Nth.
NN2: Bou, K'thpe 4B **22**
Harborough Way
NN10: Rushd 4E **33**
Harcourt Sq. NN6: E Bart 3G **41**
Harcourt St. NN9: Raun 3D **14**
Harcourt Way NN4: N'ton 6G **51**
HARDINGSTONE 3F **59**
Hardingstone La.
NN4: H'stone 3D **58**
Harding Ter.
NN1: N'ton 1B **4** (2C **52**)
Hardlands Rd. NN5: Dus 1E **51**
(not continuous)
Hardwater Rd.
NN29: Gt Dod, Woll 2C **42**
Hardwick Cl. NN8: Well 6E **17**
Hardwick Hall Way NN11: Dav . . .1D **6**
Hardwick Rd. NN4: N'ton 3C **58**
NN8: Well 3A **16**
(not continuous)
NN9: H'wick 3A **16**
Hardy Dr. NN4: H'stone 4F **59**
Harebell Sq. NN3: Ect B 5H **39**
Harefield NN4: Gra P 2F **65**
Harefield Rd. NN3: N'ton 2F **39**
Harefoot Cl. NN5: Dus 1D **50**
Harksome Hill NN4: N'ton 1G **57**
HARLESTONE 1B **34**
Harlestone Ct. NN5: N'ton 2H **51**
Harlestone Heath Nature Reserve
. . . . .1D **34**
Harlestone Ho. NN5: N'ton 2A **52**
Harlestone Rd.
NN5: Dus, Lwr H, N'ton 1A **34**
NN7: Lwr H 1A **34**
Harmans Way NN7: Weed 5B **46**
Harold St.
NN1: N'ton 3F **5** (3E **53**)
HARPOLE 3G **49**
Harrier Pk. NN4: N'ton 3B **58**
Harrington Dr. NN5: Upton 5E **51**
Harrington Rd. NN9: Irth 6A **12**
Harris Cl. NN4: Woot 4F **59**
NN9: Raun 2D **14**
Harrison Cl. NN8: Well 6D **16**
Harrold Rd. NN29: Boz 5H **45**
Harrowden La. NN9: Fine 6A **10**
Harrowden Rd. NN4: Brack 1H **59**
NN8: Well 3E **17**
Harrowick La. NN6: E Bart 2G **41**
Harrow La. NN11: Dav 1F **7**
Harrow Way NN2: K'thpe 1H **35**
Harry Brown Cl. NN5: Dus 1F **51**
Hartburn Cl. NN3: Gt Bil 1G **55**
Hartwell Cl. NN2: K'thpe 2D **36**
Harvest Cl. NN11: Dav 1F **7**
Harvest Way NN2: K'thpe 2H **35**
Harvey Cl. NN9: Raun 4B **14**
Harvey La. NN3: Moul 5H **23**
Harvey Reeves Rd.
NN5: N'ton 4A **52**
Harvey Rd. NN8: Well 2E **29**
NN10: Rushd 6D **32**
Haselrig Sq. NN4: N'ton 1H **57**
Hassocks Hedge NN4: N'ton 1E **57**
Hastings Rd. NN2: K'thpe 3D **36**
Hatfield Cl. NN4: N'ton 3C **58**
NN8: Well 4C **16**
Hatton Av. NN8: Well 6F **17**
Hatton Cl. NN3: N'ton 1G **37**
Hatton Hall NN8: Well 6F **17**
HATTON PARK 6E **17**
Hatton Pk. Rd. NN8: Well 6E **17**
Hatton St. NN8: Well 5F **17**
Havelock St. NN8: Well 6G **17**
Haven Cl. NN5: N'ton 2A **52**
Hawke Rd. NN11: Dav 6G **7**
Hawkins Cl. NN11: Dav 5G **7**
Hawkridge NN4: N'ton 2H **57**
Hawksbeard Pl. NN3: Ect B 5G **39**
Hawkshead NN8: Well 2B **28**
Hawksmoor Way NN5: Dus 6F **35**
Hawksnest NN4: N'ton 3A **58**
Hawkstone Cl. NN5: Dus 2F **51**
Hawthorn Dr. NN11: Dav 3E **7**
Hawthorne Rd. NN9: Fine 5E **11**
Hawthorn Rd. NN3: N'ton 6G **37**
Hawthorns, The NN10: High F . . .5D **20**
Hawthorn Way NN8: Well 6E **17**
Hawtin Cl. NN2: N'ton 6E **37**
Hay Cl. NN10: Rushd 5D **32**
Haycroft Wlk. NN2: K'thpe 2A **36**
Hayden Av. NN9: Fine 4E **11**
Hayden Rd. NN10: Rushd 3E **33**
Haydown Grn. NN5: Dus 1F **51**
Hayeswood Rd. NN3: N'ton 3D **38**
Hay La. NN9: Irth 2A **20**
Hayride, The NN4: N'ton 4A **58**
Haystack, The NN11: Dav 1F **7**
Hayway NN9: Irth 2A **20**
NN10: Rushd 1C **32**
Hazel Copse NN4: Gra P 4F **65**
Hazelden Cl. NN29: Woll 6B **44**
Hazeldene Rd. NN2: N'ton 5E **37**
Hazelwood Rd.
NN1: N'ton 4E **5** (4D **52**)
Headingley Rd. NN10: Rushd . . .3F **33**
Headlands, The NN3: N'ton 6A **38**
NN8: Well 5F **17**
Healey Cl. NN3: N'ton 3H **39**
Hearden Ct. NN8: Well 2E **29**
Heartlands Bus. Pk. NN11: Dav . . .2C **6**
Heatherbreea Gdns.
NN10: Rushd 2B **32**
Heather Ct. NN4: N'ton 1A **58**
NN10: Rushd 3C **32**
Heatherdale Way NN2: N'ton 4E **37**
Heather La. NN3: N'ton 3C **38**
Heathers, The NN29: Woll 5C **44**
Heathfield Way NN5: N'ton 5A **36**
Heath Grn. NN5: N'ton 6H **35**
Heath Ri. NN8: Well 5D **16**
Heathville NN5: N'ton 6H **35**
H E Bates Way NN10: Rushd 3B **32**
Hecham Way NN10: High F 4D **20**
Hedge End NN4: N'ton 5C **58**
Hedgely Ct. NN4: N'ton 1A **58**
Hedgerow Dr. NN2: K'thpe 2A **36**
Hedgerow La. NN3: West F 5E **39**
Hedgerow Way NN11: Dav 1E **7**
Hedges, The
NN10: High F, Rushd 1E **33**
Hedgeway NN4: N'ton 5C **58**
Hellidon Cl. NN2: K'thpe 3E **37**
Helmdon Cres. NN2: K'thpe 2C **36**
Helmdon Rd. NN2: K'thpe 2C **36**
Hemans Rd. NN11: Dav 3D **6**
Hembury Pl. NN4: N'ton 6H **51**
Hemmingwell Lodge Way
NN8: Well 4G **17**
Hemmingwell Rd. NN8: Well 4G **17**
Henley Cl. NN8: Well 5C **16**
Henry Bird Ct.
NN4: N'ton 6D **4** (5D **52**)
Henry Bird Way
NN4: N'ton 6D **4** (5D **52**)

Henry Smith Ho. NN11: Dav 4D 6
(off Queens Rd.)
Henry St. NN1: N'ton ...1G 5 (2E 53)
Henshaw Rd. NN8: Well 2D 28
Hensmans La. NN29: Boz ...5H 45
Herbert St. NN1: N'ton ...2B 4 (3C 52)
Hereward Rd. NN4: Far C 1B 58
Heritage Farm Cl.
  NN4: H'stone 3F 59
Heritage Way NN9: Raun ...2E 15
Hermitage Way NN4: Woot ...5D 58
Hernhill Ct. NN4: N'ton ...1G 57
Heron Cl. NN8: Well 4G 17
Heron Cl. NN11: Dav 4E 7
Heronsford NN4: N'ton ...3G 57
Heron Way NN8: Well 4H 17
Herriotts Ct. NN8: Well 6G 17
(off Herriotts La.)
Herriotts La. NN8: Well 6G 17
Hertford Cl. NN3: West F ...6E 39
  NN11: Dav 2E 9
Hervey Cl. NN3: N'ton ...5B 38
Hervey St. NN1: N'ton ...1E 5 (2E 53)
Hesperus NN8: Well 1B 28
Hester St. NN2: N'ton ...1C 52
Hever Cl. NN10: Rushd ...5E 33
Hewlett's Cl. NN29: Boz ...6H 45
Hexham Cl. NN4: N'ton ...1A 58
Heyford La. NN7: Weed ...6E 47
Heyford Rd. NN5: Dus 1B 50
Hiawatha NN8: Well 1B 28
Hibiscus Cl. NN3: N'ton ...3A 54
Hickmire NN29: Woll 4B 44
Hidcote Cl. NN4: N'ton ...4C 58
  NN8: Well 3D 28
Hidcote Way NN11: Dav ...1C 6
Higgins Sq. NN4: N'ton ...1H 57
HIGHAM FERRERS 5D 20
Higham Rd. NN8: Well 4H 29
  NN9: Stanw 6H 13
  NN10: Rushd 2D 32
  NN15: Bur L 1A 10
  NN29: Irch 4H 29
High Barns Cl. NN4: Gra P ...3E 65
Highdown Cl. NN4: N'ton ...6G 51
Highfield Cl. NN6: Brix ...2A 22
Highfield Pl. NN11: Dav 4D 6
Highfield Rd. NN1: N'ton ...6G 37
  NN6: Mears A 3E 27
  NN8: Well 6H 17
  NN9: Irth 1B 20
  NN10: Rushd 4A 32
  NN11: Dav 4D 6
Highfields NN6: Brix 2A 22
Highfield St. NN9: Fine ...4F 11
High Greeve NN4: Woot ...5G 59
Highgrove Ct. NN10: Rushd ...3D 32
Highlands Av. NN3: N'ton ...3G 37
Highlands Dr. NN11: Dav 2D 6
High March NN11: Dav 1G 9
High March Cl. NN11: Dav ...1G 9
High March Ind. Est.
  NN11: Dav 1G 9
Highslade NN6: Brix 3B 22
High St. NN2: K'thpe 4B 36
(not continuous)
  NN3: Gt Bil 5G 39
  NN3: Moul 4A 24
  NN3: West F 1B 54
  NN4: Col 2C 64
  NN4: Gt Hou 6C 54
  NN4: H'stone 3E 59
  NN4: Woot 5D 58
  NN5: Upton 4E 51
(not continuous)
  NN6: Brix 1A 22
  NN6: E Bart 3G 41
  NN6: Ect 3B 40
  NN6: Pits 1C 22
  NN7: Blis 6E 63
  NN7: Flore 4E 47
  NN7: G'ton 3A 62
  NN7: Harp 3F 49
  NN7: Kisl 5H 49
  NN7: Mil M 2G 63
  NN7: Weed 5A 46
  NN8: Well 6F 17
  NN9: Fine 4D 10
  NN9: Irth 2A 20
  NN9: Raun 3D 14
  NN9: Stanw 6H 13
  NN10: High F 6D 20
  NN10: Rushd 2D 32
  NN11: Dav 5E 7
  NN14: Lit A 1D 10
  NN29: Boz 6H 45
  NN29: Gt Dod 1E 43
  NN29: Irch 5F 31
  NN29: Woll 5B 44

High St. Mews NN8: Well 1F 29
High St. Pl. NN8: Well 1F 29
High St. Sth. NN10: Rushd ...4D 32
High Vw. NN4: Woot 5E 59
Highwoods NN6: Syw 4H 25
Hilberry Ri. NN3: N'ton ...3H 39
Hill, The NN4: Gt Hou ...1C 60
Hillary Cl. NN11: Dav 2D 6
Hillary Rd. NN10: Rushd ...4B 32
Hill Cl. NN5: Dus 5E 35
Hill Crest NN7: Blis 4E 63
Hillcrest Av. NN3: N'ton ...4G 37
  NN15: Bur L 1A 10
Hillcrest Rd. NN7: G'ton ...4A 62
Hilldrop Rd. NN4: N'ton ...4A 58
Hill Farm Est. NN14: Lit A ...2E 13
Hill Farm Ri. NN4: N'ton ...4H 57
Hill Ho. Gdns. NN9: Stanw ...6H 13
Hillside NN11: Dav 5G 7
Hillside NN29: Boz 6H 45
Hillside Rd. NN7: Flore ...3D 46
  NN8: Well 4A 18
Hillside Way NN3: West F ...1A 54
Hillstone Rd. NN9: Stanw ...6H 13
(off Chapel La.)
Hill St. NN8: Well 1F 29
  NN9: Raun 3D 14
HILL TOP 2D 36
Hill Top NN7: Blis 4E 63
Hilltop Cl. NN6: Brix 3A 22
Hind Pl. NN11: Dav 5G 7
Hind Stile NN10: High F ...6D 20
Hinton Cl. NN2: K'thpe ...2C 36
Hinton Rd. NN2: K'thpe ...2C 36
Hinwick Rd. NN29: Woll ...5B 44
Hirondelle Cl. NN5: Dus ...6B 34
Hobby Cl. NN4: N'ton ...3B 58
Hocknell Cl. NN4: N'ton ...5F 59
Hodges La. NN7: Kisl 5H 49
Hodnet Cl. NN4: N'ton ...4C 58
Hogarth Cl. NN8: Well 4F 17
Holbein Gdns. NN4: N'ton ...3G 57
Holbush Way NN9: Irth ...6A 12
Holcot Cl. NN8: Well 3E 17
Holcot La. NN6: Syw 1H 25
Holcot Rd. NN3: Moul ...1A 24
Holcutt Cl. NN4: Woot ...4F 59
Holdenby Rd. NN4: N'ton ...3D 36
Holden Gro. NN11: Dav 5D 6
Hollies, The NN3: Moul ...3H 23
  NN8: Well 1E 29
  NN10: High F 6D 20
Hollingside Dr. NN2: N'ton ...4F 37
Hollington Rd. NN9: Raun ...3D 14
Hollow, The NN9: Stanw ...6A 14
(off Newbridge La.)
Hollow Bank NN3: Moul ...1A 38
Hollowell Cl. NN10: Rushd ...5F 33
Hollowell Ct. NN8: Well ...1F 29
Holly Lodge Dr. NN2: K'thpe ...2C 36
(not continuous)
Hollyoak Ter. NN3: West F ...6B 38
Holly Rd. NN1: N'ton ...1F 53
  NN10: Rushd 2A 32
Holly Wlk. NN9: Fine 5B 10
Holman Cl. NN3: N'ton ...5B 38
Holm Cl. NN7: Weed 6A 46
Holme Cl. NN9: Well 2E 17
Holmecross Rd. NN3: N'ton ...2C 38
Holmes Av. NN9: Raun ...4D 14
Holmfield Dr. NN9: Raun ...1E 15
Holmfield Way NN3: West F ...1A 54
Holmleigh Cl. NN5: Dus ...2E 51
Holmwood Cl. NN5: Dus ...6C 34
Holyoake Rd. NN29: Woll ...5B 44
Holyrood Cl. NN5: N'ton ...2H 51
Holyrood Rd. NN5: N'ton ...2H 51
Home Acre NN7: Lit Hou ...5F 55
Home Cl. NN4: Gra P 3E 65
  NN7: Blis 6F 63
  NN9: Irth 3A 20
Home Farm Cl. NN3: Lit B ...1F 55
  NN7: Weed 6A 46
Home Farm La. NN6: Pits ...1C 22
Homefield NN11: Dav 1E 9
Homestead Cl. NN3: Moul ...4B 24
Homestead Ct. NN2: N'ton ...6E 37
Homestead Ri. NN4: Woot ...5E 59
Homestead Way NN2: N'ton ...6E 37
Honey Holme NN6: Brix ...2A 22
Honeystones NN3: Moul ...4A 24
Honeysuckle Way NN3: N'ton ...3A 54
Honister Grn. NN3: N'ton ...4A 38
Hood Rd. NN11: Dav 5G 7
Hood St. NN1: N'ton ...2E 53
Hookhams Path NN29: Woll ...5C 44

Hope Ct. NN29: Boz 4H 45
Hopes Pl. NN2: K'thpe ...4B 36
Hope St. NN29: Boz 4H 45
Hopmeadow Cl. NN3: N'ton ...3F 39
Hopping Hill Gdns. NN5: Dus ...6F 35
Hopton Cl. NN11: Dav 1F 7
Hornbeam Cl. NN8: Well ...6E 17
Hornbeam Ct. NN3: N'ton ...4C 38
Hornby Rd. NN6: E Bart ...2G 41
Horncastle Cl. NN11: Dav ...1E 7
Horrell Ct. NN10: Rushd ...3C 32
Horse Mkt. NN1: N'ton ...4B 4 (4C 52)
Horsemoor Sq. NN3: Ect B ...5G 39
Horseshoe Cl. NN6: Brix ...1B 22
Horseshoe Cotts. NN6: Syw ...2A 26
Horseshoe St.
  NN1: N'ton 4B 4 (4C 52)
Horse Well Cl. NN3: Moul ...6A 24
Horsley Rd. NN2: K'thpe ...6C 36
Horton Rd. NN7: Braf G ...2H 61
Houghton Hill NN4: H'stone ...2F 59
Houghton La. NN4: Brack ...1A 60
Hovel Rd. NN10: Rushd ...3E 33
Howard Biley Gdns.
  NN3: N'ton 3A 38
Howard Cl. NN11: Dav 6F 7
Howard Ct. NN8: Well 6H 17
(off Mill Rd.)
Howard La. NN2: Bou 5C 22
Howard Rd. NN29: Woll ...5B 44
Howard's Ct. NN8: Well 5B 44
Howards Way NN3: N'ton ...2H 37
Howe Cres. NN11: Dav 6G 7
Hoxton Cl. NN3: N'ton ...1C 38
Hoylake Rd. NN8: Well ...4C 16
Hoylake Dr. NN2: N'ton ...4F 37
Hudson Cl. NN11: Dav 2E 7
Hudson Dr. NN4: N'ton ...2F 57
Hulme Way NN8: Well 4E 17
Humber Cl. NN5: N'ton ...5G 35
  NN11: Dav 3B 6
Humfrey La. NN2: Bou 5C 22
Hunsbarrow Rd. NN4: N'ton ...5G 51
Hunsbury Cl. NN4: N'ton ...2G 57
Hunsbury District Cen.
  NN4: N'ton 3A 58
Hunsbury Grn. NN4: N'ton ...1G 57
HUNSBURY HILL 2G 57
Hunsbury Hill Av. NN4: N'ton ...6G 51
Hunsbury Hill Country Pk.
  (Nature Reserve) 1G 57
Hunsbury Hill Rd. NN4: N'ton ...1G 57
Hunsbury Wlk. NN4: N'ton ...6H 51
Hunslet La. NN4: N'ton ...2G 57
Hunt Cl. NN6: Brix 1A 22
  NN8: Well 1G 57
Hunter Penrose Ct. NN8: Well ...6G 17
(off Great Pk. St.)
Hunters Cl. NN2: K'thpe ...1D 36
Hunter St. NN1: N'ton ...1E 5 (2D 52)
Hunters' Way NN6: Brix ...1A 22
Huntsham Cl. NN3: West F ...2B 54
Huntsmead NN3: N'ton ...3H 39
Hussar Cl. NN11: Dav 6D 6
Huxley Cl. NN8: Well 1A 28
Huxloe Ri. NN10: Rushd ...1C 38
Hyacinth Way NN10: Rushd ...6D 32
Hyde Dr. NN9: Fine 4E 11

Ibstock Cl. NN3: N'ton ...1E 39
Icknield Dr. NN4: N'ton ...2G 57
Ickworth Cl. NN11: Dav 1D 6
Icon Environmental Innovation Cen.
  NN11: Dav 5F 7
(off Eastern Way)
Ideal Bldgs. NN1: N'ton ...1C 4
Ilex Cl. NN4: H'stone ...2F 59
Imperial Ct. NN10: Rushd ...3C 32
Indmere Cl. NN4: N'ton ...2E 57
Ingleborough Way NN5: Dus ...1E 51
Inglewood Ct. NN3: Gt Bil ...6G 39
Inglewood Wlk. NN3: Gt Bil ...6G 39
Inlands, The NN11: Dav 6E 7
Inlands Cl. NN11: Dav 6F 7
Inlands Ri. NN11: Dav 6F 7
Inniskilling Cl. NN3: Moul ...4B 24
Insignia Cl. NN4: Woot ...4E 59
IRCHESTER 5F 31
Irchester Caravan Site
  NN29: Irch 5B 30
Irchester Country Park 4C 30
Irchester Country Park Vis. Cen.
  ....4B 30
Irchester Narrow Gauge Railway Mus.
  ....4A 30

Irchester Rd. NN10: Rushd ...3A 32
  NN29: Farn 4E 45
  NN29: Woll 5B 44
Irondale Cl. NN4: N'ton ...6G 51
Iron Duke Cl. NN11: Dav ...3D 6
Iron Pikes NN6: Brix 2B 22
Ironstone Cl. NN6: Brix ...1B 22
Ironstone Ct. NN9: Fine ...5D 10
Ironstone Jetty NN4: N'ton ...6H 51
(off Hembury Pl.)
Ironstone La. NN4: N'ton ...6G 51
Ironstone Way NN6: Brix ...1B 22
IRTHLINGBOROUGH 1B 20
Irthlingborough Rd.
  NN8: Well 2H 29
  NN9: Fine 4E 11
  NN14: Lit A 3D 12
ISEBROOK HOSPITAL 2H 29
Ise Valley Ind. Est. NN8: Well ...3A 18
Isham Cl. NN2: K'thpe ...3C 36
Ivy Ct. NN11: Dav 6D 6
Ivy La. NN9: Fine 5D 10
Ivy Rd. NN1: N'ton ...1F 53
Ixworth Cl. NN3: N'ton ...2D 38

J

Jackdaw Cl. NN3: Gt Bil ...1G 55
Jack English Cl. NN5: Upton ...2D 50
Jacklin Cl. NN8: Well 4C 16
Jack Parnell Cl. NN5: Upton ...2D 50
Jack Pin La. NN5: Upton ...5F 51
Jackson Cl. NN2: K'thpe ...1E 37
Jackson's La. NN8: Well ...1F 29
Jacorrin Cl. NN2: K'thpe ...1E 37
James Gribble Ct. NN9: Raun ...3D 14
James Lewis Ct. NN3: N'ton ...5A 38
James Rd. NN8: Well 3F 29
James St. NN29: Irch 6F 31
James Watt Cl. NN11: Dav ...3C 6
Jardine Cl. NN3: West F ...6B 38
Jarretts Yd. NN4: Woot ...5E 59
Jasmine Gdns. NN10: Rushd ...6D 32
Jasmine Rd. NN3: N'ton ...2G 39
Jasper Wlk. NN3: N'ton ...1B 38
Javelin Cl. NN5: Dus 1E 51
Jellicoe Cl. NN11: Dav 6G 7
Jenner Cres. NN2: K'thpe ...2B 36
Jennings Cl. NN10: High F ...6D 20
  NN11: Dav 6F 7
Jerome Cl. NN3: N'ton ...1G 39
Jersey Cl. NN8: Well 5H 17
Jersey Cl. NN3: West F ...6D 38
Jervis Cl. NN11: Dav 6G 7
Jesslyn Cl. NN3: West F ...1B 54
Jeyes Cl. NN3: Moul 5A 38
Jeyes Jetty NN1: N'ton ...4C 4 (4C 52)
Joan Pyel Cl. NN9: Irth ...3A 20
John Ashby Sports Hall, The ...3H 23
John Bowen Jones Bus. Pk.
  NN7: Blis 3F 63
John Clare Hall NN2: K'thpe ...2E 37
John Clark Way NN10: Rushd ...2D 32
John Eagle Cl. NN9: Stanw ...5H 13
John Gray Rd. NN29: Gt Dod ...1D 42
John Lea Way NN8: Well ...4F 29
John Pyel Rd. NN9: Irth ...2A 20
Johnson Av. NN8: Well 4G 29
Johnson Cl. NN11: Dav 4D 6
Johnson Ct.
  NN4: N'ton 6D 4 (5D 52)
John St. NN10: Rushd ...3A 32
John White Close, The
  NN10: High F 5E 21
John White Golf Course 6F 33
Joseph Priestley Ct. NN11: Dav ...6F 7
(off New St.)
Joshua Sq. NN4: N'ton ...1H 57
Jubilee Cl. NN4: N'ton ...6H 51
Jubilee Cres. NN8: Well ...3F 29
Jubilee Gdns.
  NN10: Rushd 5E 33
Jubilee Hill NN3: Moul ...4A 24
Jubilee Ho. NN3: West F ...5C 38
Jubilee M. NN3: N'ton ...3C 38
Jubilee Rd. NN11: Dav 5D 6
Jubilee St. NN9: Irth 1A 20
Julian Way NN2: K'thpe ...4A 36
Junction Rd. NN2: N'ton ...6E 37
Juniper Ct. NN3: N'ton ...4H 39
Juniper Thorn NN6: Brix ...2B 22
JVE Building NN1: N'ton ...1D 4

K

Kangaroo Spinney NN8: Well ...2B 30
Kealdale Rd. NN3: N'ton ...3G 37

ats Cl. NN4: Gt Hou ... 2D 60
NN6: E Bart ... 3H 41
ats Rd. NN8: Well ... 1D 28
NN11: Dav ... 4D 6
ats Way NN10: High F ... 6C 20
NN10: Rushd ... 2A 32
ble Cl. NN11: Dav ... 1D 8
dleston Cl. NN4: N'ton ... 3C 58
epers Cl. NN4: Gra P ... 2F 65
lburn Cl. NN4: N'ton ... 4B 58
lmscott Cl. NN3: N'ton ... 2E 39
lsall Cl. NN5: Dus ... 1D 50
ndal Cl. NN3: N'ton ... 3B 38
NN8: Well ... 5C 16
NN10: Rushd ... 4F 33
nilworth Cl. NN5: Dus ... 1D 50
NN10: Rushd ... 4E 33
NN11: Dav ... 6D 6
nmuir Av. NN2: N'ton ... 5F 37
nmuir Cres. NN2: N'ton ... 5F 37
nmuir Gdns. NN2: N'ton ... 5F 37
nmuir Rd. NN9: Fine ... 5D 10
nnedy Cl. NN11: Dav ... 6G 7
nnel Ter. NN6: Brix ... 1A 22
nnet Cl. NN8: Well ... 5C 16
nnet Grn. NN5: N'ton ... 5H 35
nsington Cl. NN10: Rushd ... 2A 32
nsington Ga. NN3: Gt Bil ... 4F 39
nt Cl. NN5: Dus ... 3E 51
ntford Cl. NN4: N'ton ... 3B 58
nt Rd. NN5: Dus, Upton ... 2C 50
NN8: Well ... 4F 29
NN10: Rushd ... 2E 33
ntstone Cl. NN2: K'thpe ... 2H 35
nt Wlk. NN5: Upton ... 3D 50
rfield Est. NN5: Dus ... 2D 50
ston Way NN9: Raun ... 4B 14
strel Cl. NN3: West F ... 6B 38
strel La. NN8: Well ... 4G 17
swick NN8: Well ... 6B 16
swick Dr. NN3: N'ton ... 3A 38
NN10: Rushd ... 2F 33
ttering Gdns.
NN1: N'ton ... 2F 5 (3E 53)
ttering Rd.
NN1: N'ton ... 2F 5 (3E 53)
NN2: N'ton ... 2E 53
NN3: Moul ... 4C 24
NN3: N'ton ... 2E 53
NN9: Gt Har, Lit Harr ... 1E 17
ttering Rd. Nth. NN3: N'ton ... 2A 38
ttering Town FC ... 1D 20
yham Ct. NN3: N'ton ... 2E 39
ys Cl. NN11: Dav ... 6F 7
ystone NN4: N'ton ... 2F 57
ystone Ho. NN5: Upton ... 2C 50
Bus. Cen. NN5: N'ton ... 6H 35
lborn Cl. NN8: Well ... 4E 17
lborn Rd. NN8: Well ... 5D 16
lburn Pl. NN10: Rushd ... 1D 32
lby Cl. NN8: Well ... 2D 28
ln Way NN8: Well ... 6D 16
lvey Rd. NN4: Brack ... 1G 59
mbell M. NN2: Bou ... 5C 22
mble Cl. NN4: N'ton ... 3B 58
mbolton Rd. NN10: High F ... 5E 21
ng Cup Cl. NN10: Rushd ... 6E 33
ng Edward Rd. NN1: N'ton ... 2G 53
ngfisher Cl. NN4: N'ton ... 4A 58
NN8: Well ... 4H 17
ngfisher Ct. NN6: Syw ... 5G 25
ngmaker Way NN4: N'ton ... 1A 58
ng Richard Ct. NN4: N'ton ... 5C 58
ngs Av. NN10: High F ... 4E 21
ngs Cl. NN4: Gra P ... 2F 65
ngscroft Ct. NN3: Gt Bil ... 6G 39
ngscroft Wlk. NN3: Gt Bil ... 5F 39
ngsfield Bus. Pk.
NN5: N'ton ... 6A 36
ngsfield Cen. NN3: N'ton ... 6F 23
ngsfield Cl. NN5: N'ton ... 6H 35
ngsfield Way NN5: N'ton ... 6H 35
ngs Grn. NN11: Dav ... 2E 9
NG'S HEATH ... 5H 35
ngsland Av. NN2: K'thpe ... 4C 36
ngsland Cl. NN2: K'thpe ... 4D 36
ngsland Gdns. NN2: K'thpe ... 4C 36
ng's La. NN7: Flore ... 4F 47
ngsley Av. NN11: Dav ... 6D 6
ngsley Gdns. NN2: N'ton ... 6E 37
NGSLEY PARK ... 6F 37
ngsley Pk. Ter. NN2: N'ton ... 6F 37
ngsley Rd. NN2: N'ton ... 5D 36
ngsmead NN2: K'thpe ... 2A 36
ngs Mdw. La. NN10: High F ... 3C 20
ngsmead Pk. NN10: Rushd ... 6E 33
ngsmith Dr. NN9: Raun ... 3E 15
ngs Pk. NN3: N'ton ... 1F 37
NN7: Weed ... 6A 46
King's Pk. Rd. NN3: N'ton ... 1F 37
King's Park Tennis Cen. ... 1F 37
King's Pl. NN10: Rushd ... 3E 33
King's Rd. NN10: Rushd ... 3E 33
Kings St. NN8: Well ... 6G 17
KINGSTHORPE ... 4C 36
Kingsthorpe Bowling Club ... 1B 36
Kingsthorpe Golf Course ... 5D 36
Kingsthorpe Gro. NN2: K'thpe ... 5C 36
KINGSTHORPE HOLLOW ... 6C 36
Kingsthorpe Ho. NN2: K'thpe ... 2D 36
Kingsthorpe Meadows Nature Reserve
... 5A 36
Kingsthorpe Rd.
NN2: K'thpe, N'ton ... 5C 36
Kingsthorpe Shop. Cen.
NN2: K'thpe ... 4C 36
Kingston Cl. NN11: Dav ... 4D 6
King St. NN1: N'ton ... 3C 4 (3C 52)
NN6: E Bart ... 2G 41
Kingsway NN2: K'thpe ... 3A 36
NN8: Well ... 2D 28
Kingswell Rd. NN2: K'thpe ... 4B 36
Kingswell St.
NN1: N'ton ... 4C 4 (4C 52)
Kinross Cl. NN3: N'ton ... 3G 37
Kirby Cl. NN4: Woot ... 4F 59
Kirby Row *NN5: Upton ... 5F 51*
(off Clickers Dr.)
Kirkstone Wlk. NN3: N'ton ... 3A 38
Kirton Cl. NN3: N'ton ... 2F 39
Kirton End NN3: N'ton ... 3F 39
KISLINGBURY ... 5H 49
Kislingbury Rd. NN7: Rother ... 4B 56
Kitchener Cl. NN11: Dav ... 3D 6
Kites Cl. NN4: N'ton ... 3A 58
Knaphill Cres. NN4: N'ton ... 5H 51
Knightlands Rd. NN9: Irth ... 6B 12
Knightley Rd. NN2: K'thpe ... 6C 36
Knighton Cl. NN5: Dus ... 4C 34
Knightons Way NN6: Brix ... 3A 22
Knightscliffe Way NN5: Dus ... 6F 35
Knights Cl. NN6: E Bart ... 3G 41
NN29: Boz ... 6H 45
Knights Ct. NN3: Lit B ... 6F 39
NN8: Well ... 6F 17
Knights La. NN2: K'thpe ... 4B 36
Knights M. NN10: Rushd ... 4E 33
Knole Way NN11: Dav ... 1D 6
Knoll, The NN6: Brix ... 1B 22
Knot Tiers Dr. NN5: Upton ... 4E 51
Knowle Cl. NN3: N'ton ... 3A 54
Knowles Cl. NN10: Rushd ... 2F 33
Knowle Way *NN11: Dav ... 1D 6*
(off Hidcote Way)
Knox Ct. NN8: Well ... 1H 29
Knox Rd. NN8: Well ... 1H 29
KNUSTON ... 4H 31
Knuston Dr. NN10: Rushd ... 3B 32
Knuston Rd. NN29: Knus ... 4H 31
Knuston Spinney NN29: Knus ... 4A 32
Kynnesworth Gdns.
NN10: High F ... 5E 21
Kyoto Cl. NN3: N'ton ... 1G 37

L

Laburnum Cl. NN8: Well ... 6E 17
Laburnum Cres. NN3: N'ton ... 5G 37
Laceby Wlk. NN3: N'ton ... 1D 38
Lacemakers Ct. NN10: Rushd ... 5E 33
Lacing La. NN5: Upton ... 5E 51
Ladder Maker Yd.
NN1: N'ton ... 2C 4 (3C 52)
Ladybridge Dr. NN4: N'ton ... 2F 57
Lady Cl. NN11: Newn ... 6F 9
Lady Cft. NN11: Dav ... 6D 6
Ladyfield NN7: Blis ... 5F 63
Lady Hollows Dr. NN4: Woot ... 5G 59
Ladymead Cl. NN4: N'ton ... 2F 57
Lady's La. NN1: N'ton ... 2C 4 (3C 52)
NN6: Mears A ... 3D 26
Lady Smock Cl. NN4: Gra P ... 3F 65
Ladywell Ct. NN8: Well ... 4G 17
(not continuous)
Lady Winefride's Wlk.
NN3: Gt Bil ... 5F 39
Lake Cres. NN11: Dav ... 5C 6
Lakes, The NN4: N'ton ... 5A 54
Lakeside NN6: Over ... 6E 25
NN9: Irth ... 3H 19
Lakeside Dr. NN3: Ect B ... 4H 39
Lakeview Ct. NN3: West F ... 5E 39
Lakeview Grn. NN3: N'ton ... 3A 38
Lake Wlk. NN4: Col ... 1C 64
Lalgates Ct. NN5: N'ton ... 2H 51
Lambrook Dr. NN4: N'ton ... 4C 58
Lamport Ct. NN11: Dav ... 2C 6
Lamport Dr. NN11: Dav ... 2C 6
Lancaster Cl. NN29: Woll ... 4A 44
Lancaster St. NN10: High F ... 5E 21
Lancaster Way NN4: N'ton ... 1A 58
NN10: Rushd ... 2E 33
Lancers Way NN7: Weed ... 5B 46
Lanchester Way NN11: Dav ... 4B 6
Lancum Ho. NN8: Well ... 6E 17
Landcross Dr. NN3: N'ton ... 2A 54
Landimore Rd. NN4: H'stone ... 4G 59
Landor NN8: Well ... 1C 28
Landsdown Dr. NN3: West F ... 5C 38
Landseer Cl. NN8: Well ... 3F 17
Lane, The NN7: Rother ... 5D 56
Lanercost Wlk. NN3: N'ton ... 3A 38
Laneside Hollow NN4: N'ton ... 5C 58
Langdale Ct. NN8: Well ... 6D 16
Langdale Rd. NN2: K'thpe ... 4D 36
Langdon Cl. NN11: Dav ... 2D 6
Langford Dr. NN4: Woot ... 6D 58
Langham Pl. NN2: N'ton ... 1C 52
Langham Rd. NN9: Raun ... 2D 14
Langley Cl. NN4: N'ton ... 6G 51
Langley Cres. NN9: Irth ... 4D 12
Langsett Cl. NN3: West F ... 6D 38
Lansdown Cl. NN11: Dav ... 2F 7
Lapstone Ho. *NN5: N'ton ... 4A 52*
(off Byfield Rd.)
Lapwing Cl. NN4: N'ton ... 4A 58
Larch Cl. NN29: Irch ... 6D 30
Larch Dr. NN11: Dav ... 2E 7
Larch La. NN5: Dus ... 5C 34
Larchwood Cl. NN8: Well ... 6E 17
Larkhall La. NN7: Harp ... 3G 49
Larkhall Way NN7: Harp ... 2G 49
Larkhill NN10: Rushd ... 1C 32
Larkin Gdns. NN10: High F ... 6C 20
Lark La. NN4: Gra P ... 2F 65
Lark Ri. NN3: N'ton ... 3E 39
Larwood Cl. NN2: K'thpe ... 2A 36
Lasham Ct. NN3: Gt Bil ... 6G 39
Lasham Wlk. NN3: Gt Bil ... 6F 39
Latymer Ct. NN1: N'ton ... 2C 4 (3C 52)
Lauderdale Av. NN4: N'ton ... 1A 58
Launcelot Ct. NN5: Dus ... 2C 50
Laureate Ho. NN11: Dav ... 3D 6
Laurel Cl. NN6: Brix ... 2A 22
Laurel Ct. NN3: N'ton ... 4C 38
Laurels, The NN3: Moul ... 3H 23
NN6: Ect ... 4B 40
Laurel Valley NN4: Col ... 1D 64
Lavant Wlk. NN3: N'ton ... 2F 37
Lavender Way NN10: Rushd ... 5E 33
Lavenham Cl. NN3: N'ton ... 2D 38
Lawns, The NN5: Dus ... 1G 51
Lawrence Cl. NN9: Raun ... 4B 14
Lawrence Ct.
NN1: N'ton ... 1C 4 (2C 52)
Laws La. NN9: Fine ... 5D 10
Lawson Cres. NN3: Gt Bil ... 6G 39
Lawson St. NN9: Raun ... 3D 14
Lawton Rd. NN10: Rushd ... 2E 33
Laywood Cl. NN9: Raun ... 2C 14
Laywood Way NN9: Irth ... 3A 20
Leafields NN3: West F ... 1D 54
Leah Bank NN4: N'ton ... 1A 58
Leam, The NN11: Dav ... 6B 6
Leamington Way NN11: Dav ... 6B 6
Lea Rd. NN1: N'ton ... 1F 53
Leatherworks Way
NN3: West F ... 5E 39
Lea Way NN8: Well ... 1D 28
Leben Sq. NN3: N'ton ... 2G 39
Ledaig Way NN3: N'ton ... 3G 37
Lees St. NN9: Irth ... 2A 20
Lee Way NN9: Raun ... 2D 14
Leicester Pde. *NN2: N'ton ... 1C 52*
(off Barrack Rd.)
Leicester St. NN1: N'ton ... 2C 52
Leicester Ter. NN2: N'ton ... 2C 52
Leighton Cl. NN8: Well ... 3F 17
Leighton Pl. NN8: Well ... 1F 29
Leith Ct. NN4: N'ton ... 6G 51
Lennox Wlk. NN5: Dus ... 6F 35
Leonard La. NN3: Moul ... 4A 24
Leslie Rd. NN2: N'ton ... 2B 52
Lesson Rd. NN6: Brix ... 2A 22
Letts Rd. NN4: Far C ... 6B 52
Lewis Rd. NN5: N'ton ... 2H 51
Lewis Ter. NN5: N'ton ... 2A 52
Lexden Cl. NN4: Woot ... 4F 59
Leyland Dr. NN2: K'thpe ... 2A 36
Leyland Trad. Est. NN8: Well ... 1B 30
Leyland Vw. NN8: Well ... 1B 30
Leys, The NN2: K'thpe ... 5B 36
Leys Ct. NN8: Well ... 6H 17
Leys Gdns. NN8: Well ... 5H 17
Leyside Ct. NN3: N'ton ... 2F 39
Leys La. NN4: Gt Hou ... 2D 60
Leys Rd. NN6: E Bart ... 3F 41
NN8: Well ... 6H 17
Leyswell Ct. NN3: Lit B ... 1E 55
Liberty Dr. NN5: Dus ... 6E 35
Lichfield Cl. NN7: Kisl ... 6H 49
Lichfield Dr. NN4: N'ton ... 4B 58
Liddington Way NN2: K'thpe ... 2C 36
Lilac Ct. NN8: Well ... 6E 17
Lilac Gro. NN10: Rushd ... 6D 32
Liliput Rd. NN4: Brack ... 6H 53
Lilley Ter. NN9: Irth ... 1B 20
Lime Av. NN3: N'ton ... 6G 37
Lime Ct. NN9: Irth ... 1B 20
Lime Farm Way NN4: Gt Hou ... 1D 60
Limefields Way NN4: N'ton ... 5D 58
Lime Gro. NN8: Well ... 4G 17
NN10: Rushd ... 1D 32
Limehurst Cl. NN5: Dus ... 6D 34
Limehurst Rd. NN5: Dus ... 1E 51
Limehurst Sq. NN5: Dus ... 6E 35
Lime St. NN9: Irth ... 1B 20
NN10: Rushd ... 1C 32
Lime Ter. NN9: Irth ... 1B 20
Limlow Cl. NN4: N'ton ... 6G 51
Limoges Ct. NN5: New D ... 5C 34
Linacre Cl. NN3: N'ton ... 1D 38
Lincoln Rd. NN5: N'ton ... 4A 52
Lincoln St. NN2: K'thpe ... 4C 36
Lincoln Way NN11: Dav ... 1E 9
Lindale Cl. NN3: N'ton ... 4H 37
Linden Av. NN10: High F ... 4D 20
Linden Rd. NN3: N'ton ... 6G 37
Lindens, The NN1: N'ton ... 4G 5
Lindisfarne Way NN4: N'ton ... 3C 58
Lindrick Cl. NN11: Dav ... 5G 7
Lindsay Av. NN3: N'ton ... 5G 37
Lindsay Ter. NN3: N'ton ... 5G 37
Lingfield Ter. NN2: N'ton ... 6F 37
Lings Forum Leisure Cen. ... 5D 38
Lings Local Cen. *NN3: N'ton ... 4D 38*
(off Billing Brook Rd.)
Lings Way NN3: N'ton ... 2E 39
Lings Wood Nature Reserve ... 3E 39
Lingswood Pk. NN3: N'ton ... 4E 39
Link Rd. NN2: K'thpe ... 1A 36
NN10: Rushd ... 6D 32
Links Rd. NN8: Well ... 3H 17
Linley Grn. NN5: Dus ... 1F 51
Linnet Cl. NN8: Well ... 4G 17
Linnetts La. NN10: High F ... 6D 20
Lion Ct. NN4: N'ton ... 6D 4 (5D 52)
Lismore Cl. NN3: Gt Bil ... 5G 39
Lister Dr. NN4: N'ton ... 2G 57
Lister Rd. NN8: Well ... 6G 17
Litchfield Cl. NN6: Brix ... 1A 22
LITTLE ADDINGTON ... 1D 12
LITTLE BILLING ... 5E 39
Lit. Billing Way NN3: Lit B ... 5E 39
Little Cl. NN29: Boz ... 6G 45
Lit. Cross St.
NN1: N'ton ... 3A 4 (3B 52)
Littledale NN8: Well ... 5D 16
Little Fld. NN4: Gra P ... 1F 65
Lit. Greeve Way
NN4: Woot ... 5G 59
Lit. Gull Cl. NN3: N'ton ... 1D 38
LITTLE HOUGHTON ... 5E 55
LITTLE IRCHESTER ... 4A 30
Little La. NN4: Gt Hou ... 1C 60
NN7: Blis ... 5F 63
NN11: Dav ... 5E 7
NN29: Woll ... 4B 44
Lit. Park St. NN8: Well ... 6G 17
Lit. Priel Rd. NN7: Weed ... 5B 46
Little St. NN10: Rushd ... 4E 33
Littlewood Cl. NN5: N'ton ... 1A 52
LITTLE WYMINGTON ... 6C 32
Livingstone Rd. NN11: Dav ... 3E 7
LivingWell Health Club
Collingtree ... 2D 64
Lloyd Cl. NN8: Well ... 3H 17
Loach Ct. NN3: N'ton ... 1G 37
Loake Cl. NN4: Gra P ... 3D 64
Lockcroft Sq. NN3: Ect B ... 5H 39
Lockgate Rd. NN4: N'ton ... 2F 57
Lockwood Cl. NN2: K'thpe ... 3C 36
Lodge Av. NN4: Col ... 1C 64
Lodge Cl. NN4: Gra P ... 2F 65
NN5: Dus ... 6D 34
NN7: Lit Hou ... 6F 55
Lodge Ct. *NN8: Well ... 6H 17*
(off York Rd.)
LODGE FARM ... 5E 35
Lodge Farm Ind. Est.
NN5: Dus ... 5E 35
Lodge Rd. NN7: Lit Hou ... 5E 55
(not continuous)
NN10: Rushd ... 5C 32
NN11: Dav ... 5E 7

Lodge Way NN5: Dus 4D **34**
NN9: Irth 4H **19**
Lodore Gdns. NN3: N'ton 4A **38**
Logwell Ct. NN3: West F 6D **38**
Loire Cl. NN5: New D 5C **34**
Lombardy Ct. NN3: N'ton 4B **38**
London End NN6: E Bart 3G **41**
NN29: Irch 6F **31**
London Rd.
NN4: Far C, Del, Woot, Col 6C **52**
NN7: Court, Roa 6C **64**
NN8: Irch, Lit I, Well 1G **29**
NN9: Raun 1C **14**
NN11: Dav 6E **7**
NN29: Boz 4G **45**
NN29: Irch 4A **30**
NN29: Strix, Woll 5A **44**
Lone Pine Ct. NN6: Brix 1A **22**
Long Acre NN7: Braf G 6H **55**
Longacres NN4: N'ton 3B **58**
Long Acres Dr. NN9: Irth 6A **12**
Long Buckby Rd. NN11: Dav 4G **7**
Longfellow Rd. NN8: Well 1B **28**
Longford Av. NN3: Lit B 1E **55**
Longland Ct. NN3: N'ton 5H **37**
Longland Rd. NN3: N'ton 5H **37**
Longleat Ct. NN4: N'ton 3C **58**
Long Mallows Ri. NN3: Ect B 5G **39**
Long March NN11: Dav 1F **9**
Long March Ind. Est.
NN11: Dav 1F **9**
Long Marsh Sq. NN3: N'ton 1E **39**
Longmead Ct. NN3: N'ton 3F **39**
Longmeadow NN4: Woot 5H **59**
Longmynd Dr. NN5: Dus 1F **51**
Longueville Ct. NN3: N'ton 3C **38**
Lordswood Cl. NN4: Woot 5G **59**
Lorne Rd. NN1: N'ton 1C **4** (2C **52**)
Lorraine Cres. NN3: N'ton 2H **37**
Lorraine Dr. NN3: N'ton 2A **38**
Loseby Cl. NN10: Rushd 5C **32**
Louisa Lilley Homes, The
NN9: Irth 1B 20
(off High St.)
Louisberg Cl. NN4: Woot 4E **59**
Louise Rd. NN1: N'ton 2D **52**
Louth Dr. NN10: Rushd 5F **33**
Lovat Dr. NN5: N'ton 2G **51**
Lovell Cl. NN9: Stanw 5A **14**
Lovell Ct. NN9: Irth 1B **20**
Lowbury Ct. NN4: N'ton 6G **51**
Lwr. Adelaide St. NN2: N'ton 2C **52**
Lwr. Bath St.
NN1: N'ton 2A **4** (3B **52**)
Lwr. Cross St.
NN1: N'ton 3A **4** (3B **52**)
Lwr. Ecton La. NN3: Gt Bil 1H **55**
LOWER END 6H **55**
Lwr. Farm Rd. NN3: N'ton 6F **23**
Lowergrass Wlk. NN3: West F 6D **38**
Lwr. Harding St.
NN1: N'ton 2B **4** (3C **52**)
LOWER HARLESTONE 1A **34**
Lwr. Hester St. NN2: N'ton 2B **52**
Lwr. Meadow Ct. NN3: N'ton 2C **38**
Lower Mounts
NN1: N'ton 2E **5** (3D **52**)
Lwr. Priory St.
NN1: N'ton 1A **4** (2B **52**)
Lower Rd. NN7: Mil M 1G **63**
Lower St. NN29: Gt Dod 1E **43**
Lwr. Thrift St.
NN1: N'ton 2H **5** (3F **53**)
LOWER WEEDON 6C **46**
Low Farm Pl. NN3: N'ton 6F **23**
Low Greeve NN4: Woot 5G **59**
Lowick Cl. NN8: Well 4D **16**
Lowick Ct. NN3: Moul 6A **24**
Lowlands Cl. NN3: N'ton 2G **39**
Low March NN11: Dav 2F **9**
Low March Ind. Est. NN11: Dav 2F **9**
Lowry Cl. NN3: N'ton 3H **37**
NN8: Well 4E **17**
Loxton Cl. NN5: Dus 6E **35**
Loyd Rd. NN1: N'ton 2G **53**
Lucas Cl. NN9: Irth 3A **20**
Lucas Ct. NN3: Moul 5A **24**
Ludlow Cl. NN3: N'ton 6E **25**
Lumbertubs La. NN3: N'ton 2A **38**
Lumbertubs Ri. NN3: N'ton 2B **38**
Lumbertubs Way
NN3: N'ton, West F 1B **38**
Lunchfield Ct. NN3: Moul 4A **24**
Lunchfield Gdns. NN3: Moul 4A **24**
Lunchfield La. NN3: Moul 4A **24**
Lunchfield Wlk. NN3: Moul 4A **24**
Lundie Cl. NN9: Raun 2D **14**
Lutterworth Rd. NN1: N'ton 2G **53**
Lydia Ct. NN10: Rushd 3C **32**
Lyle Ct. NN8: Well 4C **16**
Lyncrest Av. NN5: N'ton 2G **51**
Lyncroft Way NN2: K'thpe 6B **36**
Lynford Way NN10: Rushd 5B **32**
Lynmore Cl. NN4: N'ton 2E **57**
Lynmouth Av. NN3: N'ton 2A **54**
Lynton Av. NN2: K'thpe 1B **36**
Lytham Cl. NN2: N'ton 4E **37**
Lytham Ct. NN8: Well 4C **16**
Lyttleton Rd. NN5: N'ton 2A **52**
Lyveden Rd. NN4: Brack 2G **59**

M

Macadam Cl. NN11: Dav 2B **6**
McGibbon Wlk. NN9: Irth 3H **19**
McInnes Way NN9: Raun 2D **14**
Mackenzie Rd. NN9: Raun 4C **14**
Mackintosh Centre, The *3B 22*
(in Brixworth Country Pk. Vis. Cen.)
Mackintosh Sq.
NN3: West F 6A **38**
Mackworth Dr. NN9: Fine 5C **10**
Mackworth Grn. NN9: Fine 5D **10**
Maclean Cl. NN3: N'ton 2A **54**
Macmillan Way NN3: N'ton 3H **37**
Macon Cl. NN5: Dus 5B **34**
Magdalen Cl. NN11: Dav 1D **8**
Magee St. NN1: N'ton 2F **53**
Magellan Cl. NN11: Dav 2E **7**
Magistrates' Court
Northampton 1D **4** (2D **52**)
Wellingborough 1H **29**
Magnolia Cl. NN3: N'ton 3B **54**
Magnolia Dr. NN10: Rushd 6D **32**
NN11: Dav 3E **7**
Maida Cl. NN4: Woot 4E **59**
Maidencastle NN3: N'ton 4F **39**
Main Rd. NN4: Far C 6A **52**
(not continuous)
NN5: Dus 5D **34**
NN6: E Bart, Wilby 2E **41**
NN7: Up Hey 5A **48**
NN8: Wilby 6A **28**
Main St. NN11: Badby 6B **8**
Malabar Flds. NN11: Dav 1D **8**
Malcolm Dr. NN5: N'ton 2G **51**
Malcolm Rd. NN2: N'ton 5F **37**
Malcolm Ter. NN2: N'ton 5G **37**
Malesoure Wlk. NN3: N'ton 1G **39**
Malham Ct. NN8: Well 5D **16**
Mallard Cl. NN4: N'ton 1H **57**
NN6: E Bart 2G **41**
NN10: High F 3E **21**
Mallery Cl. NN10: Rushd 2F **33**
Mallory Wlk. NN3: N'ton 2F **37**
Mallory Way NN11: Dav 2D **6**
Mallows Dr. NN9: Raun 2C **14**
Mallows Yd. NN29: Boz 5H **45**
Malpas Dr. NN5: Dus 1D **50**
Malthouse Cl. NN4: N'ton 5D **52**
NN9: Irth 1B **20**
Maltings, The NN29: Woll 4B **44**
Malvern Cl. NN8: Well 4D **28**
Malvern Gro. NN5: Dus 1F **51**
Malzor La. NN7: Mil M 1G **63**
Manchester Rd. NN29: Woll 4A **44**
Mandarin St. NN4: N'ton 3G **57**
Mander Cl. NN5: Dus 1B **50**
Manderville Cl. NN3: N'ton 3H **37**
Manfield Health Campus
NN3: N'ton 3H **37**
Manfield Rd. NN1: N'ton 2G **53**
Manfield Way NN3: N'ton 2H **37**
Manning Ct. NN3: Moul 6A **24**
Manningham Rd. NN9: Stanw 5A **14**
Manning Rd. NN3: Moul 6A **24**
Mannings Ri. NN10: Rushd 4E **33**
Manning St. NN10: Rushd 4E **33**
Mannington Gdns. NN4: N'ton 4C **58**
Mannock Rd. NN8: Well 2E **29**
Manor Cl. NN7: Harp 3G **49**
NN9: Gt Har 1D **16**
NN29: Boz 5H **45**
NN29: Irch 5F **31**
Manor Ct. NN2: K'thpe 4B **36**
NN8: Well 6H 17
(off Strode Rd.)
NN10: Rushd 5E **33**
Manor Dr. NN9: Irth 1C **20**
Mnr. Farm Rd. NN3: Gt Bil 5F **39**
NN9: Raun 3E **15**
Manorfield Cl. NN3: Lit B 1F **55**
Manorfield Rd. NN3: Lit B 1E **55**
Manor Gdns. NN9: Stanw 6A **14**
Manor Ho. Cl. NN6: E Bart 2G **41**
Manor Ho. Gdns. NN9: Raun 3D **14**
Manor La. NN6: E Bart 2G **41**
NN11: Newn 5G **9**
Manor Pk. NN7: Neth H 6A **48**
Manor Rd. NN2: K'thpe 4B **36**
NN3: Moul 5A **24**
NN6: E Bart 2G **41**
NN6: Mears A 3D **26**
NN6: Pits 1D **22**
NN7: Weed 6B **46**
NN10: Rushd 5D **32**
NN11: Dav 1F **9**
Manor St. NN9: Raun 3D **14**
Manor Way NN10: High F 6E **21**
Mansard Cl. NN5: N'ton 3G **51**
Mansard Ho. NN5: Upton 2C **50**
Manse Cl. NN10: Rushd 2E **33**
Mansfield St. NN9: Stanw 5H **13**
Mansfield Way NN29: Irch 5E **31**
Mansion Cl. NN3: N'ton 1G **37**
Manton Rd. NN9: Irth 1A **20**
NN10: Rushd 4E **33**
Manton Spinney NN29: Knus 3A **32**
Maple Bldgs. NN1: N'ton 1C **4**
Maple Ct. NN4: Col 1B **64**
Maple Dr. NN8: Well 6E **17**
Maple Rd. NN10: Rushd 3E **33**
Maples, The NN11: Dav 6F **7**
Mapletoft St. NN9: Raun 4C **14**
Maple Wood NN10: Rushd 6D **32**
Mapperley Dr. NN3: West F 1D **54**
Marble Arch
NN1: N'ton 1C **4** (2C **52**)
Marburg St. NN3: N'ton 1G **39**
Marchwood Cl. NN3: N'ton 1D **38**
Mare Fair NN1: N'ton 4A **4** (4B **52**)
Margaret Av. NN8: Well 3E **29**
Margaret Bondfield Hall
NN2: K'thpe 2E **37**
Margaret St.
NN1: N'ton 1D **4** (2D **52**)
Maritime Way NN11: Dav 6G **7**
Marjoram Cl. NN4: N'ton 5D **58**
Market Cross NN9: Irth 1B **20**
Market Sq. NN1: N'ton 3C **4** (3C **52**)
NN8: Well 1G **29**
NN10: High F 5E **21**
NN11: Dav 5E **7**
Market St. NN1: N'ton 1G **5** (2E **53**)
(not continuous)
NN8: Well 1G **29**
Market Wlk.
NN1: N'ton 3D **4** (3D **52**)
(Grosvenor Cen.)
NN1: N'ton 1G **5** (2E **53**)
(Market St.)
Mark Gro. Ho. NN10: Rushd 2E **33**
Markham Cl. NN5: Dus 6E **35**
Marks Cl. NN9: Stanw 6A **14**
Marlborough Av. NN8: Well 4D **16**
Marlborough Ho. NN1: N'ton 4E **5**
Marlborough Rd. NN5: N'ton 3A **52**
Marlow Cl. NN11: Dav 6D **6**
(not continuous)
Marlowe Cl. NN4: N'ton 4B **58**
Marlstones NN4: N'ton 1F **57**
Marnock Sq. NN4: N'ton 1H **57**
Marnock Wlk. *NN4: N'ton 1H 57*
(off Marnock Sq.)
Marquee Dr. NN3: N'ton 2C **54**
Marriott Cl. NN9: Irth 3A **20**
Marriott St. NN2: N'ton 1C **52**
Marseilles Cl. NN5: Dus 6B **34**
Marshall's Rd. NN9: Raun 3C **14**
Marsh La. NN9: Irth 1C **20**
Marshleys Ct. NN3: N'ton 2F **39**
Marshwell Ct. NN3: Lit B 1E **55**
Marston Way NN11: Dav 1F **7**
Martel Cl. NN5: Dus 1B **50**
Martin Cl. NN10: Rushd 1D **32**
Martindale NN2: K'thpe 2H **35**
Martins Ct. NN3: West F 6B **38**
Martin's La. NN4: H'stone 3D **58**
Martins Yd. NN5: N'ton 1A **4** (2B **52**)
Martlet Cl. NN4: Woot 6E **59**
Martyns Way NN7: Weed 6B **46**
Marvills Mill Rd. NN4: N'ton 5C **52**
Marwood Cl. NN3: N'ton 2H **53**
Masefield Cl. NN8: Well 1C **28**
Masefield Dr. NN10: Rushd 3A **32**
Masefield Way NN2: N'ton 5E **37**
Massey Cl. NN4: H'stone 3E **59**
Matchless Cl. NN5: Dus 6C **34**
Matson Ct. NN9: Raun 2E **15**
Maxwell Cres. NN5: Dus 2E **51**
Maxwell Wlk. NN5: Dus 2E **51**
May Bank NN11: Dav 1D **8**
May Cl. NN10: Rushd 6E **33**
Maye Dicks Rd. NN10: Rushd 5E **33**
Mayfield Dr. NN11: Dav 4D **6**
Mayfield Rd. NN3: N'ton 4H **3**
Mayor Hold NN1: N'ton 3B **4** (3C **5**
Meadow Cl. NN5: Dus 5D **3**
NN8: Well 4B **1**
NN10: High F 5C **2**
NN11: Dav 1F
Meadow Dr. NN10: High F 5D **2**
Meadow Farm Cl.
NN7: Flore 4F **4**
Meadow La. NN7: Lit Hou 5E **5**
NN9: Raun 3H **1**
Meadows, The NN4: Gra P 4F **6**
NN9: Well 2E **1**
Meadow Sweet Rd.
NN10: Rushd 6E **3**
Meadowsweet Rd. NN5: Dus 3B **5**
Meadowsweet Wlk.
NN4: Gra P 3F **6**
Meadowvale NN9: Irth 2B **2**
Meadow Vw. NN10: High F 5C **2**
Meadow Wlk. NN9: Irth 1B **2**
NN10: High F 5C **2**
Meadow Way NN9: Irth 2B **2**
Meadway NN3: West F 6B **3**
MEARS ASHBY 3D **2**
Mears Ashby Rd. NN6: E Bart 4D **2**
NN8: Wilby 3G **2**
Medbourne Cl. NN3: Moul 6H **2**
Medellin Hill NN3: N'ton 1D **3**
Medinah Cl. NN4: Col 6D **5**
Medway, The NN11: Dav 6C
Medway Cl. NN5: N'ton 5G **3**
Medway Dr. NN5: N'ton 5G **3**
NN8: Well 5C **1**
Medwin NN8: Well 1B **2**
Meeting La. NN5: Dus 2E **5**
NN9: Irth 1B **2**
Melbourne Ho. NN5: N'ton 3H **5**
Melbourne La. NN5: Dus 3E **5**
Melbourne Rd. NN5: N'ton 3H **5**
Melbourne St.
NN1: N'ton 2H **5** (3F **5**
Melbourne Wlk.
NN1: N'ton 2H **5** (3F **5**
Melbury La. NN3: N'ton 4F **3**
Melbury Pl. NN3: N'ton 4E **3**
Melchester Cl. NN4: H'stone 4E **5**
Meldon Cl. NN4: N'ton 3C **5**
Melloway Rd. NN10: Rushd 3H **3**
Melrose Av. NN5: N'ton 2G **5**
Meltham Cl. NN3: West F 6D **3**
Melton Rd. NN8: Well 6A **1**
Melton Rd. Nth. NN8: Well 6H **1**
Melville St. NN1: N'ton 1H **5** (2F **5**
Mendip Ct. NN11: Dav 2D
Mendip Rd. NN5: Dus 1F **5**
Meon Way NN5: Dus 1F **5**
Mercer's Row
NN1: N'ton 4C **4** (4C **5**
Mercia Gdns. NN3: N'ton 6A **3**
Mercury Cl. NN11: Dav 3C
Mercury Dr. NN4: Brack 1G **5**
Mere Cl. NN4: N'ton 3B **5**
NN7: Braf G 1H **6**
MEREFIELD 4B **5**
Merefields NN9: Irth 6A **1**
Mere Way NN4: N'ton 2B **5**
Merlin Gro. NN4: N'ton 3B **5**
Merrydale Sq. NN3: N'ton 1E **3**
Merryhill NN4: N'ton 1G **5**
Mersey Cl. NN4: N'ton 1A **5**
Mershe Cl. NN4: H'stone 4F **5**
Merthyr Rd. NN5: N'ton 1A **5**
Merton Rd. NN11: Dav 2D
Mescalero NN2: K'thpe 3C **3**
Meshaw Cres. NN3: N'ton 2H **5**
Methodist Homestead
NN2: N'ton 6E **3**
Mews, The NN3: West F 1B **5**
Micklewell La. NN3: N'ton 1D **3**
Middle Grass NN9: Irth 6A **1**
Middle Greeve NN4: Woot 5G **5**
Middle March NN11: Dav 1F
Middlemarch NN3: N'ton 3F **3**
Middlemead Ct. NN3: West F 6E **3**
Middlemore NN3: N'ton 1D **3**
Middle St. NN7: Neth H 6A **4**
Middleton Cl. NN2: K'thpe 2C **3**
Middleton Rd. NN11: Dav 1C
Middlewell Ct. NN3: West F 6D **3**
Middlewich Cl. NN11: Dav 1E
Midfield Ct. NN3: N'ton 2C **3**
Midland Bus. Cen.
NN10: High F 5E **2**
Midland Bus. Units NN8: Well 5A **1**
Midland Rd. NN8: Well 1G **2**
NN9: Raun 2E **1**
NN10: High F 5E **2**
NN10: Rushd 2C **3**

Midland Works Bus. Cen.—Nursery Gdns.

Midland Works Bus. Cen.
NN8: Well 5A 18
Midway *NN7: Blis 3D 62*
(off Oak Av.)
Milburn Dr. NN5: Upton 3C 50
Milbury NN6: E Bart 4H 41
Miles Cl. NN9: Raun 4B 14
Mile St. NN29: Boz 5H 45
Miles Well Ct. NN3: N'ton 4B 38
Military Ct. NN1: N'ton 1E 5 (2D 52)
Military Rd.
NN1: N'ton 1E 5 (2D 52)
Militia Cl. NN4: Woot 4E 59
Millbank NN3: Ect B 5H 39
Millbrook Cl. NN5: N'ton 4A 52
Mill Cl. NN9: Raun 3C 14
Millennium Way NN11: Dav 5E 7
Miller Hill NN4: N'ton 1G 57
Millers Cl. NN7: Kisl 6H 49
NN9: Fine 3E 11
NN10: Rushd 3B 32
Millers La. NN8: Well 5F 29
Millers Pk. NN8: Well 4G 29
Miller St. NN9: Raun 3D 14
Millers Way NN4: Gra P 2F 65
Mill Est. NN10: Rushd 6D 32
Mill Flds. NN10: High F 4D 20
Mill Ho. *NN2: N'ton 2C 52*
(off Mill Rd.)
NN4: N'ton 5C 52
(off River Vw.)
Millhouse Ct. *NN5: N'ton 4B 52*
(off Byfield Rd.)
Mill La. NN2: K'thpe 6A 36
NN2: N'ton 1A 4 (2B 52)
NN5: N'ton 1H 51
NN6: E Bart 3A 42
NN7: Kisl 6H 49
NN9: Fine 4A 10
Mill Mdw. NN2: K'thpe 2D 36
Mill Pond Dr. NN5: Upton 5E 51
Mill Rd. NN2: N'ton 2C 52
NN7: Kisl 6G 49
NN8: Well 6H 17
(Newcomen Rd.)
NN8: Well 4E 19
(Wellingborough Rd.)
NN29: Boz 6G 45
Mill Rd. Ind. Est. NN8: Well 5A 18
Mills Cl. NN6: E Bart 3H 41
Millside Cl. NN2: K'thpe 2D 36
Millstone Cl. NN4: N'ton 1F 57
Mill St. NN5: Upton 5E 51
Millway NN5: Dus 3E 51
Milner Rd. NN9: Fine 5D 10
Milton Av. NN8: Well 2C 28
Milton Bri. NN4: Woot 5G 59
Milton Ct. NN7: Mil M 2G 63
MILTON MALSOR 1G 63
Milton Rd. NN7: G'ton 3B 62
NN8: Lit I 4A 30
NN11: Dav 5D 6
Milton St. NN2: N'ton 6E 37
NN10: High F 6D 20
Milton St. Nth. NN2: N'ton 5E 37
Milverton Cres. NN3: West F 2A 54
Mimosa Cl. NN3: N'ton 3A 54
Minerva Way NN8: Well 6D 16
Minster Ho. NN1: N'ton 2D 4
Minton Bus. Cen. NN4: Far C 6A 52
Mitchell Cl. NN5: Dus 5F 35
Moat Pl. NN1: N'ton 3A 4 (3B 52)
Mobbs Miller Ho. NN1: N'ton 2G 53
Moffatt Ter. NN8: Well 6G 17
Monarch Rd. NN2: N'ton 6C 36
Monarch Ter. NN2: N'ton 1C 52
Monks Hall Rd. NN1: N'ton 2F 53
Monks Pk. Rd. NN1: N'ton 2F 53
Monks Pond St.
NN1: N'ton 2A 4 (3B 52)
Monks Rd. NN29: Woll 4B 44
Monks Way NN8: Well 2G 29
Monmouth Rd. NN5: N'ton 2A 52
Montague Cres. NN5: Dus 5F 35
Montague St. NN10: Rushd 3C 32
Montfort Cl. NN5: N'ton 3G 51
Montgomery Way NN4: Woot 4D 58
Moorcut Dr. NN5: Upton 5E 51
Moore St. NN2: N'ton 6F 37
Moorfield Sq. NN3: N'ton 1E 39
Moorland Cl. NN3: West F 5C 38
Moorlands NN8: Well 4C 16
Moorlands, The NN10: Rushd 1D 32
Moor Rd. NN10: Rushd 2C 32
Mordaunt La. NN5: Dus 6F 35
More Rd. NN11: Dav 3D 6
Moreton Av. NN8: Well 3D 28
Moreton Way NN2: K'thpe 2C 36
Morgan Cl. NN3: N'ton 3G 39

Morning Star Rd.
NN11: Dav 4C 6
Morris Av. NN10: Rushd 4B 32
Morris Cl. NN8: Well 5A 16
Morris Rd. NN2: K'thpe 4D 36
NN11: Dav 4B 6
Mortar Pit Rd. NN3: N'ton 2G 39
Mortimer Cl. NN4: N'ton 1A 58
Mortons Bush NN4: Woot 5G 59
Mosel Cl. NN8: Well 4G 29
Motspur Dr. NN2: K'thpe 6B 36
Motts, The NN7: Harp 3F 49
MOULTON 4A 24
Moulton College Sports Hall 2G 23
Moulton La. NN2: Bou 5C 22
MOULTON LEYS 6A 24
MOULTON PARK 1F 37
Moulton Pk. Bus. Cen.
NN3: N'ton 1G 37
Moulton Pk. Ind. Est.
NN3: N'ton 1G 37
Moulton Pk. Office Village
NN3: N'ton 1F 37
Moulton Rd. NN3: Pits 2D 22
NN6: Pits 1D 22
Moulton Sports Complex 4H 23
Moulton Way NN3: N'ton 1H 37
Moulton Way Nth. NN3: Moul 1A 38
Moulton Way Sth. NN3: Moul 1A 38
Mountbatten Ho. *NN11: Dav 1G 9*
(off Admirals Way)
Mountbatten Way NN9: Raun 3E 15
Mountclair Ct. NN3: West F 1C 54
Mountfield Rd. NN3: N'ton 4G 37
NN9: Irth 6B 12
Mt. Pleasant NN6: E Bart 3H 41
NN7: Harp 2G 49
Mounts Baths Leisure Centre, The
2D 4 (3D 52)
Mounts Bus. Cen. NN1: N'ton 1D 4
Mounts Ct. NN3: N'ton 4C 38
Mounts La. NN11: Newn 5G 9
Muirfield Dr. NN11: Dav 5G 7
Muirfield Rd. NN8: Well 4C 16
Mulberry Cl. NN5: N'ton 2H 51
NN8: Well 6E 17
Mullions, The NN4: Woot 6E 59
Mulso Rd. NN9: Fine 4E 11
Mumford Dr. NN7: Rother 4C 56
Muncaster Gdns. NN4: N'ton 4D 58
Murray Av. NN2: N'ton 6D 36
Murray Ho. NN1: N'ton 1F 53
Muscott Cl. NN7: Flore 3E 47
Muscott La. NN5: Dus 3D 50
Muscott St. NN5: N'ton 2A 52
Museum Way NN3: N'ton 2D 54
Musgrave Cl. NN4: Woot 4F 59
Mushroom Fld. Rd.
NN3: Ect B 5H 39
Musson Cl. NN9: Irth 1A 20

N

Nansen Cl. NN11: Dav 2E 7
Nantwich Dr. NN11: Dav 1F 7
Naomi Cl. NN3: West F 6D 38
Napier Cl. NN8: Well 1A 28
NN11: Dav 1F 9
Napleton Lodge NN9: Raun 1H 15
Narrowboat La. NN4: N'ton 2F 57
Narrow La. NN1: N'ton 2B 4 (3C 52)
Narrow Toe La. NN1: N'ton 4A 4
Naseby Cl. NN8: Well 4D 16
Naseby Dr. NN11: Dav 1E 7
Naseby St. NN2: N'ton 1C 52
Nasmyth Rd. NN11: Dav 2B 6
Navigation Row
NN1: N'ton 6C 4 (5C 52)
Neale Cl. NN3: West F 1B 54
NN29: Woll 4A 44
Nearside NN5: N'ton 3H 51
Nectar Way
NN4: Swan H, Upton 1C 56
Needham Rd. NN9: Stanw 5H 13
Neighbourhood Shop. Cen.
NN4: N'ton 5C 58
Nelson Cl. NN11: Dav 5G 7
Nelson St. NN1: N'ton 2C 52
Nene Centre, The NN4: N'ton 4F 53
Nene Cl. NN8: Well 5C 16
NN9: Raun 2D 14
Nene Ct. NN8: Well 2A 30
Nene Dr. NN5: N'ton 5H 35
Nene Ent. Cen. NN2: N'ton 1C 52
Nene Ho. NN11: Dav 3C 6
Nene Park 1D 20
Nene Pl. NN5: N'ton 5A 36
Nene Rd. NN10: High F 6D 20

Nene Side Cl. NN11: Badby 6B 8
Neneside Cl. NN7: Weed 6A 46
Nene Valley Retail Pk.
NN1: N'ton 6A 4 (5B 52)
Nene Valley Way
NN3: Gt Bil, Lit B, N'ton, West F
6G 39
NN4: Del, N'ton 2D 58
Nene Vw. NN9: Irth 1B 20
Nene Wlk. NN5: N'ton 5H 35
NN11: Dav 6C 6
Nene Way NN5: N'ton 5A 36
NN7: Kisl 6G 49
Nene Whitewater Cen. 5G 53
Nesbitt Cl. NN3: West F 2C 54
Nest Farm Cres. NN8: Well 3G 17
Nest Farm Rd. NN8: Well 3F 17
Nest Farm Way NN8: Well 4G 17
Nest La. NN8: Well 5H 17
Nether Jackson Ct.
NN3: N'ton 3F 39
Nether La. NN7: Flore 5E 47
Nethermead Ct.
NN3: N'ton 3D 38
Nettlebush NN8: Well 5A 18
Nettle Gap Cl. NN4: Woot 5F 59
NEW BARTON 2G 41
Newbridge La. NN9: Stanw 6A 14
Newbury Cl. NN10: Rushd 2F 33
Newbury Dr. NN11: Dav 1E 7
Newby Ct. NN3: N'ton 4A 38
Newcombe Rd. NN5: N'ton 2A 52
Newcomen Rd. NN8: Well 6H 17
New Cft. NN7: Weed 6B 46
NEW DUSTON 5D 34
New Forest Way NN11: Dav 3D 6
New Hall NN11: Dav 2D 8
Newington Rd. NN2: K'thpe 3C 36
Newland NN1: N'ton 2C 4 (3C 52)
Newlands NN6: Brix 1A 22
NN11: Dav 6E 7
Newland Sq. NN2: K'thpe 3C 36
Newland Wlk. NN1: N'ton 3D 4
Newlife Apartments
NN1: N'ton 2B 4
Newman St. NN10: High F 4E 21
NEWNHAM 5F 9
Newnham Dr. NN11: Dav 2C 6
Newnham Rd. NN2: K'thpe 4D 36
NN11: Badby, Newn 5C 8
Newport Pagnell Rd.
NN4: Woot, H'stone 3D 58
NN7: Pres D 5A 60
Newport Pagnell Rd. W.
NN4: Woot 3D 58
Newport Rd. NN5: N'ton 2A 52
New Rd. NN4: Woot 5E 59
New South Bri. Rd.
NN4: N'ton 5D 52
Newstead Cl. NN3: Ect B 4H 39
Newstone Cres. NN4: N'ton 5G 51
New St. NN6: Brix 1A 22
NN6: E Bart 3H 41
NN7: Weed 6B 46
NN8: Well 6G 17
NN9: Irth 1B 20
NN11: Dav 6E 7
NN29: Irch 5F 31
Newton Cl. NN8: Well 5B 16
NN10: Rushd 4F 33
NN11: Dav 3C 6
Newton Rd. NN5: Dus 6E 35
NN10: High F, Rushd 5E 21
(not continuous)
NN10: Rushd 3D 32
NN29: Woll 5B 44
Newtown Rd.
NN1: N'ton 2H 5 (3F 53)
NN8: Lit I 4A 30
NN9: Raun 4E 15
Nicholas Rd. NN9: Irth 2A 20
Nicholas Way
NN10: Rushd 2B 32
Nicholls Ct. NN3: N'ton 2C 38
Nichols Way NN9: Raun 2C 14
Nielson Rd. NN8: Well 3A 18
Nightingale Cl. NN11: Dav 1E 7
Nightingale La. NN8: Well 4H 17
Niort Way NN8: Well 5B 16
Nippendale NN10: Rushd 3E 33
Noble Av. NN9: Irth 4C 12
Nobottle Rd. NN5: New D 6A 34
NN7: New D 6A 34
Norfolk St. NN2: N'ton 1C 52
Norfolk Ter. NN2: N'ton 1C 52
Normal Boot & Shoe Factory, The
NN1: N'ton 1G 5
Norman-D-Gate
NN1: N'ton 5G 5 (4E 53)

Norman-D-Gate Ind. Est.
NN1: N'ton 5G 5 (4E 53)
Norman Rd. NN3: N'ton 6H 37
Norman Snow Way NN5: Dus 2E 51
Norman Way NN8: Well 3D 28
NN29: Irch 5G 31
Normead Sq. NN3: Ect B 5H 39
Norris Way NN10: Rushd 2A 32
Norris Way Ind. Est.
NN10: Rushd 2A 32
NORTHAMPTON 4D 4 (4D 52)
Northampton & District Indoor
Bowling Association 3B 36
Northampton Boat Club 3C 54
Northampton Bus. Cen.
NN1: N'ton 2A 4
Northampton Central Museum &
Art Gallery 4C 4 (4D 52)
NORTHAMPTON GENERAL HOSPITAL
4F 5 (4E 53)
Northampton Golf Course 2A 34
Northampton Ho.
NN1: N'ton 3D 4 (3D 52)
Northampton Indoor Karting 4H 51
Northampton International Raceway
6H 61
Northampton La. Nth.
NN3: Moul 5A 24
Northampton La. Sth.
NN3: Moul 1H 37
Northampton Rd. NN6: Brix 2A 22
NN6: E Bart 2F 41
NN6: Ect 3B 40
NN7: Blis 4F 63
NN7: Harp 4G 49
NN8: Well 3C 28
NN10: High F, Rushd 2G 31
Northampton Saints RFC
(Franklin's Gardens) 3H 51
Northampton Science Pk.
NN3: N'ton 1F 37
NORTHAMPTON SERVICE AREA
4E 57
Northamptonshire
County Cricket Club 1G 53
Northamptonshire County Golf Course
1E 35
Northamptonshire Ironstone
Railway Trust 1G 57
Northampton Station (Rail)
4A 4 (4B 52)
Northampton Town FC 4F 51
Northampton Water Ski Club 6F 53
Northcote St. NN2: N'ton 2C 52
North End NN10: High F 5D 20
Northen Way NN8: Well 3E 17
Northern Way NN11: Dav 1E 7
Northfield Rd. NN5: Dus 6D 34
Northfield Way NN2: K'thpe 3B 36
Nth. Hayes Ct. NN3: N'ton 2D 38
Nth. Holme Ct. NN3: N'ton 2B 38
Nth. Leys Ct. NN3: Moul 6A 24
North Mdw. Vw. NN5: Dus 3B 50
North Oval NN5: N'ton 5H 35
Nth. Paddock Ct. NN3: N'ton 3D 38
Nth. Portway Cl. NN3: N'ton 6D 24
Nth. Priors Ct. NN3: N'ton 3E 39
North Rd. NN3: N'ton 1F 37
NN6: E Bart 2G 41
North St. NN6: Mears A 3D 26
NN7: Rother 5C 56
NN8: Well 6F 17
NN9: Raun 2D 14
NN10: Rushd 2D 32
NN11: Dav 5E 7
Northumbria Gdns.
NN3: N'ton 6H 37
Nth. Western Av.
NN2: K'thpe 3A 36
Northwood Rd. NN3: N'ton 5H 37
Norton Cl. NN11: Dav 5F 7
Norton Rd. NN2: K'thpe 4C 36
NN11: Dav 5F 7
(not continuous)
Norwood Rd. NN5: Dus 2B 50
Notre Dame M.
NN1: N'ton 2E 5 (3D 52)
Nuffield Health Club
Northampton 3G 51
Nunn Mills Rd.
NN1: N'ton 6F 5 (5E 53)
Nurseries, The
NN1: N'ton 5H 5 (4F 53)
NN3: Moul 4A 24
Nursery Cl. NN7: Lit Hou 5E 55
NN11: Dav 2D 6
Nursery Ct. NN6: Mears A 3D 26
Nursery Dr. NN8: Well 4H 17
Nursery Gdns. NN9: Irth 1A 20

A-Z Northampton 77

Nursery La. NN2: K'thpe 5C **36**
Nuthall Cl. NN3: West F 1D **54**

O

Oak Av. NN7: Blis 3D **62**
Oak Cl. NN29: Irch 6E **31**
Oakfield NN10: Rushd 1C **32**
Oak Gro. NN3: N'ton 6A **38**
NN11: Dav 2E **7**
Oakgrove Pl. NN4: N'ton 5D **58**
Oakham Cl. NN3: Moul 6H **23**
NN10: Rushd 5C **32**
Oaklands NN7: Weed 6A **46**
Oaklands Dr. NN3: West F 6B **38**
Oakleigh Cl. NN9: Raun 2C **14**
Oakleigh Dr. NN5: Dus 6E **35**
Oakley Dr. NN3: Moul 4B **24**
NN8: Well 1D **28**
Oakley Rd. NN10: Rushd 2B **32**
Oakley St. NN1: N'ton . . .1D **4** (2D **52**)
Oakmont Cl. NN4: N'ton 6C **58**
Oakpark Cl. NN3: N'ton 1E **39**
Oakpits Way NN10: Rushd 4E **33**
Oaks, The NN4: Gra P 2F **65**
Oaks Dr. NN10: High F 4D **20**
Oak St. NN1: N'ton 1C **4** (2C **52**)
NN7: Weed 6A **46**
NN10: Rushd 1D **32**
Oak Ter. NN9: Irth 1B **20**
Oak Tree Cl. NN3: Lit B 6E **39**
Oak Vw. NN9: Well 2F **17**
Oak Way NN9: Irth 1B **20**
Oakway NN8: Well 4F **17**
Oakwood Rd. NN1: N'ton 6F **37**
Oathill Cl. NN6: Brix 2A **22**
Oat Hill Dr. NN3: Ect B 5H **39**
Obelisk Centre, The 6C **22**
Obelisk Cl. NN2: Bou 5C **22**
Obelisk Ho. NN2: K'thpe 6C **22**
Obelisk Ri. NN2: K'thpe 6C **22**
Obelisk Rd. NN9: Fine 4E **11**
Octagon Way NN3: West F 5C **38**
Ogee Bus. Pk. NN8: Well 2H **17**
Old Barn Ct. NN3: N'ton 4D **38**
Old Barn Wlk. NN3: N'ton 3D **38**
Old Bedford Rd. NN4: N'ton 5H **53**
Old Carpenters Cl.
NN3: Gt Bil 5G **39**
Old Cl. NN4: Gra P 3E **65**
Old Depot, The NN7: Weed 5B **46**
Olde Forde Cl. NN6: Brix 2A **22**
Oldenmead Ct. NN3: N'ton 4D **38**
Olden Rd. NN3: N'ton 2G **39**
Old Orchard La. NN3: Moul 6H **23**
Old Quarry Ct. NN3: N'ton 3C **38**
Old School Ct. NN3: Gt Bil 5G **39**
Old Slipper Baths, The
NN4: Far C 6B 52
(off Main Rd.)
Old Towcester Rd. NN4: N'ton . . .5C **52**
Old Vineyard, The
NN10: High F 5D **20**
Old Yew Ct. NN2: K'thpe 4B **36**
Oleander Cres. NN3: N'ton 3G **39**
Oliver Cl. NN10: Rushd 3E **33**
Oliver St. NN2: N'ton 6E **37**
Olympia Cl. NN4: N'ton 3B **58**
Olympic Way NN8: Well 6C **16**
Omega Ho. NN1: N'ton 2B **4**
Oransay Cl. NN3: Gt Bil 5G **39**
Orbital Trade Pk. NN5: N'ton 6A **36**
Orchard, The NN7: Flore 4F **47**
NN7: Kisl 5H **49**
NN29: Boz 5H **45**
Orchard Cl. NN4: Woot 5E **59**
NN7: Mil M 1G **63**
NN7: Weed 6C **46**
NN9: Fine 4D **10**
NN10: Rushd 2B **32**
NN11: Badby 6B **8**
NN29: Woll 4B **44**
Orchard Cotts. NN7: Lit Hou 4E **55**
Orchard Grn. NN3: N'ton 5A **38**
Orchard Hill NN3: Lit B 6E **39**
Orchard Ho. NN8: Well 5G **17**
Orchard Pl. NN29: Irch 5E **31**
Orchard Rd. NN9: Fine 4D **10**
NN9: Raun 4B **14**
Orchard St. NN5: N'ton 3A **52**
NN11: Dav 5C **6**
Orchard Ter. NN8: Well 1F **29**
NN9: Fine 4D **10**
Orchard Way NN5: Dus 3E **51**
NN7: Harp 3G **49**
Ordnance Rd. NN7: Weed 4A **46**
Oriel Rd. NN11: Dav 2E **9**
Orient Way NN8: Well 1G **29**
Orlingbury Rd. NN9: Gt Har 1C **16**
Orton Pl. NN8: Well 4D **16**
Orwell Cl. NN8: Well 5C **16**
NN9: Raun 2D **14**
Osborn Cl. NN8: Well 2E **29**
Osborne Cl. NN10: Rushd 1F **33**
Osborne Rd. NN2: K'thpe 5C **36**
Osler Cl. NN2: K'thpe 2B **36**
Osmund Dr. NN3: N'ton 2E **39**
Osprey Dr. NN11: Dav 3E **7**
Osprey La. NN8: Well 4H **17**
Osprey Ri. NN4: N'ton 3B **58**
Oswald Rd. NN10: Rushd 3E **33**
Osyth Cl. NN4: Brack 1G **59**
Oulton Ri. NN3: N'ton 2F **37**
Oundle Dr. NN3: Moul 6H **23**
Ouse Cl. NN8: Well 5C **16**
Outlaw La. NN8: Well 6F **17**
Oval Cres. NN10: Rushd 3F **33**
Oval Rd. NN10: Rushd 3F **33**
Overleys Ct. NN3: N'ton 2F **39**
Overmead Rd. NN3: Ect B 5G **39**
Overslade Cl. NN4: N'ton 3A **58**
Overslade Ho. NN4: N'ton 3A **58**
OVERSTONE **4F 25**
Overstone Cl. NN3: Moul 4C **24**
Overstone Cres. NN6: Over 4F **25**
Overstone Hgts. NN6: Syw 2H **25**
Overstone La. NN3: N'ton 2F **39**
(Dore Cl.)
NN3: N'ton 3G **39**
(Thornapple Cl.)
NN6: Over 4C **24**
(not continuous)
OVERSTONE LODGE **1E 39**
OVERSTONE PARK **5G 25**
Overstone Park . . . . . .**5E 25 & 1F 39**
Overstone Park Golf Course **6F 25**
Overstone Rd.
NN1: N'ton 2E **5** (3D **52**)
NN3: Moul 4B **24**
NN6: Syw 3G **25**
Overstone Solarium Res. Pk.
NN6: Syw 5H **25**
Owen Cl. NN8: Well 6B **16**
Owen Ct. NN7: Braf G 6H **55**
Owen M. NN8: Well 6B **16**
Owen Way NN10: High F 6C **20**
Owl Cl. NN3: N'ton 6F **23**
Oxburgh Ct. NN4: N'ton 3B **58**
Oxford Cl. NN6: E Bart 4H **41**
NN11: Dav 6E **7**
Oxford St. NN4: Far C 6B **52**
NN8: Well 1F **29**
NN9: Fine 5E **11**
NN10: Wym 6C **32**
NN11: Dav 6E **7**
Oxwich Cl. NN4: Brack 2G **59**

P

Packwood Cl. NN11: Dav 1D **6**
Padding La. NN5: Upton 5E **51**
Paddock, The NN9: Raun 5C **14**
Paddock La. NN6: Mears A 3D **26**
Paddock Mill Ct.
NN3: N'ton 3F **39**
Paddocks, The NN3: Moul 4A **24**
Paddocks Rd. NN10: Rushd 2A **32**
Paddocks Way NN3: Lit B 6E **39**
Padwell Ct. NN3: Lit B 1E **55**
Paget Cl. NN4: Gt Hou 1C **60**
Pagnell Ct. NN4: H'stone 4G **59**
Palace Ga. NN9: Irth 1B **20**
Paling Cl. NN8: Well 5H **17**
Palk Rd. NN8: Well 1H **29**
Palmer Av. NN9: Irth 5D **12**
Palmer Cl. NN8: Well 4D **16**
Palmer Ct. *NN8: Well 6F 17*
(off Hatton Av.)
Palmer Gro. NN6: Syw 2H **25**
Palmer Sq. NN3: Gt Bil 6G **39**
Palmerston Ct.
NN1: N'ton 2G **5** (3E **53**)
Palmerston Ho. NN1: N'ton 2G **5**
Palmerston Rd.
NN1: N'ton 2G **5** (3E **53**)
Palm Rd. NN10: Rushd 2A **32**
Parade, The
NN1: N'ton 3C **4** (3C **52**)
Parade Bank NN3: Moul 4A **24**
Park Av. NN3: N'ton 1G **53**
NN5: Dus 6C **34**
NN9: Raun 4E **15**
NN10: Rushd 4B **32**
Park Av. Nth. NN3: N'ton 5G **37**
Park Av. Sth. NN3: N'ton 1G **53**
Park Circ. NN4: Swan H 3D **56**
Park Cl. NN5: Dus 6C **34**
NN6: E Bart 3F **41**
NN6: Syw 3H **25**
NN7: Braf G 1H **61**
NN11: Badby 6C **8**
Park Corner NN5: N'ton 3H **51**
Park Cres. NN8: Well 6G **17**
Park Cres. E. NN5: N'ton 5H **35**
Park Cres. W. NN5: N'ton 6H **35**
Park Dr. NN5: N'ton 6H **35**
Parkers Ter. NN9: Fine 5D **10**
Parker Way NN10: High F 3D **20**
Park Farm Ind. Est. NN8: Well . . .5B **16**
(Baird Ct.)
NN8: Well 6A **16**
(Booth Dr.)
Park Farm Sth. NN8: Well 1H **27**
Park Farm Way NN8: Well 1B **28**
Parkfield Av. NN4: Del 1C **58**
Parkfield Cres. NN4: Del 1C **58**
Parkfield Rd. NN6: Brix 2A **22**
Parkham Cen. NN10: Rushd 2H **31**
Park Hill Rd. NN3: N'ton 4B **38**
PARKLANDS **2G 37**
Parklands NN6: Syw 4H **25**
NN9: Stanw 6H **13**
Parklands Av. NN3: N'ton 2G **37**
Parklands Cres. NN3: N'ton 2G **37**
Park La. NN5: Dus 6C **34**
NN6: E Bart 3F **41**
NN7: G'ton 3A **62**
NN7: Harp 3G **49**
Park Leys NN11: Dav 1E **9**
Park M. NN8: Well 6G **17**
Park Pl. NN10: Rushd 3D **32**
Park Rd. NN8: Well 6G **17**
NN9: Irth 2A **20**
NN9: Raun 3E **15**
NN10: Rushd 3D **32**
Parkside NN3: Ect B 5H **39**
NN5: Upton 5E **51**
Park Sq. NN5: N'ton 5H **35**
Park St. NN6: E Bart 3F **41**
NN9: Raun 3E **15**
NN29: Woll 5C **44**
Park Vw. NN3: Moul 5C **24**
(not continuous)
Park Vw. Cl. NN3: Moul 4C **24**
Park Vw. Ct. NN2: K'thpe 3B **36**
Park Wlk. NN5: N'ton 6H **35**
Parkway NN3: West F 1B **54**
Parkwood St. NN5: N'ton 3B **52**
Parracombe Way NN3: N'ton 2A **54**
Parsonage Way NN10: Rushd . . .2E **33**
Parsons Cl. NN6: Ect 3B **40**
Parsons Meade NN4: N'ton 1G **57**
Parsons Rd. NN11: Dav 2B **6**
NN29: Irch 5F **31**
Partridge Cl. NN2: K'thpe 2A **36**
Parva Ct. NN3: N'ton 4C **38**
Pascal Cl. NN5: Dus 2E **51**
Pascoe Cres. NN11: Dav 3C **6**
Pasteur Cl. NN2: K'thpe 2B **36**
Pasture, The NN11: Dav 6E **7**
Pastures, The NN2: K'thpe 2A **36**
NN9: Well 2E **17**
Patenall Way NN10: High F 4C **20**
Paterson Rd. NN8: Well 3H **17**
Patterdale Wlk. NN3: N'ton 3A **38**
Patterson Cl. NN3: West F 6C **38**
Pavilion Ct. NN1: N'ton 2F **53**
NN4: Brack 2F **59**
Pavilion Dr. NN4: Brack 1F **59**
Paxford Cl. NN8: Well 4E **29**
Paxton Rd. NN3: N'ton 3B **38**
Peace Cl. NN4: N'ton 6H **51**
Pearmain Av. NN8: Well 4F **17**
Pearmain Ct. NN3: Lit B 5E **39**
Pearsons M. NN29: Woll 5B **44**
Pear Tree Cl. NN3: Lit B 5E **39**
Peartree Cl. NN11: Dav 3E **7**
NN29: Boz 5H **45**
Pebble La. NN8: Well 1G **29**
Peck Way NN10: Rushd 2D **32**
Pegasus Way NN10: Rushd 1A **32**
Pelham Ct. NN3: N'ton 3B **38**
Pell Ct. NN3: N'ton 4C **38**
Pemberton Centre, The **3B 32**
Pemberton St. NN10: Rushd 3C **32**
Pembroke Cl. NN10: Rushd 4E **33**
Pembroke Cres. NN5: N'ton 1A **52**
Pembroke Gdns. NN5: N'ton 1A **52**
Pembroke Rd. NN5: N'ton 1A **52**
Pembroke Way NN11: Dav 2D **8**
Penarth Rd. NN5: N'ton 1A **52**
Pen Ct. NN1: N'ton 6D **4** (5D **52**)
Pendered Rd. NN8: Well 4G **29**
Pendle Rd. NN5: Dus 1E **51**
Penfold Cl. NN2: K'thpe 3B **36**
Penfold Dr. NN3: Gt Bil 4F **39**
Penfold Gdns. NN3: Gt Bil 4G **39**
Penfold La. NN3: Gt Bil 4G **39**
Peninsular Cl. NN4: Woot 4E **59**
Penistone Rd. NN3: N'ton 4C **38**
Penistone Wlk. NN3: N'ton 4C **38**
NN3: West F 6D **38**
Pennard Cl. NN4: Brack 1H **59**
Penn Gdns. NN4: N'ton 4B **58**
Pennine Ct. NN11: Dav 2D **6**
Pennine Way NN5: Dus 2F **51**
Pennycress Pl. NN3: Ect B 6G **39**
Penrhyn Rd. NN4: Far C 6C **52**
Penrith Dr. NN8: Well 5D **16**
Penvale Rd. NN4: N'ton 5B **58**
Peppercorn Way NN4: N'ton 5D **58**
Perceval Cl. NN5: Dus 6F **35**
Perch Cl. NN11: Dav 1D **6**
Percy Rd. NN1: N'ton 1H **5** (2F **53**
Peregrine Pl. NN4: N'ton 3A **58**
Perkins Ct. NN8: Well 6G **17**
Perkins Rd. NN9: Irth 3A **20**
Perkins Way NN11: Newn 5G **9**
Perry La. NN9: Raun 2D **14**
Perry St. NN1: N'ton 2F **53**
Pershore Cl. NN8: Well 5E **29**
Peter Crisp Way
NN10: Rushd 2D **32**
Pevensey Cl. NN10: Rushd 4F **33**
Peverel Cl. NN10: High F 5E **21**
Peverel's Way NN5: N'ton 3G **51**
Peveril Rd. NN5: Dus 2D **50**
Pheasant Way NN2: K'thpe 2A **36**
Philip Way NN10: High F 4E **21**
PHIPPSVILLE **1G 53**
Phippsville Ct. NN2: N'ton 6F **37**
Phoenix Ct. NN8: Well 2H **29**
Phoenix St.
NN1: N'ton 3B **4** (3C **52**
Piano Factory, The NN1: N'ton . . .1D **4**
Piccadilly Cl. NN4: N'ton 1H **57**
Pickerings, The NN6: Brix 2B **22**
Pie Corner NN6: Syw 2H **25**
Pightles Ter. NN10: Rushd 4E **33**
Pightles Wlk. NN10: Rushd 4E **33**
Pike La. NN1: N'ton 3B **4** (3C **52**
Pikemead Ct. NN3: N'ton 3F **39**
Pilgrims Pl. NN4: Del 1C **58**
Pilgrim Way NN8: Well 2F **29**
Pilton Cl. NN3: N'ton 2G **39**
Pindar Ri. NN3: N'ton 1C **38**
Pindar Rd. NN8: Well 3E **29**
Pine Av. NN6: Syw 4H **25**
Pine Cl. NN4: Gra P 2F **65**
NN10: Rushd 5C **32**
NN29: Irch 6E **31**
Pine Copse Cl. NN5: Dus 5C **34**
Pine Ct. NN8: Well 1H **29**
Pine Cres. NN6: Syw 4H **25**
Pineham Av. NN2: K'thpe 1D **36**
Pine Ridge NN3: N'ton 6D **24**
Pine Trees NN3: West F 6B **38**
Pinewood Rd. NN3: N'ton 4G **37**
Pinfold Grn. NN11: Badby 6B **8**
Pioneer Cl. NN4: Woot 4E **59**
Piper Cl. NN8: Well 3F **17**
Pipers Cl. NN9: Irth 1B **20**
Pippin Cl. NN8: Well 1F **29**
NN10: Rushd 2A **32**
Pippin La. NN3: Lit B 5E **39**
Pit Field Cl. NN29: Boz 5H **45**
PITSFORD **1D 22**
Pitsford Rd. NN3: Moul 3F **23**
Pitstone Rd. NN4: N'ton 5G **51**
Pitt St. NN8: Well 1E **29**
Plantagenet Sq. NN4: N'ton 1H **57**
Plantagenet Wlk. *NN4: N'ton . . .1H 57*
(off Archangel Rd.
Pleydell Gdns. NN4: Far C 1C **58**
Pleydell Rd. NN4: Far C 1C **58**
Plough Cl. NN11: Dav 1F **7**
Plough La. NN2: K'thpe 1A **36**
Ploughmans Wlk.
NN2: K'thpe 2B **36**
Ploughmans Way NN4: Gra P . . .2F **65**
Plumtree Av. NN8: Well 4G **17**
Poachers Cl. NN4: Gra P 2F **65**
Poachers Way NN2: K'thpe 2B **36**
Poets Ct. NN2: N'ton 5F **37**
Poets Way NN11: Newn 5G **9**
Poitiers Ct. NN5: Dus 6B **34**
Polar Star Cl. NN11: Dav 3C **6**
Pomfret Arms Cl. NN4: N'ton . . .5C **52**
Pomfret Ct. *NN4: N'ton 5C 52*
(off River Vw.
Pond Bank NN7: Blis 5E **63**
Pond Farm Cl. NN5: Dus 2E **51**
Ponds Cl. NN9: Raun 3D **14**
Pond Wood Cl. NN3: N'ton 1H **37**

Poole St.—Rushden & Higham Ferrers By-Pass

Poole St. NN1: N'ton 2D 52
Pope Rd. NN8: Well 2C 28
Popham Cl. NN9: Raun 2C 14
Poplar Cl. NN10: Rushd 5C 32
NN11: Dav 2E 7
NN29: Irch 6E 31
Poplar Ct. NN3: N'ton 2B 38
Poplar Pl. *NN8: Well 1F 29*
(off West St.)
NN29: Woll 5C 44
Poplar Rd. NN9: Fine 4E 11
Poplars, The *NN2: N'ton 2C 52*
(off Barrack Rd.)
Poplars Cl. NN9: Raun 3C 14
Poplar St. NN8: Well 6G 17
Poppy Cl. NN10: Rushd 5E 33
Poppyfield Ct. NN3: N'ton 3D 38
Poppy Leys NN6: Brix 3A 22
Porlock Cl. NN5: Dus 1G 51
Portchester Gdns.
NN3: West F 1C 54
Portland Cl. NN11: Dav 6F 7
Portland Pl.
NN1: N'ton 2G 5 (2E 53)
Portland Rd. NN9: Irth 6B 12
NN10: Rushd 3D 32
Port Rd. NN5: Dus 5C 34
Portstone Cl. NN5: Dus 5C 34
Portwey Cl. NN6: Brix 2B 22
Potter Ct. NN9: Stanw 5A 14
Pound La. NN3: Gt Bil 5G 39
NN3: Moul 4H 23
NN11: Badby 6B 8
Pound Pl. NN9: Fine 5D 10
Powdertree Sq.
NN3: West F 6D 38
(off Cottagewell Ct.)
Poyntz Gdns. NN5: N'ton 1G 51
Poyntz La. NN5: N'ton 1G 51
Pratt Rd. NN10: Rushd 3E 33
Premier Ct. NN3: N'ton 6G 23
Premier Way NN9: Irth 3A 20
Prentice Ct. NN3: N'ton 2E 39
Prescott Cl. NN3: N'ton 3G 39
Presland Way NN9: Irth 2H 19
Pressland Dr. NN10: High F 5E 21
Prestbury Ct. NN5: Dus 1C 50
Prestbury Rd. NN5: Dus 1C 50
Preston Capes Rd.
NN11: Newn 6F 9
Preston Ct. NN3: N'ton 4C 38
Preston Deanery Rd.
NN7: Quin 4H 65
Preston Dr. NN11: Dav 1E 7
Prestwold Way NN3: N'ton 2F 39
Primrose Gdns. NN9: Raun 4D 14
Primrose Hill *NN2: N'ton 1C 52*
(off Kingsthorpe Rd.)
NN9: Raun 4D 14
NN11: Dav 5E 7
Primrose Pl. *NN8: Well 6A 18*
(off Elsden Rd.)
Primrose Wlk. NN4: Gra P 3F 65
Primula Cl. NN3: N'ton 3A 54
Primula Ct. NN2: N'ton 1C 52
Prince Cl. NN11: Dav 4D 6
Prince of Wales Row
NN3: Moul 4B 24
Princes Cl. NN7: Weed 6A 46
Princess Cl. NN3: N'ton 3H 53
Princess Way NN8: Well 3E 29
Prince St. NN6: E Bart 2G 41
Princes Wlk. NN1: N'ton 3C 4
Print Works, The
NN1: N'ton 1H 5 (2F 53)
Printworks, The NN1: N'ton 1D 4
Priors Cl. NN10: Rushd 5B 32
Priory Cl. NN3: N'ton 3H 53
NN11: Dav 1F 9
Priory Ct. NN3: N'ton 3A 54
NN7: Weed 6A 46
Priory Ho. NN1: N'ton 2A 4
Priory Rd. NN8: Well 2F 29
NN29: Woll 4A 44
Pritchard Cl. NN3: N'ton 1G 39
Probyn Cl. NN3: N'ton 1E 39
Promenade, The NN8: Well 6E 17
Prospect Av. NN10: Rushd 1D 32
NN29: Irch 6D 30
Prospect Cl. NN29: Woll 4B 44
Prospect Ct. NN7: Blis 5G 63
Prospect Way NN11: Dav 4B 6
Provence Ct. NN5: Dus 6B 34
Puddingbag La. NN29: Boz 5H 45
Purbeck Rd. NN10: Rushd 3H 31
Purser Rd. NN1: N'ton 1F 53
Purvis Rd. NN10: Rushd 3C 32
Pyghtle, The NN6: E Bart 2G 41
NN8: Well 5F 17
Pyghtles, The NN11: Dav 6D 6
NN29: Woll 6B 44
Pyghtle Way NN4: N'ton 4A 58
Pyket Way NN3: West F 1C 54
Pym Cl. NN8: Well 5H 17
Pyramid Cl. NN3: West F 5C 38
Pytchley Cl. NN6: Brix 1A 22
Pytchley Ri. NN8: Well 2D 28
Pytchley Rd. NN10: Rushd 2B 32
Pytchley St. NN1: N'ton 3F 5 (3E 53)
Pytchley Vw. NN3: Moul 4B 24
Pytchley Way NN5: Dus 5D 34
NN6: Brix 1A 22

Q

Quantock Cl. NN11: Dav 2D 6
Quantock Cres. NN5: Dus 1F 51
Quarry Pk. Cl. NN3: N'ton 1H 37
Quarry Rd. NN5: Dus 5D 34
NN6: Brix 1B 22
Quartercroft NN3: West F 5C 38
Quarterstone NN4: N'ton 2F 57
Quebec Cl. NN4: Woot 4E 59
Queen Eleanor Rd.
NN4: Far C, Del 1B 58
Queen Eleanor Ter. NN4: Del 1C 58
Queensbridge NN4: N'ton 6H 53
Queens Cres. NN2: K'thpe 5D 36
Queensland Gdns.
NN2: K'thpe 5C 36
Queens La. NN8: Well 1G 29
QUEENS PARK 5C 36
Queen's Pk. NN7: Weed 6A 46
Queens Pk. Ind. Est.
NN2: K'thpe 5B 36
Queens Pk. Pde. NN2: K'thpe 5C 36
Queens Rd. NN1: N'ton 1F 5 (2E 53)
NN11: Dav 4D 6
NN29: Woll 5B 44
Queen St. NN6: E Bart 2G 41
NN7: Weed 6A 46
NN8: Well 6G 17
NN9: Irth 1A 20
NN10: Rushd 3D 32
NN29: Boz 6G 45
Queensway NN8: Well 1C 28
NN10: High F 6E 21
NN15: Bur L 1A 10
Queenswood Av. NN3: N'ton 3A 38
Quernstone La. NN4: N'ton 6G 51
QUINTON 4H 65
QUINTON GREEN 6H 65
Quinton Rd. NN4: Woot 6E 59
Quintonside NN4: Gra P 2F 65
Quorn Cl. NN8: Well 1D 28
Quorn Rd. NN10: Rushd 2B 32
Quorn Way NN1: N'ton 1A 4 (2B 52)

R

Racedown NN8: Well 2B 28
Radleigh Cl. NN4: N'ton 1A 58
Radleigh Ct. NN2: N'ton 6E 37
Radstone Way NN2: K'thpe 2C 36
Raeburn Rd. NN2: N'ton 5E 37
Raglan Cl. NN10: Rushd 4F 33
Raglan St. NN1: N'ton 2F 5 (3E 53)
Ragsdale Wlk. NN3: N'ton 1C 38
Rainsborough Cres.
NN4: N'ton 5H 51
Raisins Fld. Cl. NN3: Ect B 4G 39
Rakestone Cl. NN4: N'ton 5D 58
Raleigh Ct. NN11: Dav 2D 6
Ramsay Cl. NN9: Raun 2C 14
Randall Cl. NN9: Irth 3A 20
Randall Ho. *NN1: N'ton 2F 53*
(off Monks Hall Rd.)
Randall Rd. NN2: N'ton 6E 37
Randsway NN9: Raun 4E 15
Ranelagh Rd. NN8: Well 6H 17
Ransome Rd. NN4: Far C 6D 52
RAUNDS 3D 14
Raunds Rd. NN9: Stanw 6H 13
Ravensbank NN10: Rushd 1D 32
Ravens Cft. NN4: N'ton 4A 58
Ravens Way NN3: Gt Bil, Lit B 1F 55
Rawley Cres. NN5: Dus 6C 34
Rawlings Cl. NN11: Dav 6F 7
Raymond Cl. NN29: Woll 6C 44
Raymond Rd. NN5: N'ton 2A 52
Raynsford Rd. NN5: N'ton 6H 35
Rea Cl. NN4: N'ton 4C 58
Rectory Bus. Cen.
NN10: Rushd 2D 32
Rectory Cl. NN4: Gt Hou 1C 60
NN9: Stanw 5H 13
Rectory Ct. NN10: Rushd 3D 32
RECTORY FARM 2G 39
Rectory Farm Rd. NN3: N'ton 2G 39
Rectory Gdns. NN9: Irth 1A 20
Rectory La. NN7: Mil M 2G 63
Rectory Rd. NN10: Rushd 2D 32
Redbourne Pk. NN4: Brack 6H 53
Redding Cl. NN10: Rushd 6C 32
Redgrave Ct. NN8: Well 3F 17
Red Hill Cres. NN29: Woll 4B 44
Redhill Way NN9: Well 3E 17
Red Ho. Rd. NN3: N'ton 6F 23
Redland Dr. NN2: K'thpe 3A 36
Red Row NN9: Raun 3D 14
Redruth Cl. NN4: Del 2B 58
Redwell Leisure Cen. 4E 17
Redwell Rd. NN8: Well 5F 17
Redwing Av. NN3: Moul 1A 38
Redwood Cl. NN29: Irch 6E 31
Reedham Cl. NN5: Dus 6E 35
Reedhill NN4: N'ton 2G 57
Reedway NN3: N'ton 3G 37
Regal Cl. NN3: N'ton 1F 37
Regal Ct. NN10: Rushd 4E 33
Regency Cl. NN7: Weed 5B 46
Regency Ct. NN10: Rushd 2D 32
Regent Sq. NN1: N'ton 1C 4 (2C 52)
Regent St. NN1: N'ton 2B 4 (3C 52)
NN8: Well 6G 17
NN9: Fine 5C 10
Regiment Cl. NN4: Woot 4E 59
Reg Partridge Cl. NN5: Dus 2E 51
Reims Ct. NN5: New D 5C 34
Rennishaw Way NN2: N'ton 4F 37
Repton Ct. NN3: N'ton 3B 38
Reservoir Cl. NN9: Irth 3A 20
Resthaven Rd. NN4: Woot 5D 58
Restormel Cl. NN10: Rushd 4F 33
Retford Ct. NN3: N'ton 3D 38
Reynard Way NN2: K'thpe 1D 36
Reynolds Cl. NN8: Well 4F 17
Reynoldston Cl. NN4: Brack 2A 60
Rhodes Cl. NN11: Dav 2E 7
Rhosili Rd. NN4: Brack 1F 59
Ribble Cl. NN5: N'ton 5H 35
NN8: Well 5D 16
Richardson Way NN9: Raun 2E 15
Richmond Cl. NN10: Rushd 4E 33
Richmond Ter. NN5: N'ton 3B 52
Rickyard Rd. NN3: N'ton 4B 38
Rickyard Wlk. NN4: Gra P 3F 65
Ride La. NN6: Pits 1C 22
Rides Ct. NN3: Moul 6A 24
Ridge, The NN29: Gt Dod 6E 29
Ridge Gdns. NN29: Gt Dod 6E 29
Ridge Wlk. NN3: West F 1C 54
Ridgewalk NN3: Ect B 4H 39
NN3: West F 6D 38
(not continuous)
Ridgeway NN3: West F 1A 54
NN8: Well 4F 17
Ridings, The
NN1: N'ton 3D 4 (3D 52)
NN4: Gra P 3E 65
NN6: Brix 1B 22
Ridings Arcade, The
NN1: N'ton 3E 5
Ridley Ct. NN11: Dav 5E 7
Riley Cl. NN3: N'ton 2G 39
NN11: Dav 3B 6
Rillwood Ct. NN3: N'ton 3C 38
Ringtail Cl. NN9: Irth 3A 20
Ring Way NN4: N'ton 6A 52
Ringway Ter. NN4: N'ton 6A 52
Ringwell Cl. NN9: Irth 6A 12
Ringwood Cl. NN2: K'thpe 2A 36
Ripon Cl. NN4: N'ton 1A 58
Risdene Ct. *NN10: Rushd 3D 32*
(off Newton Rd.)
Rise, The NN2: K'thpe 4B 36
Riverside Bus. Pk.
NN3: N'ton 2C 54
Riverside Cl. NN8: Lit I 4A 30
Riverside Ct. NN7: Kisl 5H 49
NN7: Weed 6B 46
Riverside Dr. NN7: Weed 6B 46
Riverside Way
NN1: N'ton 5H 5 (4F 53)
Riverside Way Ind. Est.
NN1: N'ton 5H 5 (4F 53)
Riverstone Way
NN4: N'ton 1F 57
River Vw. NN4: N'ton 5C 52
Riverwell NN3: Ect B 5H 39
Rixon Cl. NN3: West F 6C 38
Rixon Rd. NN8: Well 3H 17
Roadmender 2C 4
ROAD WEEDON 5C 46
Robb Cl. NN9: Irth 6B 12
Roberts St. NN8: Well 1E 29
NN10: Rushd 3E 33
NN29: Boz 6G 45
Robert St. NN1: N'ton 1D 4 (2D 52)
Robinia Cl. NN4: N'ton 6G 51
Robin La. NN8: Well 4G 17
Robinson Rd. NN10: Rushd 3E 33
Robinson Way NN4: Woot 6G 59
Roche Cl. NN11: Dav 1E 9
Rochelle Way NN5: New D 5C 34
Roche Way NN8: Well 5F 17
Rockcroft NN4: N'ton 5D 58
Rockingham Cl. NN11: Dav 3D 6
Rockingham Ct. NN10: Rushd 5C 32
Rockingham Rd. NN4: Del 1C 58
Rockleigh Cl. NN9: Fine 4E 11
Rock Rd. NN9: Fine 4E 11
Rock St. NN8: Well 6F 17
Roderick Way NN11: Dav 3D 6
Rodney Cl. NN11: Dav 6G 7
Roe Rd. NN1: N'ton 1F 53
Rokeby Wlk. NN5: Dus 6F 35
Roland Way NN10: High F 5D 20
Roman Cl. NN4: Woot 6F 59
Roman Way NN4: Gra P 1E 65
NN9: Raun 3E 15
NN10: High F 4D 20
NN11: Dav 2E 7
NN29: Irch 6F 31
Romany Rd. NN2: N'ton 6E 37
Romulus Cl. NN4: Woot 6F 59
Rookery, The NN4: Gra P 2E 65
Rookery La. NN2: K'thpe 2A 36
Rose Av. NN10: Rushd 4B 32
Rosebery Av. NN5: N'ton 3H 51
Rose Ct. *NN29: Irch 5F 31*
(off High St.)
Rosedale Rd. NN2: K'thpe 4D 36
Rose Hill NN9: Fine 4D 10
Roseholme Rd. NN1: N'ton 2G 53
Rosemoor Dr. NN4: N'ton 4C 58
Rosenella Cl. NN4: N'ton 6H 51
Roses Cl. NN29: Woll 4A 44
Rosette Cl. NN5: Dus 1E 51
Rosewood Cl. NN11: Dav 2E 7
Rosgill Pl. NN3: N'ton 5H 37
Ross Rd. NN5: N'ton 3G 51
Rotherhithe Cl. NN4: N'ton 1H 57
ROTHERSTHORPE 5C 56
Rothersthorpe Av. NN4: Far C 6A 52
Rothersthorpe Av. Ind. Est.
NN4: Far C 6A 52
Rothersthorpe Cres.
NN4: Far C 6A 52
Rothersthorpe La. NN4: N'ton 1A 58
Rothersthorpe Rd.
NN4: Far C, N'ton 1H 57
NN7: Kisl 6H 49
Rothesay Rd. NN2: N'ton 5F 37
Rothesay Ter. NN2: N'ton 5F 37
Rotten Row NN29: Woll 5B 44
Rotton Row NN9: Raun 2D 14
Roundel, The NN6: Over 1F 39
ROUND SPINNEY 6C 24
Round Spinney Ind. Est.
NN3: N'ton 6C 24
Roundway, The NN11: Dav 1F 7
Roundwood Way NN5: Dus 1B 50
Rowallen Way NN11: Dav 3C 6
Rowan Av. NN3: N'ton 2A 38
Rowan Cl. NN4: Gra P 3E 65
NN8: Well 6E 17
Rowans, The NN11: Dav 3E 7
Rowlandson Cl.
NN3: West F 6C 38
Rowlett Cl. NN10: High F 6E 21
Rowley Way NN2: K'thpe 1E 37
Rowtree Rd. NN4: N'ton 4H 57
Royal Theatre, The 4D 4 (4D 52)
Royal Cl. NN11: Dav 4D 6
Royal Oak Ind. Est.
NN11: Dav 4B 6
Royal Oak Way Nth.
NN11: Dav 3B 6
Royal Oak Way Sth. NN11: Dav 4B 6
Royal Star Dr. NN11: Dav 3C 6
Royal Ter.
NN1: N'ton 1C 4 (2C 52)
Ruddington Cl. NN3: West F 2C 54
Rudge M. NN5: Dus 1B 50
Rufford Av. NN3: West F 2C 54
Rugby & Daventry Sailing Club
1D 6
Rugby Rd. NN7: Lwr H 1A 34
Runnymede Gdns.
NN3: West F 6D 38
RUSHDEN 3D 32
Rushden & Higham Ferrers By-Pass
NN10: High F, Rushd 3E 21

Rushden Centre, The
NN10: Rushd *3D 32*
(off Newton Rd.)
Rushden Golf Course 4H 21
RUSHDEN HOSPITAL 5D 32
Rushden Rd. NN10: Wym 6C **32**
Rushden Station Transport Mus. 2D 32
Rushden Town Indoor Bowls Club 6B 20
RUSHMERE 3A 54
Rushmere Av. NN1: N'ton 3H **53**
Rushmere Cl. NN9: Raun 4C **14**
Rushmere Cres. NN1: N'ton 3H **53**
Rushmere Rd. NN1: N'ton 5G **53**
Rushmere Way NN1: N'ton 4H **53**
NN10: Rushd 1C **32**
Rushmills NN4: N'ton 6H **53**
Rushy End NN4: N'ton 5B **58**
Ruskin Av. NN8: Well 1C **28**
Ruskin Rd. NN2: K'thpe 3C **36**
Ruskin Way NN11: Dav 1E **9**
Russell Ct. NN10: Rushd 3D **32**
Russell Ri. NN7: Flore 4E **47**
Russell Sq. NN3: Moul 1A **38**
Russell Way NN10: High F 5D **20**
Russet Dr. NN3: Lit B 5E **39**
Rutherford Dr. NN8: Well 1A **28**
Rutherford Way NN11: Dav 3B **6**
Rutland Wlk. NN3: Moul 6H **23**
Rycroft Cl. NN8: Well 6D **16**
Rydal Mt. NN3: N'ton 4A **38**
NN8: Well 2B **28**
Rydalside NN4: N'ton 6H **51**
Ryder Vw. NN8: Well 4C **16**
Rydinghurst NN3: Moul 4H **23**
Ryeburn Way NN8: Well 6E **17**
Ryebury Hill NN8: Well 1C **18**
Rye Cl. NN10: Rushd 5E **33**
Ryehill Cl. NN5: Dus 5E **35**
NN9: Irth 3A **20**
Ryehill Ct. NN5: Dus 5E **35**
Ryehill Rd. NN3: N'ton 4D **38**
Ryeland Rd. NN5: Dus 1C **50**
Ryeland Way NN5: Dus 6C **34**
Ryland Rd. NN2: N'ton 5E **37**
NN3: Moul 5A **24**
Ryle Dr. NN8: Well 1A **28**
Rylstone, The NN8: Well 2B **28**
Ryngwell Cl. NN6: Brix 2A **22**

S

Sackville St. NN9: Raun 3D **14**
Saddleback Rd. NN5: N'ton 3F **51**
Saddlers, The NN4: Gra P 2F **65**
Saddlers Sq. NN3: N'ton 1D **38**
Saddlers Way NN9: Raun 4B **14**
Saffron Cl. NN4: N'ton 6D **58**
Saffron Rd. NN10: High F 4D **20**
Sage Cl. NN3: N'ton 3C **38**
St Alban's Cl. NN3: N'ton 4H **37**
St Albans Pl. NN29: Woll 6B **44**
St Alban's Rd. NN3: N'ton 4H **37**
St Andrews Ct. NN1: N'ton 2B **4**
St Andrews Cres. NN8: Well 4E **29**
St Andrews Dr. NN11: Dav 4G **7**
ST ANDREW'S HEALTHCARE NORTHAMPTON 4G 53
St Andrew's Ho. NN1: N'ton 3H **5**
St Andrew's Rd.
NN1: N'ton 4A **4** (4B **52**)
NN2: N'ton 1A **4** (2B **52**)
St Andrew's St.
NN1: N'ton 1B **4** (3C **52**)
St Annes Cl. NN11: Dav 1E **9**
St Anthonys Cl. NN11: Dav 1D **8**
St Augustin Way NN11: Dav 1F **9**
St Barnabas Ho. NN1: N'ton 2B **4**
St Barnabas St. NN8: Well 1E **29**
St Bartholomews Ho.
NN1: N'ton 2C **4**
St Benedict's Mt. NN4: N'ton 2G **57**
St Catherines Cl. NN11: Dav 1D **8**
St Christopher's Wlk.
NN3: N'ton 2H **53**
St Crispin Av. NN8: Well 3F **29**
St Crispin Cres. NN5: Dus 1B **50**
St Crispin Dr. NN5: Upton 3C **50**
St Crispin Retirement Village
NN5: Upton 2C **50**
(not continuous)
St Crispin Rd. NN6: E Bart 3H **41**
St Crispin Way NN9: Raun 1C **14**
St Davids Cl. NN6: Brix 2A **22**
St David's Rd. NN2: K'thpe 5C **36**
NN6: Brix 2A **22**
NN10: Rushd 2H **31**
St Dunstans Ri. NN4: N'ton 2G **57**
St Edmunds Cl. NN11: Dav 2E **9**
St Edmund's Rd.
NN1: N'ton 3F **5** (3E **53**)
St Edmund's St.
NN1: N'ton 2G **5** (3E **53**)
St Edmund's Ter.
NN1: N'ton 2F **5** (3E **53**)
St Emilion Cl. NN5: Dus 6B **34**
St Francis Av. NN5: N'ton 1A **52**
St George's Av. NN2: N'ton 1C **52**
St Georges Ho. NN1: N'ton 2C **4**
St Georges Pl. *NN2: N'ton* *1C 52*
(off Kingsthorpe Rd.)
St George's St.
NN1: N'ton 1B **4** (2C **52**)
St George's Way
NN10: Rushd 2B **32**
St Giles' Sq.
NN1: N'ton 4D **4** (4D **52**)
St Giles' St.
NN1: N'ton 4D **4** (4D **52**)
St Giles Ter.
NN1: N'ton 3E **5** (3D **52**)
St Gregory's Rd.
NN3: N'ton 4B **38**
St Hilda's Cl. NN11: Dav 1E **9**
St Hughes Cl. NN11: Dav 1E **9**
ST JAMES' 4A 52
St James Cl. NN10: Rushd 1D **32**
NN11: Dav *6E 7*
(off Newlands)
St James Mill Bus. Pk.
NN5: N'ton 4H **51**
St James' Mill Rd.
NN5: N'ton 4A **52**
St James' Mill Rd. E.
NN1: N'ton 6A **4** (5B **52**)
St James' Mill Rd. Ind. Est.
NN5: N'ton 6A **4** (5A **52**)
St James' Pk. Rd. NN5: N'ton 3A **52**
(not continuous)
St James' Retail Pk.
NN1: N'ton 5A **4** (4B **52**)
St James' Rd.
NN5: N'ton 4A **4** (3A **52**)
ST JAMES'S END 3A 52
St James St.
NN1: N'ton 5C **4** (4C **52**)
NN11: Dav 6E **7**
St James Trade Pk.
NN5: N'ton 4A **52**
St John's Av. NN2: K'thpe 1C **36**
St Johns Cl. NN7: Rother 5C **56**
NN11: Dav 1D **8**
St Johns Ct. NN1: N'ton 5D **4**
St Johns Ho. NN1: N'ton 2B **4**
NN8: Well *6F 17*
(off St John's St.)
St John's Sq. NN11: Dav 5E **7**
St Johns Sta. Pas. NN1: N'ton 5D **4**
St John's St.
NN1: N'ton 5C **4** (4C **52**)
NN8: Well 6F **17**
St John's Ter.
NN1: N'ton 4D **4** (4D **52**)
St Johns Wlk. NN3: West F 6B **38**
St Julien Cl. NN5: New D 5C **34**
St Katharine's Way
NN29: Irch 4E **31**
St Katherine's Ct. NN1: N'ton 3B **4**
St Katherine's Sq.
NN1: N'ton 3B **4** (3C **52**)
St Katherine's St.
NN1: N'ton 4B **4** (4C **52**)
St Laurence Way
NN9: Stanw 5H **13**
St Lawrence Ho. NN1: N'ton 2C **4**
St Leonards Ct. NN4: Far C 6C **52**
St Leonard's Rd. NN4: Far C 6C **52**
St Lukes Cl. NN5: Dus 1B **50**
St Lukes Ho. NN1: N'ton 2B **4**
St Margarets Av.
NN10: Rushd 4B **32**
St Margaret's Gdns.
NN5: N'ton 6H **35**
St Mark's Cl. NN10: Rushd 3A **32**
St Mark's Cres. NN2: K'thpe 1B **36**
St Marks Ho. NN1: N'ton 2B **4**
St Martins Cl. NN2: K'thpe 3C **36**
St Martins Ho. NN1: N'ton 2C **4**
St Mary's Av. NN9: Fine 4D **10**
NN10: Rushd 4C **32**
St Marys Ct. NN1: N'ton 3B **4**
NN7: G'ton 3A **62**
NN9: Fine *5C 10*
(off Church St.)
NN14: Lit A 1D **12**
St Mary's Paddock NN8: Well 1A **30**
St Marys Rd. NN29: Boz 6H **45**
NN29: Woll 5C **44**
St Mary's St.
NN1: N'ton 3A **4** (3C **52**)
St Mary's Way NN7: Weed 6B **46**
St Matthew's Pde.
NN2: N'ton 1F **53**
St Michael's Av. NN1: N'ton 2E **53**
St Michael's La. NN29: Woll 5B **44**
St Michael's Mt.
NN1: N'ton 1G **5** (2E **53**)
St Michael's Rd.
NN1: N'ton 2E **5** (3D **52**)
St Nicholas Ct. *NN29: Gt Dod* *1E 43*
(off High St.)
St Nicholas Rd.
NN29: Gt Dod 1D **42**
St Patrick St. NN1: N'ton 1B **4**
St Pauls Ct. *NN2: N'ton* *1C 52*
(off Norfolk Ter.)
St Pauls Rd. NN2: N'ton 1C **52**
St Paul's Ter. NN2: N'ton 1C **52**
St Peter's Av. NN10: Rushd 2B **32**
St Peters Cl. NN11: Dav 1D **8**
St Peters Ct. NN9: Raun 3D **14**
St Peters Gdns. NN1: N'ton 4B **4**
NN3: West F 6B **38**
St Peter's Ho. NN1: N'ton 3B **4**
St Peters Sq. NN1: N'ton 4B **4**
St Peter's St.
NN1: N'ton 4A **4** (4B **52**)
St Peters Wlk.
NN1: N'ton 4C **4** (4C **52**)
St Peter's Way
NN1: N'ton 4A **4** (4B **52**)
NN7: Weed 6B **46**
NN9: Irth 1B **20**
St Peter's Way Retail Pk.
NN1: N'ton 4B **4** (4C **52**)
St Rochus Dr. NN8: Well 4G **29**
St Stephens Ho. NN1: N'ton 2B **4**
St Thomas Rd. NN7: Braf G 6H **55**
Salcey Cl. NN11: Dav 3D **6**
Salcey Ct. *NN5: Upton* *5F 51*
(off Webb Dr.)
Salcey St. NN4: Del 1C **58**
Salem La. NN8: Well 6F **17**
Salisbury Rd. NN8: Well 6A **18**
Salisbury St. NN2: N'ton 1B **52**
Sallow Av. NN3: N'ton 4G **39**
Salthouse Rd. NN4: Brack 1G **59**
Salt Pikes NN6: Brix 3A **22**
Saltwell Sq. NN3: Ect B 5G **39**
Sam Harrison Way NN5: Dus 2E **51**
Samuels Cl. NN9: Stanw 6H **13**
Samwell La. NN5: Upton 4E **51**
Samwell Way NN4: N'ton 2E **57**
Sanders Cl. NN8: Well 3H **17**
Sanders Lodge Ind. Est.
NN10: Rushd 2H **31**
Sanders Pk. NN8: Well 2H **17**
Sanders Rd. NN8: Well 2G **17**
Sandfield Cl. NN3: N'ton 1H **37**
Sandhill Rd. NN5: N'ton 3A **52**
(not continuous)
Sandhills Cl. NN2: K'thpe 1B **36**
Sandhills Rd. NN2: K'thpe 1B **36**
Sandhurst Cl. NN4: N'ton 3B **58**
Sandiland Rd. NN3: N'ton 5H **37**
Sandover NN4: N'ton 5D **58**
Sandpiper La. NN8: Well 4G **17**
Sandringham Cl. NN1: N'ton 2H **53**
NN8: Well 3D **28**
NN10: Rushd 4C **32**
Sandringham Rd. NN1: N'ton 2G **53**
Sandy Cl. NN8: Well 5F **17**
Sandy Hill La. NN3: Moul 4C **24**
Sandy La. NN5: Dus, New D 1B **50**
NN7: Harp 4A **50**
Sandy La. Link Rd.
NN7: Harp 2A **50**
Sandy Way NN4: Gra P 1E **65**
Saneco La. NN6: Brix 1A **22**
Sansom Ct. NN3: N'ton 4B **38**
Sarek Pk. NN4: N'ton 4H **57**
Sargeants La. NN4: Col 1C **64**
Sartoris Rd. NN10: Rushd 3B **32**
Saruman La. NN3: N'ton 1F **39**
Sassoon Cl. NN8: Well 5C **16**
Sassoon M. NN8: Well 6B **16**
Savill Cl. NN4: N'ton 4C **58**
Saxby Cres. NN8: Well 1A **30**
Saxon Av. NN4: Gra P 3D **64**
Saxon Cl. NN10: High F 4D **20**
Saxon Ct. NN8: Well 2G **17**
Saxon Hgts. NN6: Brix 3A **22**
Saxon La. NN5: Upton 4E **51**
Saxonlea Cl. NN10: Rushd 2A **32**
Saxon Lodge NN6: E Bart 3G **41**
Saxon Ri. NN5: Dus 2D 5
NN6: E Bart 3G 4
NN29: Irch 5G 3
Saxon St. NN3: N'ton 6H 3
Saxon Way NN9: Raun 3E 1
Scaldwell Rd. NN6: Brix 1B 2
Scarborough St. NN9: Irth 1A 2
Scarletwell St.
NN1: N'ton 2A **4** (3B 52
Scarletwell Ter.
NN1: N'ton 2A **4** (3B 52
Scarplands, The NN5: Dus 3E 5
Scharpwell NN9: Irth 6A 1
Scholars Ct.
NN1: N'ton 5E **5** (4D 52
Scholey Cl. NN4: Woot 6D 5
School Hill NN11: Newn 5F
NN29: Irch 5F 3
School La. NN3: Moul 4A 2
NN4: Gra P 2E 6
NN7: Harp 3F 4
NN7: Kisl 5H 4
NN7: Quin 4H 6
NN10: High F 4D 2
NN11: Badby 6B
NN29: Irch 5E 3
School Rd. NN29: Irch 5E 3
School St. NN11: Dav 5C
School Wlk. NN8: Well 4G 2
School Way NN3: N'ton 5A 3
Scirocco Cl. NN3: N'ton 1E 3
Scotia Cl. NN4: Brack 1A 6
Scotney Cl. NN4: N'ton 3C 5
Scotsmere NN9: Irth 6H 1
Scott Cl. NN11: Dav 3E
Scott Rd. NN8: Well 2C 2
Scribers Dr. NN5: Upton 5E 5
Scribers M. NN5: Upton 5E 5
Scully Cl. NN4: Woot 4E 5
Scythe Rd. NN11: Dav 1E
Seagrave Ct. NN3: N'ton 2F 3
Sears Cl. NN7: Flore 3E 4
Sears Ho. *NN1: N'ton* *2F 5*
(off Lea Rd
Seaton Dr. NN3: West F 6D 3
Second Av. NN8: Well 2C 2
Second La. NN5: N'ton 3H 5
Sedgemoor Ct. NN11: Dav 1E
Sedgemoor Way NN11: Dav 1E
Sedgwick Ct. NN3: N'ton 4D 3
Seedfield Cl. NN3: West F 6C 3
Seedfield Wlk. NN3: West F 1D 5
Selby Gdns. NN29: Boz 6G 4
Selston Wlk. NN3: N'ton 2B 5
Selwyn Cl. NN11: Dav 2E
SEMILONG 1C 5
Semilong Ho. NN2: N'ton 2C 5
Semilong Rd. NN2: N'ton 2C 5
Sentinel Rd. NN4: N'ton 2G 5
Sentry Cl. NN4: Woot 4D 5
Senwick Dr. NN8: Well 1A 3
Senwick Rd. NN8: Well 1A 3
Sepals Way NN4: Upton 2C 5
Serve Cl. NN8: Well 4G 2
Severn, The NN11: Dav 6C
Severn Cl. NN8: Well 5C 1
Severn Dr. NN5: N'ton 5H 3
Sexton Cl. NN11: Dav 4D
Seymour St. NN5: N'ton 3A 5
Shackleton Dr. NN11: Dav 2D
Shadowfax Dr. NN3: N'ton 2F 3
Shakespeare Av. NN11: Dav 5D
Shakespeare Ho.
NN1: N'ton 1F **5** (2E 53
Shakespeare Rd. NN1: N'ton 2E 5
NN8: Well 2B 2
NN10: Rushd 3A 3
Shale End NN5: Dus 4C 3
Shankley Way NN5: N'ton 2A 5
Shannon Cl. NN10: Rushd 2F 3
Shap Grn. NN3: N'ton 3A 3
Shard Cl. NN4: N'ton 5C 5
Sharman Cl. NN11: Dav 2E
Sharman Rd. NN5: N'ton 4A 5
NN8: Well 1F 2
Sharrow Pl. NN3: Ect B 5H 3
Sharwood Ter. NN29: Irch 5F 3
Shatterstone NN4: N'ton 5D 5
Shaw Cl. NN8: Well 6B 1
Sheaf Cl. NN5: Dus 5D 3
Sheaf St. NN11: Dav 6E
Shearwater La. NN8: Well 4G 1
Shedfield Way NN4: N'ton 5C 5
Sheep St. NN1: N'ton 2C **4** (3C 52
NN8: Well 1G 2
Sheerwater Dr. NN3: Ect B 4H 3
Sheffield Ct. NN9: Raun 4C 1
Sheffield Way NN6: E Bart 4G 4
SHELFLEYS 3G 5

Shelford Cl.—Swansea Cres.

elford Cl. NN3: N'ton ... 2F 39
elley Cl. NN11: Dav ... 5D 6
elleycotes Rd. NN6: Brix ... 2A 22
elley Dr. NN10: High F ... 6C 20
elley Rd. NN8: Well ... 1B 28
elley St. NN2: N'ton ... 6F 37
elmerdine Ri. NN9: Raun ... 3D 14
elsley Dr. NN3: N'ton ... 3F 37
elton Ct. *NN29: Woll ... 5B 44*
(off St Michael's La.)
elton Rd. NN9: Raun ... 5E 15
epherd Cl. NN2: K'thpe ... 2A 36
epherds Hill NN29: Woll ... 6D 44
epherds Wlk. NN7: Harp ... 3G 49
epperton Cl. NN3: Gt Bil ... 5G 39
eraton Cl. NN3: N'ton ... 5A 38
eraton M. NN3: N'ton ... 5A 38
eriff Rd. NN1: N'ton ... 2F 53
erwood Av. NN2: K'thpe ... 1H 35
erwood Dr. NN11: Dav ... 3D 6
ipton Way NN10: Rushd ... 2G 31
ire Pl. NN3: N'ton ... 2F 39
irley Rd. NN10: Rushd ... 2D 32
oal Creek NN4: Col ... 6C 58
oemakers Cl. NN6: E Bart ... 4G 41
oemakers Ct. NN10: Rushd ... 2D 32
ortlands, The NN9: Irth ... 5D 12
ort La. NN8: Well ... 6F 17
ort Stocks NN10: Rushd ... 2F 33
ortwoods Cl. NN9: Raun ... 4D 14
urville Cl. NN6: E Bart ... 4H 41
bley Rd. NN9: Fine ... 5E 11
ddeley Way NN11: Dav ... 4B 6
ddons Way NN3: Moul ... 4B 24
debrook Ct. NN3: N'ton ... 2D 38
degate La. NN8: Well ... 2C 18
dings, The NN9: Irth ... 3H 19
gma Ho. NN1: N'ton ... 2B 4
vanus Pk. NN5: N'ton ... 4H 51
lverdale Gro. NN10: Rushd ... 3A 32
lverdale Rd. NN3: N'ton ... 5B 38
lverstone Cl. NN2: K'thpe ... 2D 36
lver St. NN1: N'ton ... 3C 4 (3C 52)
NN8: Well ... 1G 29
mon de Senlis Ct.
NN1: N'ton ... 1D 4
mon Senlis Hall
NN3: K'thpe ... 1E 37
mon's Wlk.
NN1: N'ton ... 3B 4 (3C 52)
mpson Av. NN10: High F ... 4E 21
nclair Dr. NN8: Well ... 5A 16
r John Pascoe Way
NN5: Dus ... 1E 51
ward Vw. NN5: Dus ... 5F 35
x Acre Wlk. NN3: Ect B ... 5G 39
xfields Athletics Stadium ... 4G 51
xfields Leisure ... 4G 51
xfields Stadium ... 4F 51
awle Ct. NN3: N'ton ... 4D 38
elton Wlk. NN3: N'ton ... 3A 38
etty Cl. NN4: Brack ... 2A 60
iddaw Wlk. NN3: N'ton ... 3A 38
inner Av. NN5: Upton ... 4F 51
inner's Hill NN10: Rushd ... 3D 32
ipton Cl. NN4: N'ton ... 4B 58
ade, The NN11: Dav ... 6E 7
adeswell Ct. NN3: Lit B ... 1D 54
aters Cl. NN10: Rushd ... 3F 33
ip, The NN6: Brix ... 1B 22
ips, The
NN9: Gt Har ... 1E 17 & 6A 10
ipton Wlk. NN3: N'ton ... 2G 39
mith Ct. NN9: Raun ... 4D 14
mithfield Pl. NN9: Raun ... 4C 14
miths Ct. NN4: N'ton ... 6D 4 (5D 52)
mithy, The NN3: West F ... 6C 38
myth Ct. NN3: N'ton ... 4C 38
apewood Wlk. NN3: N'ton ... 3G 39
etterton Cl. NN3: N'ton ... 3F 37
owbell Sq. NN3: Ect B ... 4G 39
owshill Cl. *NN11: Dav ... 1D 6*
(off Hidcote Way)
ane Cl. NN8: Well ... 3F 17
l Central ... 4B 4 (4C 52)
merford Rd. NN8: Well ... 5E 17
merset St.
NN1: N'ton ... 1E 5 (2D 52)
merville Rd. NN11: Dav ... 1D 8
pwith Way NN11: Dav ... 3C 6
rrel Cl. NN4: Woot ... 6E 59
theby Ri. NN3: Ect B ... 4H 39
urton Pl. NN11: Dav ... 1F 7
uthampton Rd. NN4: Far C ... 6C 52
uth Bern NN4: N'ton ... 6A 52
uthbridge Ct.
NN4: N'ton ... 6D 4 (5D 52)
UTHBROOK ... 5F 7
uth Cl. NN10: Rushd ... 4E 33
South Copse NN4: N'ton ... 4B 58
Southcourt NN3: Moul ... 6H 23
Southcrest NN4: N'ton ... 2G 57
Southfield Av. NN4: Far C ... 6D 52
Southfield Rd. NN5: Dus ... 2D 50
SOUTHFIELDS ... 6D 24
Southfields NN10: Rushd ... 4E 33
Southfields Ho. NN3: N'ton ... 1E 39
Sth. Holme Ct. NN3: N'ton ... 2C 38
South March NN11: Dav ... 1F 9
South Mdw. Cl. NN5: Upton ... 3C 50
South Mdw. Rd.
NN5: Dus, Upton ... 2C 50
South Mdw. Vw. NN5: Upton ... 3C 50
South Oval NN5: N'ton ... 6H 35
Sth. Paddock Ct.
NN3: N'ton ... 3D 38
South Pk. NN10: Rushd ... 4D 32
South Pl. NN11: Dav ... 5D 6
Sth. Portway Cl.
NN3: N'ton ... 1D 38
Sth. Priors Ct. NN3: N'ton ... 4E 39
South St. NN1: N'ton ... 2H 5 (3F 53)
NN7: Weed ... 6C 46
NN29: Woll ... 5B 44
South Ter. NN1: N'ton ... 2H 5 (3F 53)
South Vw. NN6: Brix ... 2A 22
NN7: Kisl ... 4A 50
South Way NN11: Dav ... 5F 7
Southwood Hill NN4: N'ton ... 1H 57
Sovereign Ct. NN3: N'ton ... 6D 24
NN10: Rushd ... 2D 32
Spanslade Rd. NN3: West F ... 6E 39
Sparke Cl. NN8: Well ... 4D 16
Spartan Cl. NN4: Woot ... 6F 59
Spectacle La. NN3: Moul ... 3F 23
Speke Dr. NN11: Dav ... 2E 7
Spelhoe St. NN3: N'ton ... 1D 38
Spencelayh Cl. NN8: Well ... 4F 17
SPENCER ... 2A 52
Spencer Bri. Rd.
NN5: N'ton ... 1A 4 (3A 52)
Spencer Cl. NN6: E Bart ... 3H 41
Spencer Ct. NN10: Rushd ... 2C 32
Spencer Gdns. NN29: Boz ... 6H 45
Spencer Haven NN5: N'ton ... 2A 52
Spencer Pde.
NN1: N'ton ... 3E 5 (3D 52)
NN9: Stanw ... 6H 13
Spencer Perceval Hall
NN3: K'thpe ... 1E 37
Spencer Rd. NN1: N'ton ... 1F 5
NN8: Well ... 4F 29
NN9: Irth ... 2A 20
NN10: Rushd ... 1C 32
Spencer St. NN5: N'ton ... 4A 52
NN9: Raun ... 3E 15
Spenfield Ct. NN3: N'ton ... 4D 38
Spenser Cres. NN11: Dav ... 4C 6
Spey Cl. NN8: Well ... 5C 16
Spinney, The NN4: Gra P ... 3E 65
Spinney Cl. NN2: Bou ... 6C 22
NN10: Rushd ... 3B 32
Spinney Dr. NN4: Col ... 1C 64
SPINNEY HILL ... 4G 37
Spinney Hill Cres. NN3: N'ton ... 3G 37
Spinney Hill Rd. NN3: N'ton ... 3F 37
Spinney La. NN8: Wilby ... 3C 28
Spinney Ri. NN11: Dav ... 6E 7
Spinney Rd. NN3: N'ton ... 1H 37
NN9: Irth ... 1B 20
NN10: Rushd ... 4B 32
Spinneyside Wlk. NN3: N'ton ... 3E 39
(not continuous)
Spinney St. NN9: Raun ... 3D 14
Spinney Ter. NN9: Irth ... 1B 20
Spinney Way NN3: N'ton ... 2G 37
Spire Rd. NN10: Rushd ... 1E 33
Splash Leisure Pool ... 2C 32
Sportsmans Cl. NN7: Cog ... 3H 55
Spratton Rd. NN6: Brix ... 1A 22
Springbanks Way NN4: N'ton ... 3B 58
Spring Cl. NN2: Bou ... 4C 22
NN9: Irth ... 1B 20
NN11: Dav ... 1E 9
Springer Straight
NN4: N'ton ... 6H 51
Springfield NN4: Woot ... 4E 59
NN7: Flore ... 4E 47
Springfield Ct. NN3: N'ton ... 4D 38
Springfield Rd. NN10: Rushd ... 5E 33
Spring Gdns.
NN1: N'ton ... 3E 5 (4D 52)
NN6: E Bart ... 3H 41
NN8: Well ... 1F 29
NN10: High F ... 5D 20
NN11: Dav ... 6E 7
Spring Ho. *NN8: Well ... 1F 29*
(off Hill St.)
Spring La. NN1: N'ton ... 2A 4 (3B 52)
NN7: Flore ... 4E 47
NN8: Well ... 1G 29
SPRING PARK ... 2A 36
Springs, The NN4: N'ton ... 6A 52
Spring St. NN9: Irth ... 1B 20
Springs Walk, The
NN4: N'ton ... 6A 52
(off The Springs)
Spring Ter. NN9: Irth ... 1B 20
Springwell Cl. NN4: Gra P ... 2E 65
Springwood Ct. NN3: N'ton ... 2D 38
Spruce Ct. NN3: N'ton ... 4C 38
Spur Rd. NN8: Well ... 4F 29
Spyglass Hill NN4: N'ton ... 5B 58
Square, The NN4: Gra P ... 2F 65
NN5: Upton ... 5E 51
NN6: E Bart ... 3G 41
NN6: Pits ... 1C 22
NN9: Raun ... 3D 14
Squires Wlk. NN3: N'ton ... 4H 37
Squirrel Cl. NN4: Gra P ... 3F 65
Squirrel La. NN5: Dus ... 2E 51
Stable Ct. NN2: K'thpe ... 4C 36
Stable La. NN6: Pits ... 1D 22
Stafford Ct. NN11: Dav ... 2F 7
Stafford Pl. NN3: N'ton ... 6F 23
Stagshaw Cl. NN4: N'ton ... 3C 58
Staines Cl. NN5: N'ton ... 3G 51
Standens Barn Local Cen.
NN3: West F ... 6D 38
(off Topwell Ct.)
Standens Barn Rd.
NN3: West F ... 1D 54
Standing Stones NN3: Gt Bil ... 4F 39
Standside NN5: N'ton ... 3H 51
Stanfield Rd. NN5: Dus ... 3E 51
Stanford Way NN4: N'ton ... 4C 58
Stanhope Rd. NN2: N'ton ... 6C 36
Stanley M. NN8: Well ... 6H 17
Stanley Rd. NN5: N'ton ... 3A 52
NN8: Well ... 6H 17
Stanley St. NN2: N'ton ... 1B 52
Stanley Way NN11: Dav ... 2E 7
Stannard Way NN6: Brix ... 1A 22
Stanton Av. NN3: N'ton ... 3G 37
Stanton Cl. NN8: Well ... 3H 17
Stanwell Way NN8: Well ... 2C 28
(not continuous)
STANWICK ... 6A 14
Stanwick Lakes ... 5F 13
Stanwick Lakes Vis. Cen. ... 5F 13
Stanwick Rd. NN9: Raun ... 5B 14
NN10: High F ... 4E 21
(not continuous)
Star Ho. *NN8: Well ... 6H 17*
(off York Rd.)
Starmers La. NN7: Kisl ... 5H 49
Starmer's Yd. NN5: Dus ... 2E 51
Station App. *NN10: Rushd ... 2D 32*
(off John Clark Way)
Station Cl. NN3: Gt Bil ... 6G 39
NN11: Dav ... 5F 7
Station End NN3: Gt Bil ... 6G 39
Station M. NN3: Gt Bil ... 5G 39
Station Rd. NN3: Gt Bil ... 6G 39
NN6: Brix ... 1A 22
NN6: E Bart ... 3G 41
(not continuous)
NN7: Blis ... 3D 62
(not continuous)
NN7: Cog, Lit Hou ... 3G 55
NN7: Gren ... 6H 41
NN9: Fine ... 2A 10
NN9: Irth ... 1B 20
(not continuous)
NN9: Raun ... 3G 15
NN10: High F ... 3D 20
NN10: Rushd ... 3C 32
NN29: Irch ... 5F 31
Staverton Park Golf Course ... 1A 8
Staverton Rd. NN11: Dav ... 1A 8
(not continuous)
Steele Rd. NN8: Well ... 1D 28
Steene St. NN5: N'ton ... 3A 52
STEFEN HILL ... 1D 8
Stefen Hill Sports Ground Track
... 2E 9
Stefen Way NN11: Dav ... 6B 6
Stenson St. NN5: N'ton ... 3A 52
Stephen Bennett Cl.
NN5: Dus ... 1E 51
Stephenson Cl. NN11: Dav ... 3B 6
Sterling Bus. Pk. NN4: Brack ... 1A 60
Stevens Ct. NN6: E Bart ... 2H 41
Stevenson St. NN4: Del ... 1C 58
Stewart Cl. NN3: Moul ... 3H 23
Stewarts Rd. NN8: Well ... 2G 17
Stile Cl. NN11: Dav ... 5C 6
Stimpson Av.
NN1: N'ton ... 1H 5 (1F 53)
Stirling St. NN5: N'ton ... 2H 51
Stirrup Ho. *NN5: N'ton ... 4B 52*
(off Byfield Rd.)
Stitchman Ho. *NN5: N'ton ... 3A 52*
(off Byfield Rd.)
Stockley St.
NN1: N'ton ... 3G 5 (3E 53)
(not continuous)
Stockmead Rd. NN3: Lit B ... 1E 55
Stocks Hill NN3: Moul ... 4A 24
NN9: Fine ... 5C 10
Stockwell Av. NN4: Woot ... 6D 58
Stockwell Rd. NN7: Mil M ... 1H 63
Stockwell Way NN7: Mil M ... 1H 63
Stoke Firs Cl. NN4: Woot ... 5F 59
Stoke Rd. NN7: Blis ... 6F 63
Stonebridge Ct. NN3: N'ton ... 4D 38
Stonebrig La. NN9: Lit Harr ... 1A 16
Stone Circ. Rd. NN3: N'ton ... 1B 38
Stone Cl. NN8: Well ... 3F 17
NN29: Woll ... 5B 44
Stone Hill Ct. NN3: N'ton ... 4B 38
Stonehill Way NN6: Brix ... 2A 22
Stonelea Rd. NN6: Syw ... 2H 25
Stoneleigh Chase NN5: Dus ... 6F 35
Stone Way NN5: Dus ... 2D 50
Stoneway NN11: Badby ... 6B 8
Stonewold Cl. NN2: K'thpe ... 3A 36
Stoneyhurst NN4: N'ton ... 6H 51
Stoney Piece Cl. NN29: Boz ... 6G 45
Stook, The NN11: Dav ... 1E 7
Storton's Pits Nature Reserve
... 4G 51
Stour, The NN11: Dav ... 1C 8
Stourhead Dr. NN4: N'ton ... 4C 58
Stour Rd. NN5: N'ton ... 3H 51
Stourton Cl. NN8: Well ... 4D 28
Stow Cl. NN8: Well ... 4D 28
Stowe Wlk. NN3: N'ton ... 2F 37
NN11: Dav ... 1D 6
Stradlers Cl. NN4: Woot ... 6E 59
Stratford Dr. NN4: Woot ... 5D 58
Stratton Cl. NN3: N'ton ... 2B 54
Strawberry Hill NN3: N'ton ... 4G 39
Straws Cl. NN9: Irth ... 2A 20
Straws Yd. NN9: Irth ... 2A 20
Stream Bank Cl. NN8: Well ... 1D 28
Streambank Rd. NN3: N'ton ... 1C 38
Streatfield Rd. NN5: N'ton ... 1A 52
Streather Ct. NN9: Raun ... 4D 14
(not continuous)
Streeton Way NN6: E Bart ... 2G 41
Strelley Av. NN3: West F ... 1D 54
Strobel Dr. NN5: Upton ... 5E 51
Strobel M. NN5: Upton ... 5E 51
Strode Rd. NN8: Well ... 6H 17
Stuart Cl. NN4: N'ton ... 4H 57
Stubble Cl. NN2: K'thpe ... 1A 36
Stubbs Cl. NN8: Well ... 4F 17
Studland Rd. NN2: K'thpe ... 6B 36
Sturdee Cl. NN11: Dav ... 6F 7
Style Way NN4: Upton ... 2B 56
Sulby Rd. NN3: N'ton ... 1C 38
Sulgrave Rd. NN5: N'ton ... 2H 51
Summerfields NN4: N'ton ... 1G 57
Summerhouse Pl. NN3: N'ton ... 1G 37
Summerhouse Rd.
NN3: N'ton ... 1G 37
Summerlee Rd. NN9: Fine ... 5D 10
Summer Leys Local Nature Reserve
... 3F 43
Summit Ri. NN4: N'ton ... 4D 58
Sunderland St. NN5: N'ton ... 3A 52
Sundew Ct. NN4: N'ton ... 2F 57
Sunningdale Cl. NN2: N'ton ... 5E 37
Sunningdale Dr. NN10: Rushd ... 5F 33
NN11: Dav ... 4G 7
Sunny Side NN6: E Bart ... 3F 41
Sunnyside NN4: Woot ... 5E 59
NN6: Ect ... 3B 40
Sunset Ct. NN3: Lit B ... 5E 39
Sussex Cl. NN5: Dus ... 3E 51
Sussex Ct. NN1: N'ton ... 2C 4
Sussex Pl. NN10: Rushd ... 1D 32
Sutton Acre NN7: Flore ... 4E 47
Sutton Cl. NN2: K'thpe ... 1D 36
Sutton St. NN7: Flore ... 4E 47
Swain Ct. NN3: N'ton ... 4C 38
Swale Dr. NN5: N'ton ... 5H 35
NN8: Well ... 5C 16
Swallow Cl. NN4: N'ton ... 4A 58
NN8: Well ... 4H 17
Swallow Dr. NN10: Rushd ... 1D 32
Swan Cl. NN9: Raun ... 3E 15
Swann Dale NN11: Dav ... 6F 7
Swann Dale Cl. NN11: Dav ... 6F 7
Swansea Cres. NN5: N'ton ... 2A 52

A-Z Northampton 81

Swansea Rd. NN5: N'ton 1A **52**
Swansgate Centre, The
NN8: Well 1G **29**
Swans La. *NN8: Well 1G 29*
(off Market St.)
Swansnest NN6: Brix 1A **22**
Swanspool Ct. NN8: Well 1G **29**
Swanspool Pde. NN8: Well 2G **29**
Swan St. NN1: N'ton 4D **4** (4D **52**)
Swans Way NN10: High F 3E **21**
SWAN VALLEY 2D **56**
Swan Valley Ind. Est.
NN4: Swan H 2D **56**
Swan Valley Office Village
NN4: Swan H 3E **57**
Swan Valley Way
NN4: N'ton, Swan H 2D **56**
Swan Yd. NN1: N'ton 3C **4** (3C **52**)
Swedish Houses
NN7: Up Harl 3A **34**
Swift Cl. NN4: Gra P 2F **65**
Swift Ct. NN4: N'ton 3G **57**
Swinburne Rd. NN8: Well 1B **28**
Swinford Hollow NN3: Lit B 1E **55**
Sycamore Cl. NN10: Rushd 3E **33**
NN11: Dav 2E **7**
Sycamore Dr. NN6: Syw 5H **25**
Sycamore Rd. NN5: Dus 2E **51**
Sylmond Gdns. NN10: Rushd 5B **32**
Sylvanus Ho. NN8: Well 6D **16**
Symington St. NN5: N'ton 2A **52**
Syresham Way NN2: K'thpe 2C **36**
SYWELL 2A **26**
Sywell Airport Bus. Pk.
NN6: Syw 1B **26**
Sywell Av. NN8: Well 5D **16**
Sywell Aviation Mus. 1B **26**
Sywell Country Park 5B **26**
Sywell Country Park Vis. Cen.
6C **26**
Sywell La. NN6: Ect 2A **40**
Sywell Rd. NN6: Mears A 4C **26**
NN6: Over 4D **24**
NN8: Mears A, Well 5A **16**
Sywell Way NN8: Well 5D **16**

T

Taborley Cl. NN3: West F 6C **38**
Tadcaster Cl. NN11: Dav 1E **7**
Tainty Cl. NN9: Fine 4C **10**
Talan Ri. NN3: N'ton 2F **39**
Talavera Cl. NN11: Dav 6C **6**
Talavera Way
NN3: Moul, N'ton 1H **37**
Talbot Rd. NN1: N'ton 1G **5** (2E **53**)
NN8: Well 6A **18**
NN10: Rushd 4B **32**
Talbot Rd. Nth. NN8: Well 5A **18**
Tall Trees Cl. NN4: N'ton 3H **57**
Tallyfield End NN4: N'ton 6G **51**
Tamar Cl. NN5: N'ton 5G **35**
Tamarisk Dr. NN3: Moul 1A **38**
Tamar Sq. NN11: Dav 6C **6**
Tancred Cl. NN4: Woot 4E **59**
Tanfield La. NN1: N'ton 4H **53**
Tanglewood NN4: Col 1D **64**
Tanner St. NN1: N'ton 5B **4** (4C **52**)
Tannery Cotts. NN9: Irth 3A **20**
Tann Rd. NN9: Fine 4D **10**
Tansy Cl. NN4: N'ton 2F **57**
Tantree Way NN6: Brix 1B **22**
Tapeley Gdns. NN4: N'ton 4D **58**
Taper Way NN11: Dav 4C **6**
Tarn Cft. NN3: N'ton 4H **37**
Tarragon Way NN4: N'ton 5D **58**
Tarrant Cl. NN3: Moul 4B **24**
Tarrant Way NN3: Moul 4B **24**
Tate Gro. NN4: H'stone 4E **59**
Tattersall Cl. NN3: N'ton 3G **37**
Taunton Av. NN3: N'ton 2A **54**
Tavern La. NN11: Dav 6E **7**
Tavistock Cl. NN3: Ect B 5H **39**
Taylor Av. NN3: N'ton 6A **38**
Taylor Cl. NN8: Well 4C **16**
Teal Cl. NN4: N'ton 3F **57**
NN10: High F 3E **21**
NN11: Dav 3E **7**
Teal La. NN8: Well 4H **17**
Teasel Cl. NN10: Rushd 6E **33**
Teasle Cl. NN5: Dus 3B **50**
Tebbutt's Yd. NN6: E Bart 3G **41**
Tees Cl. NN8: Well 5C **16**
Teesdale NN3: N'ton 1D **38**
Telford St. NN5: Upton 5E **51**
Telford Way NN5: Upton 5F **51**
Temperance Cotts.
NN9: Raun 3D **14**
Templar Dr. NN2: K'thpe 3A **36**
Temple Bar
NN1: N'ton 1C **4** (2C **52**)
Temple Ct. NN10: High F 4D **20**
Temple Gdns. NN10: Rushd 1E **33**
Tenby Rd. NN5: N'ton 1A **52**
Tennyson Cl. NN5: N'ton 1H **51**
Tennyson Rd. NN8: Well 2D **28**
NN10: Rushd 3B **32**
NN11: Dav 4C **6**
Tenpin
Northampton 3F **51**
Ten Pines NN3: N'ton 6D **24**
Tenter Cl. NN10: High F 6D **20**
Tenter La. NN9: Fine 4D **10**
Tenter Rd. NN3: N'ton 6F **23**
Tesla Cl. NN5: Dus 1E **51**
Teviot Cl. NN5: N'ton 5G **35**
Tewkesbury Cl. NN4: N'ton 2A **58**
NN8: Well 5D **16**
Tewkesbury Dr. NN10: Rushd 5F **33**
Thames Rd. NN4: N'ton 4B **58**
NN8: Well 5C **16**
NN11: Dav 6B **6**
Thatchwell Ct. NN3: West F 1D **54**
The ....
Names prefixed with 'The'
for example 'The Albany' are
indexed under the main name
such as 'Albany, The'
Thebwell Rd. NN3: West F 6D **38**
Thenford St.
NN1: N'ton 3F **5** (3E **53**)
Third Av. NN8: Well 2D **28**
Thirlestane Cres. NN4: Far C 6B **52**
Thirlestane Rd. NN4: Far C 6B **52**
Thirlmere NN8: Well 6C **16**
Thirlmere Av. NN3: N'ton 4A **38**
Thirlmere Cl. NN11: Dav 5C **6**
Thistle Ct. NN4: N'ton 6A **52**
Thistleholme Cl. NN2: N'ton 4E **37**
Thomas Chapman Gro.
NN4: N'ton 5D **52**
Thomas Flawn Rd. NN9: Irth 3H **19**
Thomas St. NN1: N'ton 1D **4**
(not continuous)
NN8: Well 6H **17**
Thomas Webb Cl. NN11: Dav 5F **7**
Thompson Cl. NN5: Upton 3C **50**
Thorburn Rd. NN3: West F 1C **54**
Thornapple Cl. NN3: N'ton 3G **39**
Thornbridge Cl. NN10: Rushd 4C **32**
Thornby Dr. NN2: K'thpe 4B **36**
Thornfield NN3: N'ton 3G **39**
Thorn Hill NN4: N'ton 6H **51**
Thorn Hill Wlk. *NN4: N'ton 6A 52*
(off Bern Side)
Thornton Cl. NN7: Flore 4F **47**
NN11: Newn 6F **9**
Thornton Hall Cl. NN2: K'thpe 5B **36**
Thornton Rd. NN2: K'thpe 6B **36**
Thorpe Cl. NN8: Well 6C **16**
Thorpe Rd. NN4: Del 6C **52**
NN6: E Bart 5G **41**
Thorpe St. NN9: Raun 4D **14**
Thorpeville NN3: Moul 6B **24**
(not continuous)
THORPLANDS 2C **38**
Thrapston Rd. NN9: Fine 4E **11**
Three Mile Wlk. NN3: Ect B 4G **39**
THREE SHIRES BMI HOSPITAL
4F **53**
Thrift St. NN10: High F 6D **20**
NN29: Irch 5E **31**
NN29: Woll 5B **44**
Thrupp Bri. NN4: Woot 5G **59**
Thrush La. NN8: Well 5G **17**
Thruxton Dr. NN3: N'ton 3F **37**
Thursby Rd. NN1: N'ton 2H **53**
Thurspit Pl. NN3: Ect B 5H **39**
Thwaite Wlk. NN3: West F 6E **39**
Thyme Ct. NN3: N'ton 4C **38**
Tideswell Cl. NN4: N'ton 3H **57**
Tiffany Gdns. NN4: N'ton 5C **58**
Tiffield Rd. NN7: G'ton 4A **62**
Tiller Way NN4: N'ton 2F **57**
Timken Cl. NN5: Dus 2F **51**
Timken Wlk. NN5: Dus 2F **51**
Timken Way NN11: Dav 3C **6**
Timken Way Nth. NN5: Dus 2E **51**
Timken Way Sth. NN5: Dus 2E **51**
Tingdene Rd. NN9: Fine 4D **10**
Tinkers Cres. NN6: Mears A 3D **26**
Tinsley Cl. NN3: N'ton 4F **39**
Tintagel Cl. NN10: Rushd 5F **33**
Tintern Av. NN5: N'ton 2A **52**
Tiptoe Cl. NN3: N'ton 3G **39**
Tithe Barn Cl. NN9: Raun 2E **15**
Tithe Barn Rd. NN8: Well 1G **29**
Tithe Barn Way NN4: Swan H 3E **57**
(Cygnet Dr.)
NN4: Swan H 3D **56**
(Park Circ.)
Tithe Rd. NN7: Weed 6A **46**
Titley Bawk Av. NN6: E Bart 1H **41**
Titty Ho NN9: Raun 4C **14**
Tiverton Av. NN2: K'thpe 6B **22**
Tollbar NN10: High F, Rushd 6D **20**
Tollgate Cl. NN2: K'thpe 5B **36**
Tollgate Way NN5: Dus, N'ton 3F **51**
Toms Cl. NN4: Col 2C **64**
Tonmead Rd. NN3: N'ton 3C **38**
Tonmead Wlk. NN3: N'ton 4C **38**
Top End NN14: Lit A 2D **12**
Top Farm La. NN29: Gt Dod 6E **29**
Topgrass Wlk. *NN3: West F 6D 38*
(off Logwell Ct.)
Top Meadow Wlk. NN3: N'ton 4E **39**
Topnotch Health Club
Northampton 4B 4
(in Sol Central)
Topwell Ct. NN3: West F 6D **38**
Torrington Cres. NN8: Well 5E **17**
Torrington Grn. NN8: Well 5E **17**
Torrington Rd. NN8: Well 5D **16**
Torrington Way NN8: Well 5E **17**
Toulouse Cl. NN4: Woot 4E **59**
Touraine Cl. NN5: New D 5B **34**
Tourist Info. Cen.
Daventry 5E **7**
Northampton 4D **4** (4D **52**)
Tovey Dr. NN11: Dav 5F **7**
Towcester Rd.
NN1: N'ton 5A **4** (6B **52**)
NN4: Mil M, N'ton, Del, Far C
3G **63**
NN7: Blis 6D **62**
NN7: Mil M 3G **63**
Tower Cl. NN9: Fine 5F **11**
Tower Ct. NN6: Over 6F **25**
NN29: Woll 4D **44**
Tower Fld. Sq. NN3: N'ton 1E **39**
Tower Hill Cl. NN4: N'ton 6G **51**
Tower Sq. NN5: N'ton 3H **51**
Tower St. NN1: N'ton 2B **4** (3C **52**)
Tower Works *NN9: Fine 4D 10*
(off Well St.)
Town Corner NN5: N'ton 3H **51**
Townley Way NN6: E Bart 2G **41**
Townsend Cl. NN8: Well 1F **29**
Townsend Leys NN10: High F 4D **20**
Townwell La. NN29: Irch 5F **31**
Towpath Av. NN4: N'ton 2E **57**
Towton Ct. NN4: N'ton 2A **58**
Trafalgar Way NN11: Dav 6G **7**
Trafford Rd. NN10: Rushd 3E **33**
Treetops NN3: N'ton 2E **39**
Trefoil Cl. NN10: Rushd 6E **33**
Trelawney NN8: Well 6B **16**
Trenery Way
NN4: N'ton 6D **4** (5D **52**)
Trent Cl. NN5: N'ton 5G **35**
NN8: Well 5C **16**
Trentham Cl. NN4: N'ton 4C **58**
Trent Wlk. NN11: Dav 6B **6**
Tresham Grn. NN5: Dus 6F **35**
Trevor Cl. NN5: N'ton 2G **51**
Trevor Cres. NN5: N'ton 2G **51**
Trimley Cl. NN3: N'ton 3B **54**
Trinity Av. NN2: N'ton 6D **36**
Trinity Cen. NN8: Well 4A **16**
Trinity Cl. NN11: Dav 1D **8**
Triumph Gdns. NN5: Dus 1B **50**
Trojan Cen. NN8: Well 3G **17**
Troon Cres. NN8: Well 4C **16**
Troutbeck Wlk. NN3: N'ton 3A **38**
Trundle Jetty *NN4: N'ton 6H 51*
(off Pitstone Rd.)
Trussell Rd. NN3: Gt Bil 6G **39**
Tudely Cl. NN4: Woot 4F **59**
Tudor Ct. NN4: Woot 5F **59**
Tudor Rd. NN1: N'ton 5G **37**
Tudor Wlk. NN10: Rushd 2E **33**
Tudor Way NN8: Well 4E **17**
Tulip Dr. NN10: Rushd 5D **32**
Turnberry Ct. NN8: Well 4C **16**
Turnberry La. NN4: Col 6B **58**
Turnbrook Cl. NN9: Irth 6A **12**
Turnells Mill La. NN8: Well 4G **29**
Turner Rd. NN8: Well 4F **17**
Turners Ct. NN4: Woot 4D **58**
Turners Gdns. NN4: Woot 4D **58**
Turner St. NN1: N'ton 2F **53**
Turn Furlong NN2: K'thpe 2A **36**
Turrets, The NN9: Raun 4D **14**
Tweed Cl. NN11: Dav 1C **8**
Tweed Cres. NN10: Rushd 1E **33**
Tweed Rd. NN5: N'ton 3G **51**
Twigden Rd. NN7: Kisl 6H
Twyford Av. NN9: Raun 3C
Twyford Cl. NN3: Lit B 1E
Tyebeck Ct. NN2: K'thpe 4B
Tyes Ct. NN3: N'ton 4D
Tyne Cl. NN8: Well 5C
Tyne Rd. NN5: N'ton 3G
NN11: Dav 1
Tyne Way NN10: Rushd 1E
Tyringham Cl. NN3: West F 6B

U

Ullswater Cl. NN8: Well 6C
NN10: High F 3D
Ultra Cl. NN8: Well 2A
Underbank La. NN3: Moul 1A
Union St. NN1: N'ton 3D **4** (3D
NN9: Fine 4E
Unity Cl. NN29: Woll 4A
University Cl. NN2: K'thpe 1E
University of Leicester
Institute of Lifelong Learning
1C
(off Barrack R
University of Northampton
Avenue Campus 6D
Park Campus 2F
Upland Rd. NN3: N'ton 5A
Up. Bath St.
NN1: N'ton 3B **4** (3C
(not continuo
Up. Cross St.
NN1: N'ton 3B **4** (3C
Up. George St. NN10: High F 4E
Up. Glen Av. NN7: Blis 3D
UPPER HARLESTONE 3A
Up. Havelock St. NN8: Well 6G
UPPER HEYFORD 5A
Up. High St. NN7: Harp 3G
Up. Kings Av. NN10: High F 4E
Upper Mounts
NN1: N'ton 2D **4** (3D
Up. Park Av. NN10: Rushd 4B
Up. Priory St.
NN1: N'ton 1B **4** (2C
Up. Queen St. NN10: Rushd 2E
Up. Thrift St.
NN1: N'ton 2H **5** (3F
UPPER WEEDON 6A
Uppingham St.
NN1: N'ton 1A **4** (2B
UPTON 4F
Upton Cl. NN2: K'thpe 1D
Upton Hall La. NN5: Upton 5E
Upton La. NN5: Upton 4D
Upton Valley Way E.
NN4: N'ton, Upton 2D
Upton Valley Way Nth.
NN4: Upton 4B
NN5: Upton 4B
Upton Way NN5: N'ton 4F
Usher Ho. NN2: K'thpe 2D

V

Vale, The NN1: N'ton 6F
Valemead Wlk. NN3: N'ton 3E
(not continuo
Valentine Way NN3: Gt Bil 4G
Valley Cres. NN3: Lit B 6F
Valley Rd. NN3: Lit B 6F
NN8: Well 3F
Vantage Mdw. NN3: Ect B 4H
Vardon Cl. NN8: Well 4C
Varley Cl. NN8: Well 3E
Vaux Rd. NN8: Well 2G
Velocette Way NN5: Dus 6B
Verdant Va. NN4: N'ton 5D
Vernier Cl. NN11: Dav 4
Vernon Cl. NN11: Dav 1
Vernon Ct. NN1: N'ton 3
Vernon St. NN1: N'ton 2H **5** (3F
Vernon Ter. NN1: N'ton 3H **5** (3F
Vernon Wlk.
NN1: N'ton 2H **5** (3F
Verwood Cl. NN3: N'ton 2D
Veteran Cl. NN4: Woot 4E
Vicarage Cl. NN2: K'thpe 4A
NN8: Well 5D
Vicarage Farm Rd. NN8: Well 5D
Vicarage Hill NN11: Badby 6
Vicarage La. NN2: K'thpe 4A
NN6: Mears A 3D
Vicarage Rd. NN5: N'ton 2A
NN10: Rushd 2E
Vicar La. NN11: Dav 5

eroy Cl. NN9: Raun ... 3E 15
toria Bus. Pk. NN5: N'ton ... 3B 52
NN8: Well ... 3B 30
(Claudius Way)
NN8: Well ... 3H 29
(Whitworth Way)
toria Cl. NN6: E Bart ... 2G 41
NN10: Rushd ... 2D 32
toria Ct. NN10: Rushd ... 2D 32
toria Gdns.
NN1: N'ton ... 5C 4 (4D 52)
toria Ho. NN1: N'ton ... 3G 5
toria Prom.
NN1: N'ton ... 5C 4 (4D 52)
toria Rd. NN1: N'ton ... 2F 5 (3E 53)
NN8: Well ... 1G 29
NN9: Fine ... 4D 10
NN10: Rushd ... 2D 32
toria St. NN1: N'ton ... 2D 4 (3D 52)
NN6: E Bart ... 2H 41
NN9: Irth ... 2A 20
nne Cl. NN5: Dus ... 1B 50
lagers Cl. NN4: Woot ... 6E 59
la La. NN9: Stanw ... 6H 13
la Ri. NN10: High F ... 4D 20
la Way NN4: Woot ... 6F 59
ncent Cl. NN5: Dus ... 1B 50
ne Hill Cl. NN10: High F ... 5C 20
ne Hill Dr. NN10: High F ... 5D 20
gin Active
Collingtree ... 6C 58
Northampton ... 3D 54
scount Rd. NN3: N'ton ... 1G 39
vian Rd. NN8: Well ... 6H 17
kes Cl. NN3: Lit B ... 6E 39
lunteer Cl. NN4: Woot ... 5E 59
e Cinema
Northampton ... 4B 4
(in Sol Central)
lcan Cl. NN11: Dav ... 3C 6
se Rd. NN2: Bou ... 6B 22

W

ade Mdw. Ct. NN3: N'ton ... 3D 38
ade Mdw. Wlk. NN3: N'ton ... 4D 38
adham Ct. NN11: Dav ... 2E 9
aendel Leisure Cen. ... 6H 17
agtail Cl. NN3: Moul ... 6A 24
aingrove NN3: N'ton ... 3F 39
ake Cl. NN8: Well ... 4F 29
akefield NN8: Well ... 1C 28
akefield Rd. NN2: K'thpe ... 3D 36
akehurst Dr. NN4: N'ton ... 4C 58
ake Way NN4: Gra P ... 3E 65
algrave Cl. NN3: Lit B ... 1F 55
alker Sq. NN8: Well ... 4C 16
alkers Way NN4: Woot ... 6E 59
NN9: Fine ... 5D 10
allace Gdns. NN2: N'ton ... 5F 37
allace Rd. NN2: N'ton ... 5F 37
allace Ter. NN2: N'ton ... 5F 37
allbeck Cl. NN2: K'thpe ... 3C 36
alledwell Ct. NN3: West F ... 6D 38
allingford End NN3: Lit B ... 1E 55
allis Cl. NN8: Well ... 1A 28
almer Cl. NN10: Rushd ... 4F 33
alnut Tree Ct. NN10: High F ... 4D 20
alter Tull Way NN5: N'ton ... 4F 51
alton Heath Way NN2: N'ton ... 4E 37
ansford Wlk. NN3: N'ton ... 1C 38
antage Cl. NN3: Moul ... 4C 24
antage Pl. NN29: Irch ... 5F 31
antage Rd. NN1: N'ton ... 1G 53
NN29: Irch ... 5F 31
ardens Cl. NN9: Irch ... 6A 12
ardens Lodge *NN11: Dav ... 5E 7*
(off North St.)
ardington Ct. NN2: K'thpe ... 3B 36
ardlow Cl. NN4: N'ton ... 3H 57
ARMONDS HILL ... 1C 32
armonds Hill NN10: High F ... 6D 20
arners Hill NN29: Boz ... 6H 45
arnham NN8: Well ... 6B 16
arren, The NN4: H'stone ... 4F 59
arren Cl. NN29: Irch ... 6G 31
arren Rd. NN5: N'ton ... 2H 51
arrens Cl. NN9: Irth ... 1B 20
arth Ho. NN9: Raun ... 2B 14
arth Pk. Way NN9: Raun ... 2B 14
arwick Cl. NN5: Dus ... 1D 50
NN9: Raun ... 4D 14
arwick Ct. *NN11: Dav ... 6D 6*
(off Warwick St.)
arwick Rd. NN8: Well ... 3G 29
arwick St. NN11: Dav ... 6D 6
ashbrook Cl. NN3: Lit B ... 6F 39
ashbrook La. NN6: Ect ... 2B 40

Washbrook Rd. NN10: Rushd ... 2C 32
Washington St. NN2: K'thpe ... 4B 36
Waterfowl Wlk. NN3: Lit B ... 6F 39
Watering La. NN4: Col ... 1C 64
Water La. NN4: Woot ... 5E 59
Waterlee Furlong NN6: Brix ... 2B 22
Waterloo NN11: Dav ... 6E 7
Waterloo Way NN9: Irth ... 3A 20
Waterloo Yd. NN8: Well ... 1F 29
Waterlow Bri. NN9: Fine ... 4D 10
Watermeadow Dr. NN3: N'ton ... 2D 38
Water Pike NN6: Brix ... 1B 22
Waterpump Ct. NN3: N'ton ... 2C 38
Waterside Way NN4: N'ton ... 5H 53
Watersmeet NN1: N'ton ... 3A 54
Waterview Wlk. NN3: N'ton ... 2C 38
Watervill Way NN14: Lit A ... 1D 12
Waterworks La. NN8: Well ... 4C 16
Watkin Ct. *NN1: N'ton ... 2D 52*
(off Watkin Ter.)
Watkin Ter. NN1: N'ton ... 2D 52
Watling St. NN7: Broc, Weed ... 1A 46
Watson Cl. NN5: Dus ... 1E 51
NN8: Well ... 4C 16
Watts Cl. NN7: Kisl ... 6H 49
Waveney Cl. NN11: Dav ... 1C 8
Waveney Way NN5: N'ton ... 6H 35
Waverley Rd. NN2: N'ton ... 6E 37
Waypost Ct. NN3: N'ton ... 4D 38
Wayside Acres NN4: N'ton ... 3B 58
Weavers, The NN4: N'ton ... 4C 58
Weavers Leisure Cen. ... 1D 28
Weavers Rd. NN8: Well ... 1D 28
Webb Dr. NN5: Upton ... 5E 51
Webb Rd. NN9: Raun ... 2C 14
Webbs Factory NN2: N'ton ... 6D 36
Webbs La. NN6: Syw ... 2G 25
Webster Cl. NN9: Raun ... 2D 14
Weddell Way NN4: Brack ... 1A 60
Wedmore Cl. NN5: Dus ... 2F 51
WEEDON BEC ... 5B 46
Weedon La. NN7: Dod ... 3A 46
Weedon Rd.
NN5: Upton, Dus, N'ton ... 4E 51
(not continuous)
NN7: Kisl, Up Hey ... 5D 48
NN7: Neth H ... 6G 47
NN11: Newn ... 5G 9
Weedon Rd. Ind. Est.
NN5: N'ton ... 3G 51
Weekly Cl. NN14: Lit A ... 1D 12
Weggs Farm Rd. NN5: Dus ... 1B 50
Weighbridge Way NN9: Raun ... 4C 14
Weir, The *NN11: Dav ... 1D 6*
(off Buscot Pk. Way)
Weir Cl. NN8: Well ... 5F 17
Welbourne Cl. NN9: Raun ... 3C 14
Weldon Cl. NN8: Well ... 4D 16
Welford Av. NN9: Irth ... 4D 12
Welford Cl. NN9: Irth ... 4D 12
Welford Rd.
NN2: Chap B, K'thpe ... 1H 35
Welland Cl. NN9: Raun ... 2C 14
NN11: Dav ... 6B 6
Welland Grn. NN5: N'ton ... 5H 35
Welland Wlk. NN5: N'ton ... 5H 35
Welland Way NN5: N'ton ... 5H 35
WELLINGBOROUGH ... 1G 29
Wellingborough Bus. Cen.
NN8: Well ... 3H 29
Wellingborough Golf Course ... 1E 17
Wellingborough Heritage Centre
... *1G 29*
(off Tithe Barn Rd.)
Wellingborough Indoor Bowls Club
... 6F 17
Wellingborough Mus. ... 1H 29
Wellingborough Rd.
NN1: N'ton ... 2F 5 (3E 53)
NN3: N'ton, West F ... 1H 53
NN6: E Bart ... 2H 41
NN6: E Bart, Ect ... 3A 40
NN6: Mears A ... 3D 26
NN6: Syw ... 2A 26
NN8: Well ... 3B 18
NN9: Fine ... 6C 10
NN9: Gt Har, Well ... 1D 16
NN9: Irth ... 4F 19
NN10: Rushd ... 2H 31
NN29: Woll ... 4A 44
Wellingborough Squash Club
Diana's Health & Fitness
... 4A 18
Wellingborough Station (Rail)
... 6A 18
Wellington Pl. NN1: N'ton ... 1C 4
Wellington Rd. NN9: Raun ... 4C 14
Wellington St.
NN1: N'ton ... 3D 4 (3D 52)

Wells, The NN9: Fine ... 4D 10
Wells Ct. NN3: Moul ... 5A 24
Wellspring NN7: Blis ... 6F 63
Well St. NN9: Fine ... 5D 10
Well Yd. NN2: K'thpe ... 4B 36
Welton La. NN11: Dav, Welt ... 2F 7
Welton Rd. NN11: Dav ... 3E 7
(not continuous)
Wenlock Way NN5: Dus ... 1F 51
Wensleydale NN2: K'thpe ... 2H 35
Wentworth Av. NN8: Well ... 5C 16
Wentworth Cl. NN11: Dav ... 4G 7
Wentworth Rd. NN9: Fine ... 4E 11
NN10: Rushd ... 3C 32
Wentworth Way NN2: N'ton ... 4E 37
Wessex Way NN3: N'ton ... 6H 37
West Bank NN3: N'ton ... 1C 38
West Brook NN7: Blis ... 5F 63
NN11: Newn ... 5F 9
Westbrook NN8: Well ... 1C 28
Westbury Cl. NN5: Dus ... 2F 51
W. Cotton Cl. NN4: N'ton ... 5C 52
Westcott Way NN3: West F ... 2B 54
West Ct. NN11: Dav ... 6E 7
West Cres. NN10: Rushd ... 3A 32
Westerburg Sq. NN11: Dav ... 1E 9
Westerdale NN2: K'thpe ... 2H 35
Western Av. NN11: Dav ... 5D 6
Western Cl. NN11: Dav ... 5D 6
Western Vw.
NN1: N'ton ... 4A 4 (4B 52)
Western Way NN8: Well ... 2D 28
Westfield Av. NN9: Raun ... 5B 14
NN10: Rushd ... 3A 32
Westfield Dr. NN9: Raun ... 5B 14
Westfield Pl. NN10: Rushd ... 3B 32
Westfield Rd. NN5: Dus ... 1D 50
NN5: N'ton ... 3H 51
NN8: Well ... 1E 29
Westfields Av. NN10: High F ... 6D 20
Westfields St. NN10: High F ... 6D 20
Westfields Ter. NN10: High F ... 6D 20
Westgate Ind. Est. NN5: N'ton ... 3F 51
Westgate Rd. NN5: N'ton ... 3F 51
Westlea Rd. NN6: Syw ... 2H 25
Westleigh Cl. NN1: N'ton ... 1F 53
Westleigh Office Pk.
NN3: N'ton ... 1E 37
W. Leys Ct. NN3: Moul ... 6A 24
West March NN11: Dav ... 2F 9
W. March Ind. Est. NN11: Dav ... 1F 9
W. Mead Ct. NN3: West F ... 6D 38
Westminster Rd. NN8: Well ... 4D 16
Westone Av. NN3: West F ... 6B 38
WESTON FAVELL ... 1B 54
Weston Favell Shop. Cen.
NN3: West F ... 5D 38
Weston Mill La. NN3: West F ... 2C 54
Weston Way NN3: West F ... 1A 54
Weston Wharf
NN1: N'ton ... 5B 4 (4C 52)
West Oval NN5: N'ton ... 6H 35
W. Paddock Ct. NN3: N'ton ... 3D 38
West Pl. *NN11: Dav ... 5E 7*
(off West Ct.)
W. Priors Ct. NN3: N'ton ... 3D 38
West Ridge NN2: K'thpe ... 4D 36
West Rising NN4: N'ton ... 4D 58
West St. NN1: N'ton ... 2H 5 (3F 53)
NN3: Moul ... 4H 23
NN5: Upton ... 5E 51
NN6: E Bart ... 3F 41
NN6: Ect ... 4B 40
NN7: Weed ... 6B 46
NN8: Well ... 1F 29
NN9: Raun ... 3D 14
NN9: Stanw ... 6G 13
NN10: Rushd ... 3D 32
West Vw. NN8: Lit I ... 4A 30
NN11: Dav ... 6D 6
West Vw. Ct. *NN8: Well ... 1F 29*
(off West St.)
Westvilla Cotts. NN8: Well ... 1F 29
W. Villa Rd. NN8: Well ... 1F 29
West Way NN6: E Bart ... 2F 41
NN7: Weed ... 6B 46
Westway, The NN11: Dav ... 1F 9
Westwood Way NN3: N'ton ... 6B 38
Wetenhall Rd. NN9: Stanw ... 5A 14
Wetheral Cl. NN3: N'ton ... 3A 38
Whaddon Cl. NN4: N'ton ... 2G 57
Whaddon Fld. NN6: Brix ... 2B 22
Wharf Grn. NN5: N'ton ... 5H 35
Wharf Rd. NN10: High F ... 5C 20
Wharton Cl. NN8: Well ... 6F 17
Wheat Cl. NN11: Dav ... 1E 7
Wheatcroft Gdns.
NN10: Rushd ... 3D 32
Wheatens Cl. NN6: Brix ... 3B 22

Wheatfield Cl. NN3: N'ton ... 6H 37
Wheatfield Gdns. NN3: N'ton ... 6H 37
Wheatfield Rd. NN3: N'ton ... 6H 37
Wheatfield Rd. Nth.
NN3: N'ton ... 5H 37
Wheatfield Rd. Sth.
NN3: N'ton ... 6H 37
Wheatfield Ter. NN3: N'ton ... 6H 37
Wheelwright Cl. NN9: Raun ... 2E 15
Wheelwrights Yd. NN29: Boz ... 6H 45
Whernside NN8: Well ... 5D 16
Whernside Way NN5: Dus ... 1E 51
Whilton Rd. NN2: K'thpe ... 3D 36
Whistlefield Cotts. NN6: Over ... 6G 25
Whistlets Cl. NN4: N'ton ... 2F 57
Whiston Rd. NN2: K'thpe ... 3D 36
White Delves NN8: Well ... 4E 17
White Doe Dr. NN3: Moul ... 6A 24
Whitefield Rd. NN5: Dus ... 6D 34
Whitefield Way NN9: Raun ... 2C 14
Whitefriars NN10: Rushd ... 4A 32
Whitegates NN4: N'ton ... 2F 57
Whiteheart Cl. NN3: Gt Bil ... 5F 39
WHITE HILLS ... 1B 36
White Hills Cres. NN2: K'thpe ... 1B 36
Whitehills Way NN2: K'thpe ... 1B 36
White Ho. Ct. *NN10: Rushd ... 4E 33*
(off Denmark Rd.)
White Ho. Ind. Est.
NN6: E Bart ... 1F 41
Whiteland Rd. NN3: N'ton ... 5A 38
Whitesands Way NN4: N'ton ... 1E 57
Whites La. NN5: Lwr H ... 4C 34
Whites Ri. NN9: Irth ... 2A 20
White Way NN6: E Bart ... 2G 41
Whitfield Way NN2: K'thpe ... 2D 36
Whiting Ct. NN3: Moul ... 5A 24
Whitley Cl. NN9: Irth ... 2H 19
Whitney Cl. NN9: Raun ... 4C 14
Whitsundale Cl. NN9: Fine ... 5D 10
Whittam Cl. NN9: Raun ... 2C 14
Whittemore Rd. NN10: Rushd ... 2F 33
Whittlebury Cl. NN2: K'thpe ... 2D 36
Whittle Cl. NN8: Well ... 5B 16
NN11: Dav ... 2C 6
Whittles Cross NN4: Woot ... 5G 59
Whitworth Cres. NN6: E Bart ... 2G 41
Whitworth Rd.
NN1: N'ton ... 1H 5 (2F 53)
NN8: Well ... 6A 18
Whitworth Way NN8: Well ... 3H 29
NN9: Irth ... 3A 20
Whytewell Rd. NN8: Well ... 5F 17
Wickery Dene NN4: Woot ... 5G 59
Wicksteed Ct. *NN5: Upton ... 5F 51*
(off Clickers Dr.)
Wilberforce St.
NN1: N'ton ... 2G 5 (3E 53)
WILBY ... 4B 28
Wilbye Grange NN8: Well ... 3D 28
Wilby La. NN29: Gt Dod ... 6D 28
Wilby Pk. Mobile Home Pk.
NN8: Wilby ... 3C 28
Wilby Rd. NN6: Mears A ... 4D 26
Wilby St. NN1: N'ton ... 2H 5 (3F 53)
Wilby Way NN8: Well ... 3D 28
Wilce Av. NN8: Well ... 4G 29
Wildacre Dr. NN3: West F ... 5E 39
Wildacre Rd. NN10: Rushd ... 3A 32
Wildern La. NN4: N'ton ... 6C 58
Wilford Av. NN3: West F ... 1D 54
Wilkie Rd. NN8: Well ... 3F 17
Wilks Wlk. NN4: Gra P ... 2E 65
William Carey Hall
NN3: K'thpe ... 1E 37
William Steele Way
NN10: High F ... 6E 21
Williams Ter. NN11: Dav ... 5D 6
William St. NN1: N'ton ... 1D 4 (2D 52)
NN9: Fine ... 5E 11
Williams Way NN4: Gra P ... 2E 65
NN10: High F ... 6D 20
NN29: Woll ... 6C 44
William Tarry Ho. NN5: N'ton ... 4A 52
William Trigg Cl. NN9: Irth ... 3A 20
Williton Cl. NN3: West F ... 2B 54
Willmott Rd. NN10: Rushd ... 5E 33
Willoughby Cl. NN11: Dav ... 4D 6
Willow Brook Sq. NN3: Ect B ... 4H 39
Willow Ct. NN1: N'ton ... 2G 53
Willow Cres. NN4: Gt Hou ... 1C 60
Willow Herb Cl. NN10: Rushd ... 6E 33
Willow Ho. *NN1: N'ton ... 2F 53*
(off Lea Rd.)
Willow La. NN4: Gt Hou ... 1C 60
Willow Ri. NN3: Lit B ... 1F 55
Willows, The NN4: N'ton ... 6H 53
NN11: Dav ... 4E 7
Willow Vw. NN7: Kisl ... 6G 49

Wilson Cl. NN11: Dav 3C **6**
Wilson Cres. NN9: Irth 2A **20**
Wilson Rd. NN10: Rushd 3C **32**
Wilson Way NN6: E Bart 4G **41**
Wimbledon St. NN5: N'ton 3A **52**
Wimborne Cl. NN3: Ect B 4H **39**
Wimborne Pl. NN11: Dav 2E **7**
Wimpole NN8: Well 1C **28**
Wincely Cl. NN11: Dav 1E **7**
Winchester Cl. NN4: Del 2C **58**
Winchester Rd. NN4: Del 2C **58**
   NN10: Rushd 4E **33**
Windermere Cl. NN11: Dav 5D **6**
Windermere Dr. NN8: Well 6C **16**
   NN10: High F 3D **20**
Windermere Way NN3: N'ton . . .3A **38**
Windflower Pl. NN3: Ect B 5H **39**
Windingbrook La.
   NN4: Col, N'ton 6C **58**
Windlass Cl. NN4: N'ton 3F **57**
Windmill Av. NN7: Blis 6F **63**
   NN9: Raun 3D **14**
Windmill Banks NN10: High F . . .4E **21**
   NN10: Rushd 3B **32**
Windmill Cl. NN8: Well 3E **29**
   NN29: Woll 5C **44**
Windmill Glade NN6: Brix 2A **22**
Windmill Gro. NN9: Raun 3D **14**
Windmill La. NN9: Raun 2C **14**
Windmill Rd. NN9: Irth 2A **20**
   NN10: Rushd 3C **32**
Windmill Ter. NN2: K'thpe 2D **36**
Windrush Rd. NN4: H'stone 3F **59**
Windrush Way NN5: N'ton 6A **36**
Windsor Cl. NN3: Gt Bil 5B **46**
   NN11: Dav 6D **6**
Windsor Cl. NN3: Gt Bil 5G **39**
Windsor Cres. NN5: N'ton 3G **51**
Windsor Ho. NN5: Dus 1E **51**
   (off Limehurst Rd.)
Windsor Rd. NN8: Well 4E **29**
   NN10: Rushd 2E **33**
Windyridge NN2: K'thpe 4D **36**

Winnington Cl. NN3: N'ton 2G **39**
Winsford Way NN3: West F 2B **54**
Winstanley Rd. NN8: Well 1H **29**
Winston Cl. NN3: N'ton 2A **38**
Wisley Cl. NN4: N'ton 4C **58**
Wisteria Cl. NN10: Rushd 6D **32**
Wisteria Way NN3: N'ton 3A **54**
Witham, The NN11: Dav 6B **6**
Witham Grn. NN5: N'ton 5G **35**
Witham Wlk. NN5: N'ton 5H **35**
Witham Way NN5: N'ton 6H **35**
Witheys, The NN4: Gra P 3F **65**
Wittlich Rd. NN8: Well 5H **17**
Witton Rd. NN5: Dus 1E **51**
Woburn Ct. NN10: Rushd 5C **32**
Woburn Ga. NN3: Ect B 4H **39**
Wollaston 5B **44**
Wollaston Ind. Est.
   NN29: Woll 6C **44**
Wollaston Mus. 5B **44**
Wollaston Rd. NN29: Boz 4G **45**
   (not continuous)
   NN29: Irch 2D **44**
Wollaton Gdns. NN3: West F . . .1D **54**
Wood Avens Cl. NN4: N'ton . . .2G **57**
Woodborough Gdns.
   NN3: West F 1C **54**
Woodcote Av. NN3: N'ton 3F **37**
Woodfields Wlk.
   NN3: N'ton 2C **38**
Woodford Chase NN6: Syw 3G **25**
Woodford Rd. NN14: Lit A 1E **13**
Woodford St.
   NN1: N'ton 3G **5** (3E **53**)
Woodford Wlk. NN1: N'ton 3G **5**
Woodgate Rd. NN4: Woot 5F **59**
Woodhall Cl. NN4: N'ton 2F **57**
Wood Hill NN1: N'ton . . .4D **4** (4D **52**)
Woodhill Rd. NN5: Dus 6D **34**
Woodland Av. NN3: N'ton 6G **37**
   NN6: Over 4F **25**
Woodland Cl. NN5: Dus 5D **34**
Woodland Rd. NN10: Rushd . . .2C **32**
Woodlands NN4: Gra P 4E **65**

Woodlands, The NN5: Dus 4D **34**
   NN9: Stanw 6A **14**
Woodlands Grange
   NN6: E Bart 3A **42**
Woodlands Rd. NN29: Irch 6D **30**
Woodland Wlk. NN3: N'ton 1F **39**
Woodlark Ct. NN4: N'ton 3G **57**
Woodley Chase NN5: Dus 6D **34**
Woodpecker Way NN4: N'ton . .4H **57**
Woodrush Way NN3: Moul 6A **24**
Woodsfield NN6: Brix 1A **22**
Woodside NN6: Syw 4H **25**
Woodside Av. NN3: N'ton 3B **38**
Woodside Cres. NN3: N'ton 3B **38**
Woodside Grn. NN5: N'ton 6H **35**
Woodside Wlk. NN5: N'ton 6G **35**
Woodside Way NN5: N'ton 6G **35**
Woodstock
   NN1: N'ton 3H **5** (3E **53**)
Woodstock Cl. NN8: Well 4E **17**
Wood St. NN1: N'ton 3D **4**
   NN8: Well 1F **29**
   NN10: High F 6E **21**
Woodward Cl. NN11: Dav 6G **7**
Wooldale Rd. NN4: Woot 6D **58**
Woolmonger St.
   NN1: N'ton 4C **4** (4C **52**)
Woolston Cl. NN3: N'ton 3H **37**
Wootton 5E **59**
Wootton Brook Cl. NN4: N'ton . .5C **58**
Wootton Flds. Cen.
   NN4: Woot 5F **59**
Wootton Hall Pk. NN4: N'ton . . .3C **58**
Wootton Hill Farm NN4: N'ton . .3H **57**
Wootton Hope Dr. NN4: Woot . .4F **59**
Wootton Rd. NN7: Gra P, Quin . .1F **65**
Wootton Trad. Est. NN4: Woot . .5F **59**
Worcester Cl. NN3: Gt Bil 5B **46**
Worcester Way NN11: Dav 2E **9**
Wordsworth Rd. NN8: Well 2B **28**
   NN11: Dav 4D **6**
Works, The NN1: N'ton 3G **5**
Wrekin Cl. NN4: N'ton 6G **51**
Wrenbury Rd. NN5: Dus 1B **50**

Wren Cl. NN4: Gra P 2F
Wrights La. NN7: G'ton 1A
Wroe, The NN10: High F 4D
Wychwood Cl. NN5: Dus 6C
Wyckley Cl. NN9: Irth 6A
Wycliffe Rd. NN1: N'ton 2G
Wye, The NN11: Dav 1
Wye Cl. NN8: Well 5C
Wykeham Rd. NN10: High F 4E
Wyman Cl. NN29: Boz 6H
Wymersley Cl. NN4: Gt Hou 1D
Wymington Pk. NN10: Rushd . . .4D
Wymington Rd. NN10: Rushd . . .6D
Wysall Rd. NN3: N'ton 2E

Y

Yardley Dr. NN2: K'thpe 1D
Yarrow NN8: Well 2B
Yarrow Cl. NN10: Rushd 6E
Yarwell Sq. NN4: N'ton 1H
Yelden Cl. NN10: Rushd 3B
Yeldon Ct. NN8: Well 2H
Yelvertoft Rd. NN2: K'thpe 4C
Yeoman Dr. NN2: K'thpe 2F
Yeoman Mdw. NN4: N'ton 3H
Yeomanry Cl. NN11: Dav 6L
Yeomanry Way NN11: Dav 5C
Yewtree Ct. NN3: N'ton 2B
Yew Tree Gdns. NN7: Flore 4E
Yew Tree Gro. NN11: Dav 1L
York Cl. NN10: High F 4E
Yorke Cl. NN9: Fine 4C
York Ho. NN1: N'ton . . . . .4+
York Ride *NN7: Weed* 5B
   (off Gloucester C
York Rd. NN1: N'ton 3E **5** (3D **5**
   NN8: Well 6H
   NN10: High F 4E
   NN10: Rushd 4E
York Way NN9: Raun 2C
   NN11: Dav 2C

The representation on the maps of a road, track or footpath is no evidence of the existence of a right of way.

The Grid on this map is the National Grid taken from Ordnance Survey® mapping with the permission of the Controller of Her Majesty's Stationery Office.

Copyright of Geographers' A-Z Map Company Ltd.

No reproduction by any method whatsoever of any part of this publication is permitted without the prior consent of the copyright owners.

SAFETY CAMERA INFORMATION

PocketGPSWorld.com's CamerAlert is a self-contained speed and red light camera warning system for SatNavs and Android or Apple iOS smartphones/tablets. Visit www.cameralert.co.uk to download.

Safety camera locations are publicised by the Safer Roads Partnership which operates them in order to encourage drivers to comply with speed limits at these sites. It is the driver's absolute responsibility to be aware of and to adhere to speed limits at all times.

By showing this safety camera information it is the intention of Geographers' A-Z Map Company Ltd., to encourage safe driving and greater awareness of speed limits and vehicle speed. Data accurate at time of printing.